QUANTUM MAN

QUANTUM MAN

THE UNDISCOVERED SEX

Ken Fegradoe

BLOOMSBURY

First published 1992
Copyright © 1992 by Ken Fegradoe

The moral right of the author
has been asserted

Bloomsbury Publishing Ltd, 2 Soho Square, London W1V 5DE

A CIP catalogue record for this book
is available from the British Library

ISBN 0 7475 1166 7

10 9 8 7 6 5 4 3 2 1

Printed in England by Clays Ltd, St Ives Plc

For S.W.

ACKNOWLEDGEMENTS

The speculations in this book were inspired by many writers and thinkers; among them are Jane Roberts (see her series of 'Seth Books', Prentice Hall, USA), Fritjof Capra, Carlos Castaneda, Danah Zohar, Lyall Watson, Carl Sagan, Robert Anton Wilson, Henry Miller, C. G. Jung and Jean-Paul Sartre. Any inaccuracies should be ascribed to this author rather than to the integrity of their work.

ONE

This is the meaning of loneliness: that you can go through your entire life without ever seeing the one pair of eyes that will stop your heart dead as a stone, hurl you instantaneously to paradise, then bring you back knowing that what you were till that moment might just as well have been a corpse. I had lived with loneliness but never quite believed in it. I had been a counter of carcasses, a flaw in a production line, a porter of vats of soup, a packer of effluent, a moulder of ersatz Wedgwoods, a dopehead, an invisible voice, a digger of mental graves and a card-carrying gynophobe who drifted laterally into a sinecure as a third-rate wordchurner in an advertising agency in the desert, into which, by a concatenation of events beyond all recounting, she had walked – looking for a job.

The moment I saw her eyes I knew.

We were thrown to work together on a project. It could have been about the Second Coming for all I cared. I was spilling out the old word-magic, pitching my voice a tone lower, sitting up straight like my mother told me. My muscles had turned to abalone, clinging to my skeleton for fear I would fly apart. She must have seen straight through me. Under the desk our ankles touched.

Weeks later we made a pact in a bar that was a regurgitation of the wooden interior of a ship that could never have existed. It was always full of lonely men striking unlikely poses. We hardly noticed. I introduced her to the five-to-one Martini and we had seventeen between us. Seventeen. I had a drinking habit in those days. Home at the crack of dawn, I would line up the empties after dripping each one down my gullet and then blow them to nirvana with my trusty Diana. My carpets were mined with shards of glass.

She wore a tight white dress of something crisply textured. It slipped over her knees when she sat down. Sometimes I noticed her figure: she was a perfect miniature. When I thought of her I didn't think of making love to her. Falling asleep alone, I tried hard to fantasize that side of things with her. But she overwhelmed me.

We made a pact. Those were the early days of my quantum awareness, so I invented a metaphor, boring in retrospect but elevated by circumstance. We were particles generated by the same benign force, traversing the cosmos in separate but parallel paths. How else shall lovers cease attempting to own each other? There would be no effort to be together, no tampering with our lives, no pledges. We might be destined to be mundanely partnered in some subsequent lifetime. It didn't matter. We could never be apart. Our origins were common. Our destination was shared. The journey was irrelevant.

I escorted her home, staggered out to the desert shore and fell asleep in the faint shadow of a moonlit dune. Moon, dune.

A year later she left town.

It is not enough to be delivered from corpsehood: the repose of Lazarus must have held its own solitary compensations. After she left I felt as if I had been reborn into nothing. Born again to no avail, O Lord! Thump me a Bible, send me a signal, let me bleed into my surplice every *Götterdämmerung*! And to be delivered from corpsehood is not to be delivered from one's fellow ghoulies, Ah yes, the walking dead.

From out of the throng of inconsequential people around me one like-minded soul had emerged. Now she had gone and my evidence that there could be so momentous and beguiling a thing as the conjunction of souls had gone with her. There is a misconception that a man is nobler alone and profits by self-sufficiency, but it is all a sham. The contact that denies the hunger for a committed and dependent love is a sham, of the same order as all shams and arid self-deceptions: the sham of mutual possession, the sham of work for the sham of money, the sham of ambitions for accomplishments that can never be shared.

In the light of our insubstantial encounter I began to understand that to be undivided as a soul was to be blind and dead. You cannot aspire to a discrete existence once you have discovered tenderness. I had found the very thing I had refused to believe did not exist; goddamn, I was right! Infected once, the soul divides with the same urgent compulsion as the zygote, releasing you from the pressure of what you are. It grants you the possibility of reprieve from the self that you have carefully nurtured and defined, and of which you were unknowingly weary. You may be capable of growing old alone, but the hunger to become someone else by loving someone other than yourself will never leave you. Either that or you must take care to ascertain whether you have been buried alive.

TWO

Though no corpse, my friend Rostand was a typical example of the kind of man I had begun to leave behind in myself. Is it blasphemy to say that the camaraderie of men is merely a substitute for the comfort of women? I speculated that lovers together in the proper way must create a third sex, or depending upon your proclivities a fourth sex, but certainly one which engenders a new being – separate from each person yet containing them. This becomes possible when you have gathered enough of another to be able to reconstitute yourself into a whole, and when you have given enough of yourself to have lightened your own burden.

Rostand was, I believe, no different from any other male conditioned to be a man. He hungered like the rest of us but was imbued with the myth of manly solitude. Men fool themselves into thinking that they are alone, weep for it, then cut each other's hearts out to prove that they have risen above emotion. What is above emotion I do not know: Elsinore, Shangri-La, the Black Hole of Calcutta, My Lai; it is an unnamed place, a province of Anaesthesia, perhaps. But under Rostand's bloodhound, blood-shot exterior beat the tenderest heart that ever was. He had been conditioned to think of women as denizens of a lower territory, a separate species in whom the prospect of kindredness was hardly the point.

In the desert town, desperate men together, we would drive our cars into creeks and leave them to drown. Lurching home, he would weep and giggle at some concocted malaise while I savoured the divinity of having known *her*. He thought me something of a tenderfoot, without the calluses that protect men from their lovers, wives, mothers, daughters. To him this was a sign of immaturity rather than depth. Ah well, he was a good man to drink with. We used to shoot up the empties together. He had met her briefly.

One night after an automotive joust we scurried back to my place, breathless and glad to be alive. 'What's wrong with you?' he asked, noting a lack of my usual enthusiasm for our encounters with destiny.

'I've had it, Rostand,' said I.

'Had what, bastard?'

Gruff expletives were his way of showing affection. In a room of people he liked he was a volcano of profanity. You could judge your place in his affections by the severity of epithet applied to you. Cursing your near relatives was as good as saying he would die for you. He cursed in three languages, a hybrid invective that he was glad to translate into surreal images for his victims. There was one about your mother being able to accommodate, in a delicate part of her person, the bed on which he would . . .

'Had it with this way of living,' I replied. 'It's a sham. I'm broke. I drink my money and spew out dead brain cells in the morning.'

'So what else is new, fucker?' He lay in the middle of my living-room with a whisky balanced on his forehead.

'I am sick of enjoying myself. I don't enjoy it any more,' I whinged.

Rostand haw-hawed and pooh-poohed, his prone form undulating. The whisky toppled and he licked his streaming cheeks. 'Of course you don't enjoy *it*! You're not getting any of *it*!'

'I am interested in only one woman, Rostand.'

'You should get yourself checked,' he said, but in a kindly tone. Then he exhibited what might after all be a virtue of ennobled solitude: tenacity – the egoism of bending the world to one's intentions. 'Cocksucker! You have decided that you will never see her again. This is information from Zarathustra, of course, which you have romanticked into a tragedy with your nit-picker poncy little intellect . . . ' He paused for effect, glowering at me from under Semitic eyebrows. 'Don't lie around whimpering like a tool. Go out there and bring her back!' Then he complained to an invisible presence, his voice trailing off in profanity, a thorny weed tumbling into the distance.

I was left to think. *Go out there and bring her back.* I'll be damned! What could be simpler? It conjured pictures of club-wielding primitives but it made visceral sense. I had covered my ineptitude with reticence. I could talk a woman into bed, but that presupposed her disposition to listen. Logic is no ally of hormones, and hormones unassuaged will turn love into a narcotic – idealized, absent, neither genitalic nor a sustainable source of literature. Ha, ha, ha. I had probably talked more women out the door than I had into bed. It took a gentle Neanderthal like Rostand to curse me out of my slumber. However, it had slipped my mind that the last thing I wanted to do with her was to talk her into bed. That would occur at an appropriate stage, sex being only a component of something larger, something underrated. Perhaps I had better get myself checked.

In the company of Rostand and others like him I was weak-kneed enough to revert to the conquering male. I would grunt and posture as well as the next man; never mind she was the gentlest woman in creation and offspring of a shared deity – I would go out there and *get* her.

The trouble was I hadn't the faintest notion of where she was and knew nobody who could tell me. Rostand's little implant of baboon blood wore thin in a matter of days. My reticence was in the best taste. I had been a fool to forget that time and distance were nothing compared with The Pact of the Seventeen Martinis. Metaphysical love was preferable to the grind and tedium of the allegedly real thing. You could keep your nose clean and your pants on and avoid complicating your illusions. You could shift your weight from foot to foot. You could live your sham liberation and exercise your quantum choice, being in turn and as necessary the club-wielder or the reticent, the boozer, the profaner, the self-proclaimed metaphysician, the air-pistol packer, the disingenuous tenderfoot. La di da.

Then, like a particle booming out of the void, her letter arrived.

THREE

On the birthing bed her belly, strapped for the monitor, shone like the pate of a bottled-nosed dolphin. In my non-discriminating quantum world, made vivid by twenty-eight hours of starvation and wakefulness, her beautiful belly *was* the pate of the bottled-nosed dolphin. Her belly-button, stretched into a tiny smile by the distension of her belly skin, was the proud, puckered blowhole of *Tursiops truncatus*.

Ah, for the uninformed male mind a woman's body is explored for sex. That is like landing in Cape Cod and proclaiming America. There are nuances, undulations, atmospherics about a woman's body. The male's mechanistic physicality is impoverished in its senses next to the woman's Vulcanic organism, so it is an appropriate mission for him to discover what he can of a woman's body. No more than one reciprocating woman is needed.

If we had not lost our primeval nose we might have embarked on low-flying reconnaissances of clefts and dips, valleys and shorelines that each hold their own thaumaturgic airs. If we had not lost the focus of our touch in a world where we brush past each other, we might have made the pilgrimage to the Musée Rodin to trace surreptitiously the tips of our fingers over his reclining *Camille*, then rushed home to revive the vanishing sensations on our own loves. In the forecleft of the hip, a line swoops down to the mons veneris and vanishes like a diving swallow. Behind the clavicle there is an oasis from which sediments may be licked. The swell of the deltoid muscle stalls the hand gently as it caresses the shoulder. The tracery of upturned creases under the breasts and belly forms a concert of living smiles with the smile above. The backs of the knees dimple and undimple in semaphore. Below the sternum is a veiny triangle of membrane under which tremors can be felt. The inward curve of the waist shelves out over the hip, a soft ledge for the respite of hands and thighs.

I could go on. I could create a twenty-volume parallel anatomy of women that would make all other anatomies obsolete, granting men whatever knowledge they need to nurture this other species of themselves, were they so inclined. Yet, of all things, we lack even first-hand experience, and women are reticent for having been pecked or prodded. The woman's body is an area of tenderness, where men can recover their sensitivities; all our emotions arise from it, can be traced back to it; it is an embodied emotion, our first world, where before we learnt to think we found ourselves capable of being inseparably in love with some-thing outside ourselves.

We have forgotten.

The birthing room was undoubtedly conceived by a man who couldn't tell a woman from a block of masonry. A cell of stainless-steel prods and bathroom tiles dripping with formaldehyde. Lighting of the kind used to interrogate prisoners. Left alone, V and I extinguished the lights and opened the windows for fresh air. The night before, the duty nurse had probed V until she screamed and screamed again, pronouncing her dilation insuf-ficient in the manner of someone reading a railway timetable. We were dumped in a darkened ward with a bare table, an ancient wooden chair, a bed and a cylinder of entonox. The contractions had subsided. It looked like being a long stretch to delivery. We shared the entonox for a few seconds each. The gas kicked at my diaphragm and pushed bubbles of laughter up my throat. There was no one else around. V couldn't sleep for fright.

We were holed up at the time in two rooms on the edge of the Big City. Neither of us worked or was concerned to make money. Security was something you eked out of each day. If the wolves retreated from our door by sundown it was enough to have the peace of each evening to spend together. During the day, we worked on our dreams, but when the offices had closed, and the collectors, arbitrators, money-lenders, penny-pinchers and men in rumpled suits went home to fidget in their uneasy chairs and disembowel their children — that was when we were most at peace. The world and its work had buggered off. There was no busyness to infect the air.

All we wanted was to be together, to be able to talk, exchange our histories, share the things we made up from one moment to the next. Apart, there was nothing to engage us or make us feel as if we were alive. The pact we had made to be inseparable in spirit had evolved into the need to be materially inseparable. We gave up everything for this, but such a monumental relinquishment was easy, for being constantly together drove us divinely mad. If the object of insanity is to escape, we were nuts, we had slipped out the back door. We could have sat down from the first moment of our meeting again and talked late into the night of for ever, repeating ourselves if necessary. The verbal exchange was only the half of it: on another level we were splicing neurons, intertwining synapses and merging pineal glands. Our brains would think thoughts simply to experience the pleasure of exchanging them. What else was there that was worth achieving? It was the mental equivalent of the exchange of body fluids, but without pausing for breath. It grew and fed on itself, creating itself as it went along with no need for external stimuli. Even when we were silent, the process of mutual absorption was continuous; to have interrupted this with work, money or other people would have been like walking away from the Burning Bush. We scraped a living together day by day with our wits and a couple of typewriters, and a wild new idea every morning, all so we wouldn't have to be out of earshot of each other. Nothing frightened us more than the prospect of being separated by some irksome physical necessity. Nothing made the fearsome threats of the loveless, money-grubbing world we lived in so small and distant as each other's company. And no pinnacle of success could have given me a view so rewarding as this vast internal map of another's consciousness – this *woman* I had got to know.

Self-knowledge makes an evolutionary leap when it becomes centred upon another; it enters a relativistic universe in which it is possible to become someone else. Here nothing is measurable unless there is a fixed point from which scale may be deduced. But a fixed point is arbitrary, no more nor less significant than any other point in the universe. Likewise, no one is more or less significant than anyone else. From this knowledge we may reach an equanimity that says, I know that what I think or feel is no more important than what you think or feel: we may now change places.

Love motivates this abandoning of a limited self for a greater self that embodies, in its intentions and concerns, others. We overlap. The boundary between self-love and love for another is discarded. Our egos become multiple. It is the old gregarious spirit, perhaps. Our first communities might always have been internal. And all it takes to begin with is one other person who is willing to head the same way for a time. To V and me it wasn't something you had to cook up. We suspected that given the right chances it would come as naturally to everybody on this planet.

V pointed out that men had some catching up to do and she was right. A democracy of the spirit does not come easily to men, who are supposed to be manipulators of environments and species. Men had learned to pin down love, or to define it and bury it with the example of De Sade or Lawrence or Abelard; they had concocted harridans and gorgons and mermaids with which to dissect the history of the female spirit, then mastered women's bodies under the scalpel and speculum. Men had become gynae-cologists but were never so much explorers of the soul that they would dismantle their own personalities in order to understand – experience – the interior life of women. With me there was no choice. I was not embarking on a planned mission, like some anthropologist going off to unleave a forgotten tribe. For me to learn who I was and who she was I had to exchange my soul with this woman.

And V showed me more about the interior life of men, such as it was. Men whined because women were different: what would they rather have had, male or neutered spirits in receptive female bodies? Freud's distorted legacy has made us suspicious of women. The male assumes that in women the turmoil of the human unconscious is sooner or later a matter of biology. Men have kept the higher ground for themselves. Their inner storms are sacro-sanct because they are created in the image of God, who is assumed to possess male genitalia. The question of the nature and objectives of the Deity's sex organs would provide an interesting

study for novitiates and theologians. Furthermore, in contraven-
tion of everything we know about our organs, and in what must
have been the prototype of the political lie, it was decided that a
man gave birth to the first woman. Perhaps this is a vestigial
species memory of the protoplasmic blob that had the first erection
and so began our mammalian destiny. You could tell it was a
male gizmopod by the length of its sideburns. At any rate, it gave
the male parental rights in perpetuity. And further yet, useful
speculation that Eden was a mythic rendition of the development
of the neocortex is, obliquely, evidence of the tardiness of the
female species. It was the punishment of Eve that her pelvis failed
to evolve sufficiently to deliver the little megacephalic other than
in screaming agony. Yet another example of the defective biology
of the female, M'Lud, though of course we shall not renounce our
stated preference for the svelte-shanked nymphet with a pipette
for a vagina. And bugger the obstetric consequences.

In a male Dystopia of the future, hips shall be bound like
Chinese tootsies, mass-televised pelvic-floor exercises will give the
vagina a jawlike purchase, and the techniques of surgical interven-
tion in the birthing room will have propagated their own fund-
raising body at the United Nations. Hail, Caesar!

Each new generation of males concocts its own lies about the
irksome, clinging and feeble daughters of Eve, burying them like
bones along with all the other dark prejudices that threaten stasis
for the human psyche. No question yet of understanding women
or joining with them, other than to subsume their individuality
under the imperatives of procreation or for indiscriminate seed-
scattering. Behind it all was the fatal flaw of contemporary men:
while women struggled to sustain, men were failing the species
itself. Reducing women to instruments of their own biology, men
also misdefined their own destiny, aspiring to the condition of
machines, sterility and stasis, automotons in a Darwinist twilight.
You can see it now in the new and silent generation of control-
freaks who are downloading evolution and genetics into the
databanks of the highest bidders. If evolution was the only aspect
of nature that could not be reduced and controlled it had to be
assumed extinct: the only fitting end for the species was the
reductionist end, a great leap forward into a clockwork future,

with eugenics and conformity for all, and the soul merely an historic neurosis of which we had cleansed ourselves.

For reasons beyond me it appears that men of our century have embraced the notion that human nature does not change. And, having fulfilled this destiny by posing as unevolving, unemotional, unintuitive gizmos, they provide us with the catechism of modernity: the abandonment of human will as a quantum element in evolution, as a participant in creating the future. The interior life of men. Such as it is.

Me, I prefer the company of women. Better we hand the whole shebang over to them. Better you join me and thousands of other men who refuse to believe in loneliness and have gone off in search of a woman to inhabit. Jump ship now! Jettison your conditioning! Forget your fathers! Let us attempt to create something really important, such as a future of good relations between the sexes. Think of the fun!

V dozed. I sat propped like a Hindu corpse on the rickety chair, wide awake in the underworld of the ward. We had gone to bed that night not expecting the child for another week at least. I remembered my boyhood reading of Conan Doyle, how Holmes would starve himself to keep his head in shape for the case. Fancifully I resolved not to eat until my child was born, no matter how long it took. I needed hunger to give me a sharp focus on what was happening to us. My mind was free to roam. My body began to feel thin and light.

V's head had fallen to one side on the pillow. Her belly was monumental now under the white sheets, the great bump catching what there was of light in the empty ward. Under that belly our child was being intermittently squeezed into existence. I had read somewhere that the passage through the birth canal was like being run down by a truck, that the trauma of being born had to be exorcized in many full-grown adults. I couldn't credit it. In a universe of wondrous things it didn't make much sense that we poor creatures had evolved for millions of years only to be clobbered in the act of emerging. There had to be something wrong with our methods.

It seemed incredible that the scientists had been so slow to adjust their methods to include the comfort of the emerging child or the natural birthing abilities of the woman. In the Afrikan bush, women squatted to push, meeting gravity halfway and letting the child fall to meet the earth. But the medical scientists and their buddies in the drugs business were armed with stern statistics about natal mortality in premedical societies. Science was telling us that to live we must accept a degree of unnatural suffering. That didn't surprise me. The men who had invented scientific method were stringent in more than their methodology. Their descendants had honed the propaganda that science eliminated suffering even as they were telling us what pain was and was not permissible under science. Someone forgot to ask the women who were losing their ability to give birth as each decade passed. Their screams of pain were passed off with gruff paternal urgings to put on a brave face. You must be brave, darling: it is the fate of women to endure in childbirth pain statistically recorded by our boys in the back-room to exceed anything incurred on the battlefield or under the knife.

We were talking in bed earlier that night when the first jolt silenced V. Like hitting an iceberg in the dark. I heard her draw her breath in slowly. The axis of the world had shifted. Forces of nature that began when the universe exploded found their way into our little room. Lines of neutrinos running backwards in time to the first instant of creation made a microcosmic Big Bang inside the body of my wife. I didn't need a divine revelation to know that the force at work here had proclaimed its inexorability before the beginning of time. I felt affronted by God. I would rather we had control over our own bodies and that the time and place of the delivery were a matter of consultation.

The pregnancy had taught me something about letting go of control. It had dragged on endlessly, turning nine months into eighteen, it seemed. V's body became even more beautiful. Looking at it I saw that the Afrikan goddesses were not simply celebrations of universal abundance, they were also particular tributes to the pregnant female form. The sag and swell are authoritative. The lumbering has a benign air, the grace and slowness of a ship laden with cargo.

And the body also became wise. Subliminal directives were

13

issued to us as it grew, proving wiser than our conscious decisions. They programmed the child's nutrition in a discernible sequence, building blood, bone, tissue, keratin by sending up impatient signals for food. Bread all this week, strawberries the next, herring the week after. Because we were together night and day, I fell into the rhythms that were being imposed on V. I had to be fast on my feet, quick to set aside whatever I was engaged in. Forget routines. Stay flexible. Logic be damned. Jump up when this large, slow and demanding entity that has taken over your wife croaks plaintively. Become a lateral creature altogether and your vision shifts, your focus sharpens; your brain, dislodged, lets inspiration leak in, each act is refreshed, your energy quadruples.

Could be there's a hormone or two activated in expectant fathers as well. One day the medical boys will tell us all about it. The secret machinations of the pineal, maybe. It's all in there some place where emotions and chemicals dance their little jig together.

For V, the pregnancy brought extended periods of contemplation. That suited her fine, being a contemplative sort of woman. We kept ourselves free for just such occasions. To me, it's the work of being human. I had visions of the primeval dignity of woman with child. She told me that the contemplation was not directed, a state of being inaccessible to active verbs. Perhaps she was joining instinctively with the child, engaging with it in a collaborative mental act to create that symmetry of form and that great constellation of neurons that signifies a human being. The little boy or girl who grows up to be one of those nice Afro-Caucasians they put on the *Voyager* plaque.

It seemed curious to me that the iconic Madonnas never portrayed the prenatal Mary. There was a way in which V sat, head bowed, one arm resting on the shelf of her belly, that made her look like all the women who had ever lived. Rodin's *The Thinker*, the only equivalent icon I know for the condition of men, always looked to me as if he were about to give up grappling with his problem and go mow the lawn. V's silence and stillness were never more inviolate, like the stillness at the core of something.

And the body had its own secret hygiene as well, effected in bouts of epic nausea. I, never able to watch anyone throw up, took refuge in speculation. There were sudden deflections from whatever she happened to be doing, when the child demanded she sit down and let it feed or breathe. Her eyes would glaze over and her sharpness dissolve. She would turn into a marine mammal, a dreamy manatee preoccupied with its own slow progress through a world of refracted light and floating thoughts. The child was feeding not just on her body but on her thoughts too. The marine world was the primeval habitat brought to the surface of her terrestrial awareness by the condition of maternity. The patterns of preverbal thought being laid down in the child's neural circuits were derived from the submarine cogitations of the mother. The circle was complete.

Later I heard that the amnion resounds with sounds coming in from the outside world: traffic, the clank of dishes, the piped music of parental conversation – and that the child *listens*. In that uterine sound-sphere, those unnamed murmurs and the dance of bloodshot light must be like a dream. It seemed generous of nature that the child should spend its first months in a dream. I couldn't think of a more perfect welcome for the forming entity, and one more likely to deflect it from the rudeness of obstetrics. In the bubble V and I had created for each other the dream state seemed the most natural of all.

The dream was here now, in this drab, darkened ward with its taint of disinfectant and cabbage soup. I rose to stretch my legs and ambled towards the light of the corridor. The rows of empty beds evoked eerie absences. Torn soldiers cried out from them in newspaper etchings of the Crimean War. I stuck my head around the door. Faint voices drew me out for a moment. It would be comforting to chat with a nurse, have a cup of coffee. But I was afraid to leave V asleep alone in the empty ward. We were lost in a giant machine. We had been processed into it and we would be processed out of it. Nothing to do but wait. Birth was to be endured in hiding, in quarantine and darkness, away from voices and laughter, away from celebration. There was a monster in the labyrinth, materialized out of the echoes of screams of pain, out of the malignant thought-forms of those who had gone before, who had separated pain from emotion, had called birth shameful,

15

KEN FEGRADOE

had locked menstruating women out of temples and churches, invented hysteria, burnt the witch. If I left V alone the monster would surely pay her a visit. The dream. The nightmare.

'Call the nurse.'

I loped back to the bed. The contractions had begun again. She was groping for the entonox.

Nurse? Were there nurses in a place like this?

There was a flurry of lights and sheets when they arrived. The contractions subsided abruptly. They were kind in a perfunctory way; it was late at night; they had seen too much pain. Still some way to go, darling. You must produce, you must dilate.

V had cervical problems that had resulted in miscarriages. The cervix caused greater pain than might have been expected for a first birth, but there was no measure of pain available by which you could say to the nurses, You do not understand, this is *pain*, this pain is killing me. They had not been briefed by the statisticians. I wanted to moan and rock and jump about next to her bed, to shriek like an Arab woman ululating funereal grief. I wanted some ceremonial myth with which to chase the monster away, a burning of antimony, imprecations to banish demonic ketones ... But such things were unheard of in the empty ward.

She was asleep again. Six hours had passed.

There is always this possibility brought home to you in a hospital: that the person you love will die. The great machine, tended by people who seem themselves in need of cure, runs a byline in human and mechanical error. Lists are produced of patients who could not be saved. She succumbed to anaesthesia. She contracted pneumonia. Her blood sugar was too high. There is always a passivity in these explanations that belies the fact that you were in their hands, doing exactly what they told you to do when you had the misfortune to shuffle off. When you were being manipulated into a position that was allegedly for your own good, they were the experts. When someone blunders, they cover it up in Latin, which, being dead and sacred, has the double benefit of implying an act of God and being incomprehensible. There is nothing wrong with some hospitals that a little fellow-feeling cannot cure, but, in the rush for God knows what, fellow-feeling

16

gets thrown in the gutter. My wife and I were in the gutter along with all those other poor saps who had the nerve to get ill. And if you have the bad taste to complain or even to ask for the help we are employed to provide, well! We shall just have to treat you like a number. Pain-killers for the wimp in Number Eleven, Sister — she's down with an imminent foetus!

Kicking my heels in the monstrous great yellowing labyrinthine machine while V slept, I wondered about the role of women in all this. It occurred to me that the true culture of women — that dodo-bird of the male domain — had been subverted. How else could women be proud to send their sons off to be roasted in the wars? How else could we explain all these women who watched their men work themselves into early senility?

V had taught me that an emotional response to things was at least as valid as the rational response. You can rationalize a thing until it is wrung dry, but then you cannot dance with it. Men like Einstein had been brought to the brink of their revelations by reason, then the dance had taken over. The process was a whole process, however, not one that deployed our faculties in any willed sequence. In it, emotion and intellect, impulse and decision, myth and mentation unify to make us wholly human, that is — perfectly divine.

It could be that I was pigeonholing women a little too much here, but it seemed to me that the culture of women encouraged this felicitous state. V gave me glimpses of this. She made decisions intuitively, without the painful, linear dialectic that steals so much from men; and her decisions were often more successful, daring and productive than mine. She trusted, she danced. Her emotions were not the chained beasts of male culture, they were tools used instinctively to create her power in the world. Amen.

If female culture is dormant, it may be that it has to lie low while rust completes its work on the iron soul of post-industrial man. Certain strengths persist; patience pays off. The effect of women on the world has been limited in a history written by the conquerors, but the culture of women is larger than history and needs no static definitions of past and future. V's culture was fluid, operating in a fluid world. I was often irritated by her lack of consistency, but, aptly enough, being a fool for love enlightened me. If I slipped occasionally into damning her logical shortcomings, it was only to realize, in my relativistic way, that her female faculties endowed her with something immeasurably more valuable: open-mindedness. She appreciated life as a series of whole phenomena in which events, beliefs, definitions, ideals are part of the flux. If she woke up in the morning and denied completely the answers she had come to yesterday, it was not to invalidate them or to have made a mistake — it was to have progressed to the point where they had changed. If this was the culture of the dominated half of our species, how appropriate that their freedoms should be forbearing and internal. The intuitive flux of their reasoning made them pacific and unthreatening: they had no positions to defend. Even if Darwin was right about the survival of the fittest, they were better equipped for survival and therefore for their role as sustainers. They were moving targets.

Swallowed up in the history of blood and territory that men had written, perhaps women had been the real advancers of the human psyche: the witches and clairvoyants, the earth mothers, the Besants and Blavatskys and Pankhursts, the Kalis who destroyed the overblown powers of men, the soothers, the silent ones. V's culture was a true culture because it was inherently capable of change. Perhaps it was the culture of human antiquity, soon to be reaffirmed; the culture of the original Afrikans, who appear to have understood that imagination and emotion have a validity which is not subsumed to the intellect, with powers of their own, a progress of their own. And they are dormant cultures, not vanquished ones. How apt that the primeval mother of humankind is thought to have been an Afrikan woman. What a boot in the gonads for all held dear in the world of the Great White Western Male!

Mammy!

FOUR

Now in the dark ward, watching my precious one writhe, I realized that only the power of myth and imagination could possibly rehabilitate us. There was no rational answer to a universe in which love and pain coexist, and love contends with the possibility of death. I thought of all the rituals and ceremonies that modern man had dismissed as nonsense, all the women whose cries for peace had gone unheard. If V was typical of her sex, then women have no use for the fleeting comforts of empiricism: only an unfixed world can assuage the pain of childbirth and the indignity of domination. Perhaps men learn in wars what women know from giving birth. Perhaps the culture of women is the culture of triumph over pain, the culture of survival, sustenance and functioning myth. What men search for is under their noses, if only they would care to exchange souls!

It was six in the morning and still I felt no need of sleep. I tried to imagine what it would be like to be confronted with my child. He or she was struggling towards me now, at the end of a long destiny that would lead only as far as a beginning.

Through the term of the pregnancy V and I had felt a mystic impulse that we had been chosen for this child. We began to believe that every child and parent makes this connection in a way unknown on the physical plane. We saw that only the disaffection people in our society felt for the whole business of child-bearing made them blind to this possibility. Before we met, each of us had clung to the notion of a perfect counterpart. Our meeting in the desert was entirely implausible. It could not have been more fateful had we bumped into each other in the darkness of a minor moon of a dead planet in some undetectably distant galaxy.

From then on, nothing seemed accidental. It was impossible that our child was not a part of the collision of events that had preceded it.

At eight o'clock the staff rounds began. Nurses and doctors trundled up like bedouin out of a mirage. V saw them through a cloud of hunger and pain. She was being drawn halfway to heaven to be made ready for the arrival. For me, things looked better in the morning. One of the nurses had come to work without the mental prosthesis that forbids hospital staff from wearing real smiles. V was to be prepared for the birthing room. The nurse, noting my manic alertness, suggested home and rest. I declined; I was damned if I would leave V alone for a second. It didn't matter if she slept through the whole circus, I wanted to be there to watch her dream. The hell if I looked like someone who had tumbled out of a *gulag*. V didn't look all that great either. The child was hurtling in from oblivion to meet a couple of ragged saints of the gutter. I wanted to breathe the night air I had shared with the Monster right in the doctor's face, just to reacquaint him with the institution he ran. They had to know that only the fearsome power of myths and monsters could save us from their sterile machinations. Even if I looked like I had been assembled by a mad scientist, I was sharp as a pin. I was ready for my child's arrival in a way they could never understand. I would have been ready if it had abseiled in through the windowpanes and announced itself as the Messiah. I would have been ready if it had been borne in on the shoulders of cheering Pathans as the late lamented Akoond of Swat.

The doctor poked around inscrutably. We had warned them off any brisk rummaging the night before, following the avid ministrations of the duty nurse. This was done in the manner of talking to small children, everything repeated at least three times.

'She was in great pain at the first examination, Doctor,' I said in my we're-all-men-together-and-they're-just-women-with-waterworks voice.

'My cervix is tilted to one side,' said V through a fog of giggles – and we repeated ourselves with studied patience.

I watched the doctor's face for a glimmer of sentient life. His prosthetic was firmly in place and tightened with a monkey wrench. You don't want to give these civvies any leeway, he was thinking; I have taken the oath of Hippocrates and the power they vest in me grants me the liberty to ignore them. The learned shall always ignore those whom they consider ignorant. In a world of quantified values all human contact shall be a grudging transaction between haves and have-nots.

He mumbled something about inducing the birth and left. He said a few cursory words to me but I forgot them instantly. It is difficult to listen to people who do not extend you the same courtesy. I wondered how many years of training it had taken to deprive him of the ability to communicate with his species. This might produce interesting mutations if Charles Darwin is right: a race of experts degenerated into total aphasia. Who would know the difference? What did he do when he went shopping or to a restaurant? Did he write his orders out on a clipboard or leave it to his minions to interpret signals from the cast of his eyebrows?

Inducing the birth. I got my nouns mixed up and asked the nurse about inducement. The baby would have to be coaxed out with a triple-scoop ice-cream cone or kickbacks on commissions.

'Induction, silly!' The entonox made V strangely attentive to the trivial. Of course, if I looked like Dr Frankenstein's patchwork protégé it was only a short step to demonstrating that my brains were of the order of graveyard offal.

But the nurse would not enlighten us. There is certainly a tacit conspiracy in public institutions that information be withheld to keep the public pliable. This is the essence of bureaucracy. Nothing so undermines a person as the awareness that someone knows more about them than they do themselves. I felt like one of Kafka's Ks. I resolved to make a pretence of deaf-muteness the next time around, conveying everything in writing from a clipboard, preferably in quadruplicate. A piece of paper to a bureaucrat: like feculence to a dog.

V was fully awake now, drying out from the cold sweat of being probed. She looked at me with the wordless sympathy she had had right from the beginning. She could be falling into the abyss, but she would look at you screaming on the precipice and signal: Don't panic, I suspect the impact will be minimal.

'Well,' I said, trying to be flippant, 'another visit from the commissars. Were you able to deduce what happens next?'

'They've gone to fetch an excavator,' she replied dryly, acknowledging that for the moment we had descended to farce. 'If only I could eat! I could murder half the standing beef in Argentina! How are you supposed to push like bejesus if you don't have the strength to fart?'

I had heard that women in labour fell into a mysterious profanity. This made me nervous enough to answer even rhetorical questions. 'Beats me,' I said urbanely. I pointed at the drip that was keeping her ketones from marching up the Rhine. 'That's all the hamburger you're going to get until the little bugger is out and kicking.' She was almost a vegetarian anyway.

She drew in her breath and blew it out in a whistling O. 'God botched it up when it came to women's insides,' she complained. 'The old goat must have had other things on His mind.'

'It's all your fault for getting us kicked out of Eden,' I reminded her.

'Women are pigs!' she warbled, mopping her forehead with a hot towel I had wrung from the nurse.

'Aye!' I grunted, 'and men are sows, doctors ogres, nurses harpies, hospitals haggis factories; inductions are what they do to little babies to prepare them for military school. Do you remember that bit in the John Wayne movie when the footsoldier turns to him in the trenches and says, "It's quiet, Serge," and Big John says, "Too quiet, son," and pow-kaboom! the Boches land the big one?'

'Not at this precise moment,' she said. 'What's that got to do with anything?'

'Well, that's how I feel.'

'Thanks a lot.'

'Did you know that back in the forties or something doctors used to congregate for entonox parties? Used to blow their scientific minds, apparently.'

'Well, fan my brow! You mean they were human once?'

And so we went.

At eleven o'clock the swing doors of the ward were flung wide and V was carted off to the birthing room to be induced. I trotted along behind the trolley with the impression that it was being precipitated down the corridors until, reaching a bay, it would be upended, flinging V down a shute which would deposit her, in her hospital gown, into the midst of a fund-raising dinner for under-privileged mothers.

The porter pushing the trolley was a merry sort. He eyed me leerily. 'Been here long, then?'

'Since the beginning of time.'

'What're you expecting? Boy or girl?'

'We're not particular,' I replied.

He eyed the mound. 'Looks like a boy to me.'

'How can you tell?' I asked.

'Experience, matey.' He waved a knobbly hand in the air. 'You can tell by the wobble.'

I thought it a pity he would not be attending the birth.

The only doctor for whom I could summon any respect was an eleven-year-old boy nicknamed Doc whom V and I had met in Sri Lanka four years before. We had escaped from the desert together after I had made a brief return to bury my prequantum self. We sold everything to the first bidders and threw caution to the four winds, determined to make our way back to the West eastwards around the world. We had about enough money to get to the middle of the Bay of Bengal.

Landing in Colombo we bussed down the coast and disembarked at a town we had picked off the map for its name: Unawatuna. On the beach at Unawatuna (pronounced: Oona-wath-na, very rapidly) Doc materialized from behind a coconut palm, a gangly kid with housemaid's knees and long spatulate fingers. He hacked a coconut open and handed it to V with a straw plucked from behind his ear. V accepted it gratefully, sucking at the straw. Her first instinct was to trust strangers. I was the suspicious one. Because of the way she looked I had tried to build fences around her. She dismantled them gently.

Doc spoke to V. 'Thirstyheat in Unawatuna. Where you sleep tonight?' I restrained myself. Doc looked at me and laughed broadly, showing a prodigious overbite. He turned back to V.

'We haven't quite decided,' V replied. 'Perhaps you could help us.'

I was appalled. We had been warned off street people.

Doc scratched his head, creating a small shower of sea sand. 'You got moany?'

'Money?' V jibed. 'What's that?'

Doc seemed to get the joke. He launched into a rapid sales pitch. 'This coconut good you eat come from my father plantation half-sold because I ambition to go Germany to become doctor. Nowadays coconut not fetch much moany so father says you give free coconut for goodwill to Neckermanns on beach you get goodwill in return so bring them to our house room for rent very cheap very clean good people no daytime robbery. You come stay our house I show you big Buddha temple – you hear of Buddha? – full of mosquito nets and mother's cooking very easy on stomach. I show you moanistry. Doc look after you, you no look like Neckermanns. You call me Doc.'

V extended her hand and Doc shook it vigorously. 'What's a Neckermann, Doc?'

'Bad rich German tooriss who stay big hotels don't bring any moany to Sri Lanka poor people like my plantation father lose half because hotel man want my father land.'

'We're not rich, Doc, and we're not Neckermann.'

'Good!' said Doc, squatting at our feet and folding his spindly legs until his knees framed his face. 'Good you not Neckermann. I say you are to find out you not because Neckermann complain too much and stingy moany. Rich people always too much complain. Sri Lanka people no moany no complain. Air is free, friendships are good, fish are in the sea. You come stay Doc's house and three, four years you moany help to make me doctor come back from Germany and bring good health for Sri Lanka peoples.'

It was irresistible. V looked at me with a glint in her eye. What the hell, we thought, if it was true it was a thousand times better than lining the pocket of some billionaire hotelier with our measly takings from the desert; if it was a line it was utterly impudent and the best sales pitch in the world because it was funnier than the truth. The kid had every angle covered. He waited expectantly, keeping his eyes down and humming a tune. It was up to us.

We were shattered after the bus ride from Colombo. I had read as a boy that the entire human population of the planet could be squeezed into a box a half a mile cubed. This principle was applied in filling Sri Lankan public transport. If Doc's dad's place turned out to be a hellhole we could always light out in the morning. When we picked the town off the map I had been anxious about finding a place to sleep. V had assured me that the gods would provide. She would have slept on the beach if it were up to her, but I was a funk for tropical creepy-crawlies. I depended on her for the confidence that everything would turn out right. Rational fears constrict the future.

Doc squinted at me as if I were unworthy of the company of angels, he and V having established their common divinity. I could see his mind working. He had the psychology of adults all sized up. He had figured the woman as the soft touch, and by ignoring the man would undermine him enough to make him pliable. He had the right candidate for pliability in me. Besides, the kid was a natural linguist. I couldn't remember hearing a more useful version of the English language, the syntax agitated and compressed to convey more in a sentence than native speakers manage in several paragraphs.

Since I was probably the one with the wallet (which I was not), Doc decided to breach the gap. He couldn't have done it better.

He addressed himself to me with solemn gravity. 'I bring coconut for ladymissus now I go back you make decide come Doc's house I come maybe back half-hour bring you special drink make my father's house only up there above beach you see behind you. Very good, clean, beach convenient. You talk make decide I come back bring you mister special drink good for man but not nice for ladymissus.'

'How much will your room cost?' I ventured, instantly mortified at having brought up the subject of cost. I could feel V's disapproval of my reluctance to trust to the Fates. We had no moany anyway, what difference would it make if we spent a good wad of it now? That was V's attitude. Whatever happened we could get by, moany or no.

25

Doc was smarter than that. 'You make decide you come talk to Father he give you special rate because ladymissus so kind and talk respect to Doc not like Neckermann.'

I wondered what subspecies were the fearsome Neckermann.

V and I didn't have to make decide. She saw my caution as a specifically male symptom. Men hedge their bets to keep control of situations, the spontaneous course being fraught with unknown hazards; then when things don't work out they curse their luck, having stoutly refused to believe in luck in the first place. It is impossible to be a coward in the company of a brave woman.

So we sat in silence waiting for Doc, watching the waves of the Indian Ocean crashing against the blackened gneiss that lined the shore. We were tired and tranquil. The prospect of Doc's hospitality suddenly looked very attractive indeed.

A half-hour later to the minute, Doc materialized once more. It was almost twilight. He had changed into long black trousers and a crisp white shirt with holes in the armpits. He looked like a waiter from hell. To complete the picture he bore a grubby tray laden with coconuts and a glass of something tall and fizzy.

'Doc not break promise, see?'

I sipped the drink and discovered the Third World Martini. It was probably the local moonshine, unlicensed arak made under somebody's bed from old coconut shavings. I warmed to Doc instantly. The bite of the arak washed Colombo and six years of desert sand from my throat. My head swam. If he was going to soften me up this way, I didn't mind a bit. V tried a sip of the arak and wrinkled her nose. The dust of Colombo was still on her and her hair was windblown. She looked like Doc, half urchin, half angel. V attracted angels and swore that I was no exception, but I felt old and worldly when I saw her glowing on the beach at Unawatuna.

Doc's place was a squat vermilion stucco on the main road through Unawatuna, a sort of blend of Odeon and Hindu doubtless built by some sunstruck plantationwallah in the feverish days of the Raj. The house had no front door, a fact almost obscured by the throng of women and children spilling out of its portal as we arrived to take up residence. At least two dozen eyes followed V's every move as Doc introduced us to his father. V had wrapped herself in a sarong fished from the meagre supply of clothing we had brought, a vivid tropical print tied tight at her breasts and flapping round her knees. She looked as striking and incongruous as any white woman would who had fetched up in a Gauguin.

Though otherwise bare and threatening hidden grime, our room was dominated by a monumental bed of worked rosewood, regally tented with yellowing mosquito nets. A matrimonial bed, unveiled decades ago by some desperate colonist to coax passion from a frigid memsahib.

To orientate us in this utterly strange environment, Doc had the good sense to issue mild commands. 'You make bath, make fresh come for dinner good special Mother cook then we make party for friend Stereo I invite you ladymissus pretty kind maybe you like disco.'

Bath turned out to be a corrugated tin cubicle open to the skies, with a hose and shower-head flung over the top. Shower pressure was maintained by an overhead tank kept full by a train of children passing a bucket up and down a ladder. Dinner was served on a long table in the kitchen, where, we learnt, Doc and his siblings slept. Their original rooms were now for the tooriss. Doc's mother, a wizened but young woman for such a brood, heaped aromatic rice, fried vegetables and live yogurt on to our plates. Doc ate with us, pushing his food around his plate with his fingers to get the right mix. V followed suit gleefully. The other children gathered around us on the floor and ate with a concert of chewing and slurping reminiscent of Philip Glass. All eyes were fixed on V. Neckermann women do not go native with such abandon.

Doc continued his quest for their common divinity. 'How come you not Neckermann?' he demanded.

Doc's father had enlightened me: Neckermann was the agent who brought elderly Germans to Sri Lanka by the planeload.

V thought for a moment. 'Not all Europeans are Neckermann.'

'So you British. But British not respect Doc. Shoo! they say. Go way not pestering treat like poor boy but Doc father had big plantation and Buddhist religion very very old.'

'The British have a history of bad behaviour abroad,' said V, 'but I am not strictly British. I became British. I was born in Canada and brought up in South Africa.'

'But you not South African. *Viva* Mandela! South African not like brown people, black people.'

'This is true, Doc, but I do. It's a pity about the white South Africans, isn't it? They could have been an example to all races.'

'Sri Lankan like black people, like Bowmali. You like Bowmali?'

'The Bowmali? Are they a tribe? I've never heard of them.'

Doc almost fell off his chair. 'You say you European not hear of Bowmali? Bowmali black make reggae music world reggae king! Sri Lankan love Bowmali! After dinner we dance disco I play Bowmali!' He turned to me, framing his question with a diffidence that suggested I was to be a mere accessory in the evening's entertainment. 'You mister dance disco with ladymissus any time?'

I was daunted at the thought of V and I topping the bill in Unawatuna, and a little sorry that this gentle young man's idea of the apex of Western civilization was the disco. All the dross of the West is sold to the developing world: the bad food, the forbidden drug patents, the coprophiliac consumerism, the disco. The word had a magic in his mouth; if his Doctor story was true, all the West's neon cesspits awaited him, along with the casual inhumanity meted out to his kind in the ghettos of Europe. Some fate for an ingenuous son of Serendip!

V, as ever, was steeped in the present. To mock my unease she wrinkled her nose at me, then beamed at her audience, jiggled her boobs and wagged her shoulders in a spoof disco-frenzy. The children screamed with laughter. All of Unawatuna was alerted.

Stereo, for whom the party had been pledged, was a weather-beaten boy of about thirteen with a cleft in his upper lip. The children called him Stereo because he talked out of both corners of his mouth. Doc put Bob Marley on the communal ghetto-blaster. It seemed a prearranged signal for the whole village to congregate. Doc's old man and I had already worked our way through a bottle of his best arak and my knees refused to bend when V and I danced. She discoed, tangoed and flamencoed wildly and to thunderous applause, plucking grannies and toddlers out of the crowd and setting them awhirl like tops. The whole place was in an uproar.

That night in the colonial bed she took my mental temperature. 'It wasn't so bad, was it? I told you we'd find a decent place to stay.'

'It's bloody good. The old man's arak makes my eyes tingle.'

'They're happy at such small things.'

'Yeah,' I agreed. 'I wish we could be like that.'

Fragments of moonlight fell through the mosquito netting and darted across her cheekbones. 'Really?' she said. 'I thought we were.'

A thunderous crash burst through the walls of the room. We shot upright, clinging to each other. Inches outside the window a laden bus had plummeted past and dopplered into the night.

V first demonstrated her magic to me in those early days. The trust and fortitude she applied to every situation turned us away from many misadventures and made the ordeals we fell into seem only detours from a happier path. Without words she taught me that a change in attitude could avert pain. It was a matter of navigation. Soon, where no pain was expected, none occurred. And yet it was I, with my male logic and premeditation, who thought I could slip out from under when the booms were lowered. If you adjust your imagination you can reinterpret the world. In any given reality, facts are inconstant. My dependence on facts made me an observer and a critic. V's imaginative and emotional spontaneity made her a participant. I felt sorry for myself and for men. It is the male who must be broken by initiation and distanced from the world. Men are trusted to be creatures of discipline, and discipline is not achieved by cultivating the fluidity of one's nature. At some point, the male's spirit is undone. Even his participation is conditioned and at one remove.

As I began, in those Sri Lankan days, to look into V's world, I saw that men, clutching at facts with which to quantify, order and predicate an existence – an existence which had been cautioned out of them – could grasp only meagre solidities. The richness of the flux is forbidden them and makes them leery of optimism. V's world was not an optimistic one for the sake of it. It was so because that is the emotional tenor required to survive in a world in which pain exists. For her facts were secondary; the truth had to be felt as much as deduced. It was not an objective phenomenon, out there waiting to be discovered; it was ineluctably a part of her own emotional reaction to it.

The observed, the observer. What could be simpler? And men had torn themselves with solipsisms!

Then it dawned on me: the uncertainty principle might be written into the nature of women; Western man had succeeded in grasping it only as a set of equations.

FIVE

Now I could adjust my attitude to make this grim mausoleum of antisepsis tolerable. Men of science made little distinction between places of birth and death. In the birthing room V was strapped to a massive bed that hissed hydraulically under the mattresses. An epidural was given her, and we waited while her hips and legs went dead. As the pain faded, her face fell into repose.

Since the threat of further pain had been lifted, I too felt relieved. The lightheadedness of the night before might not have been just the entonox or the starvation. My body had been releasing chemicals to protect me from V's pain. That was a good enough myth for now. In a quantum world endorphins and antibodies might be angels of mercy. If pain was simply a biological safeguard, why did it have to be such an overwhelming sensation? Universal overkill, proof that God exists. Only a will for something could invent pain and overperfect it to this degree, then inflict it on the weak and unprepared, on those whose only recourse is God, on children supposedly still in the lap of God, on women delivering the species anew, on infants tunnelling out of God's uterine dreamworld . . .

How could this be? V was brave when she had to endure pain and grateful when there was an escape from it. A fact of life, for women. For men it is the ancient enemy confronted at initiations or courted to the death. Is this bravery or a broken spirit? Women quelled pain with chants and rituals, as midwives with instinctive soothing arts, cuddlers and strokers, ululators, mourners, brewers in the breastmilk of sedatives and antiseptics; but fathers thrash their boys for crying, and men are taught suppression of their pain. Where does it emerge, finally? We are cumulative beings, our memories of pain hurt sometimes more than the pain itself.

Perhaps there are legitimate channels for the male anguish – the anguish of skyscrapers and missiles, nerve gas, anti-personnel mines, lobotomies, circumcisions, rapes, clitoridectomies, incest, industrial slavery, brainwashing, torture, capital punishment, solitary confinement, xenophobia, economic and political theft – perhaps those channels exist in the closed-off portion of the modern male psyche where the shamans and the myths once abounded. Science has no definition of pain, it is only the enemy; but women have cultivated and seduced it, stroking away the pain of children and of men.

V's optimism was a facet of this nurtured spirit. To dance with pain do not anticipate it; to quell pain do not curse it; to accept pain do not name it the enemy; to understand pain do not imagine that the anger of God is implacable, do not imagine a perfect God. And women had had much experience of imperfect gods. In common with any who have been subjugated they could see that if the condition of life must yield to a definition it must yield to this one: To court power is to idealize pain. Men qualify themselves in this fashion and bring destruction upon themselves, they do not go beyond good and evil to find love. In the fluidity that they have lost and in their illusive primacy as observers and conquerors of nature, their love has become conditional; they seal their scriptures, circumscribe their knowledge and fight their wars that they might capture this imperfect love within the small lives of fear and suppression they have made for themselves.

I looked at V powerless in the great machine with its chemical excretions and wondered if the final tragedy for women might take place in this century of their emancipation, if they might make the same mistake as men and begin to imagine – no, *believe* – that power was the purpose of life. No, women were part of the fluid power of nature and could never become the misfits and artificers that men were. It was left only for men to rejoin the human race by learning the talent of women or remembering what equivalent of it they once possessed.

With no patriarchal God of pain to intervene, it might not matter to women whether or not they acquired the power of men, and men themselves might relinquish their conditioned and peculiar attachment to pain. It would free us all for the realization of quantum choice and become, indeed, the end of history. The exchange of souls, the non-location of the human individual, the surrender of sexual territory – if that was what was needed I was on the right track! Men had appropriated the past and future, but there was always one area of freedom in the present where women bred our comforts. That was where I was headed, backpack, bivouac bag, toilet roll, primus stove, java mug, jack-knife, spotted handkerchief, atom smasher and all!

There at the end of my mission waited V – a version of her that I had not the equipment to understand now, and also a version of myself like that time-projected avatar in Clarke and Kubrick's *2001*. I was looking back on the me who was now, planting these thoughts in my head, sharing the manifold superstrung metadimensional synapses in my brain that were stretching me out thinly across loop after (upon, behind) loop of nonexistent time, backwards, forwards, upwards, downwards, inwards, outwards, towards the event horizons of my life – death, eternity, nothingness; my centre and singularity: V!

The only sound now in the birthing room was the rustle of printout dropping in folds below the monitor. That sound originated, through electrodes, along electronic circuits, in the beating of my baby's heart. He or she was here in the room, generating a soft-shoe-shuffle, whispering, 'I am here, I am here.'

At thirteen weeks we had seen it on a scan. It floated facedown, suspended in the sac, arms folded, legs Buddhaed, eyes bulbous, waiting, watching. A complete being looking down into empty space watching a point where a world might explode into existence. The outlines were iridescent. The spine, showing most clearly against the black swim of the womb, was a downcurving crescent from which silvery haloes hung.

V gave a little gasp when the image resolved out of the blackness and twitched of its own volition. 'Like a line of fireflies!' she whispered.

The monitor turned the baby's signs of life into thin scratches on a chart which leapt into craggy peaks at each contraction. The heart beat faster under the strain. Was it all part of an inexorable biology, the squeezing of uterine walls and the cardiac reply bound together as one inseparable reflex, nature itself preserving the child by pumping blood to withstand the pressure? Or was it the child's first fear of this swamping peristalsis as its world of nine months suddenly came alive and turned hostile? Now it was no longer just V and I, but also this third presence whose struggle, conscious or not, was enacted in real time on a slow cascade of folding paper. Cranial tectonics were turning the smooth-domed foetal skull into a four-faceted steeple of parietal bones. Behind the thin, membranous fontanelle, under which the bones gather like pinching fingers, the doctors had planted a cautionary electrode. But only after a sudden and shocking alarm.

V had dozed fitfully once the epidural had taken hold. I watched every scrape of the stylus on the graph, reading a hieroglyphic biography of the child's last hours in its first world. The monitoring device that fed the signal to the graph was fastened to V's belly by a simple buckle and belt. She turned over in her sleep and the buckle slipped. The line of the stylus flattened out. Somewhere a nurse was alerted. I watched for a moment, then adjusted the belt. The signal resumed.

A nurse hurried in, peered at the graph, hurried out, came back with a doctor who checked the graph again and left mumbling words from which I caught only this heart-stopping phrase: Caesarean section.

V did not want to be unconscious in the hands of these robots. I rushed out after them. 'Look,' I said to the doctor, 'all that happened was that she turned over in her sleep and dislodged the, er, signal pick-up device microphone sensor thingy. I saw it with my own eyes. I adjusted it myself and the signal started up again.'

The doctor said nothing, in the manner of his profession. Perhaps these guys write so poorly because they'd rather not even be read. The nurse returned and rebelted the whole contraption, leaving it less stable than I had. Then she poodled off and returned with yet another doctor who, with the nonchalance of a man taking a pee, inserted the electrode into V and clamped it on the baby's scalp. There was a different doctor for every task. Electrode-clamper. Stylus-adjuster. Pillow-fluffer. Thermonuclear-burn inspector. Clipboard-scrutinizer.

They had wired up my wife and now they had wired up my

baby. The poor little bastard had to cope with grizzly hugs from the walls of the womb as well as bits of metal pinned to the apex of its skull. And while I accepted that all this was imponderably crucial and that the wonderful world of medical science made us safe, I had a few doubts about the relation between the technology and the bleary cyborgs who kept it pumped up. They relied on their instruments, but, of course, the instruments relied on them. Now was this a mutual misunderstanding? The humans appeared somewhat diminished in judgement, timing, intuition; they had been taught to respond to machines and to implement a system in which causes and effects were interpreted to a prescribed pattern. The machines, on the other hand, had not been taught not to slip off bottle-nosed dolphin bellies. Perhaps I was doing them all an injustice. They were victims of the same caution that I was trying to shrug off in my quest for V – the caution that predicts consequences and nudges us towards them in the process. My romantic absorption in the scratch of the stylus had saved V from being cut open and delivered of our child. How would you like to come into the world to find your mother steeped in oblivion?

All along, V's implicit challenge to my cautious demeanour turned me from observer to participant. Otherwise I might have assumed that the doctors knew best. In my former mode I may not have had the temerity to question their conclusions. The missing power of myth makes us all observers, to the point where we will relinquish even our bodies to a process distantly monitored by another band of observers: the 'experts'. They deprive us of the imaginative powers with which we would assist our own cures. In the hours I spent at the hospital looking after V, I became an expert for us both. By immersing myself in the process I took control of events, implanting my own spirit into the monstrous machine and accomplishing my rituals of power on an unknown, unseen level. If I lacked the sedative chants and talismans of the past, I replaced them with an equivalent force derived from my own spirit. The belt slipped again and again, and as each new nurse or doctor responded I kept fresh alarms at bay.

It struck me then that there was nothing wrong with the system or the machine, it was simply that they had not been infused by inhabitant spirits. In the magical world, machines, tools and factories are blessed and breathed into life with invocations to appropriate gods. In our world it may be hogwash to hire shamans and have them spit in the doorway, but any godless ritual with the right noises and the right morale would do the trick. It is harder to become a robot in a place explicitly dedicated to the gods or to some common good.

My love for V had awakened some inner gifts, and it came to me that that is what sex is – the larger sex, the communing between masculine and feminine spirits – an exchange of gifts of power. Not the power of our mortal pursuits, but the power to be forceful participants in events, *equal with events*, combining gifts of either sex to become the third sex, with a range of faculties that lifts us beyond the slavery of circumstance. Was it possible?

At the intersection of past and future is the moment of choice, a latent state where the force that shifts you into the future or causes you to repeat a pattern from the past is the force of will. You choose. This is identical to the precise moment a quantum particle leaps in and out of the void and changes the texture of existence, backwards and forwards into infinity. Your will moves you past the point of stillness; other influences are secondary. You move because you choose to move; you make the choice, even if it is only reflexive. This is the quantum freedom of the individual, and all fixed states are inimical to it. Our institutions, our knowledge and our ambitions as a species ought to derive from this basic awareness of the contingency of all things. Otherwise we remain merely cyclical.

V and I had come to this conclusion in a wordless way. Women may be spared the static sense of history that is enervating our male world with its male institutions. She knew, in a direct way, that only a choice has to be made for all of history to be wiped out in a flash, and this includes, if one is daring enough in the exercise of quantum freedom, our personal histories as well. She had shown me that this is in the fluidity of women's natures. You can reconcile with past selves, you can change your perception of them so that they themselves are changed. You are not fixed even in what you were! Or, you can choose to forget what you were altogether and begin to recreate yourself from this very moment and in every moment that follows it. This is possible simply if you decide it, but to be in love – with yourself, another, the universe, it doesn't matter – provides us with the unity of spirit that makes choices meaningful. And unless one is singularly unfortunate, life presents at different times the conditions to make this possible.

V and I were given the opportunity to experiment with an exchange of souls. But we had to abandon our fixed positions in relation to ourselves, the world and to each other. We felt at odds with the world because we had found in each other the beginnings of a state of benign coexistence, and to us it seemed a potential of humans everywhere. In the face of this, we were expected to conform with modes of existence concocted from fixed states and fixed assumptions – everywhere the individual in opposition to forces within and beyond himself.

Before the pregnancy had distilled V into the present, she and I had had many speculations on how our microcosmic experiment might reflect on the future of the sexes. Was there ever a man and a woman who had attempted to share, in exact measure and wherever biologically possible, all that life presented? The assumption was that there were always biological and social imperatives that forced each into separate roles. The relations of men and women had been structured on this basis, but structures themselves are obstacles to freedoms, abstractions that define what may not need defining. Common sense and mucking through can keep us going together, but if lines are drawn and roles assigned the trap slams shut – we circumscribe individual freedoms in deference to some weird abstraction and become the fodder our societies feed on. And we die as half-men and half-women, having sold our souls and the possibility of kindredness to this abstraction, supposedly to advance the spirits and the materiality of those who follow. How can it be?

So history be damned; whatever the structures and precedents there was no reason why a man and a woman could not undefine the limitations of their sex and fly headlong towards each other. And damn reticence, damn old moralities, damn conditioning – it could all be cast off with a shrug of the shoulders and with the conviction that love and kindredness had to be cultivated, that the whole universe had to be reconstituted in the image of the unified individual who lives on equal terms with life and death.

So much for the world, but our personal histories can also damn us all to hell when we attempt to share our lives. You can get to the point where nothing is transacted between you without the pain of your shared past creeping in. After a few weeks in each other's company you will have defined and fixed each other a thousand times: you will be lumbered with a history of yourself, of the other person, of the two of you jointly, of the other person's perception of you, as well as the other person's versions of all these histories. The only way to wriggle free is to remember that you can obliterate all of it simply by deciding to do so – by making the choice. Then you are free in the quantum sense because you have recognized that all of these histories are merely fixed positions. Your relationship with the other person may then reveal its potential to be what you will it to be in every succeeding moment. V and I began to understand what we felt for each other when we reached that point. It was extremely pleasurable because we could feel our future selves calling. But it wasn't easy heeding the call.

Abandon your respective positions! You cannot dance if either of you stands in one place. In the beginning V moved towards me naturally. It was part of her nature to be obliging. I didn't have to shift myself much, and besides, when you know you are loved, you fall in love with yourself – you don't see much call for change.

This was how we were shortly after we hitched up and went back to the desert to inter our old selves. The desert had little refinement and V needed a few small reminders of civilization. Among these was a set of the most fragile underwear in the entire galaxy. They fluttered erotically on the washing line after each careful wash V gave them, until my brace of black Labradors ripped them off and chewed them to pathetic shreds.

V went ape. Her mask slipped. Every exalted image I had of her was shattered as she rounded on the dogs and then on me. A harridan had burst into our home and taken her over. A fishwife had sprouted out of her, casting off the V I knew like a sloughed skin. I thought it was the beginning of the end. People like us didn't lose our tempers over lingerie. Material possessions. Trivia. My male conditioning required a certain decorum in women.

Even after V had forgotten the whole thing I moped around, thinking the bubble had burst.

Well, men lose their tempers, but women get hysterical. An aggressive show of rage from a woman makes men so insecure, so undermines their stereotypes, that they have to attribute it to her biology. Men may roar and spit as they please, throw global tantrums, slobber and whine, foam and thrash; but a woman's right to rage is consigned to the subterrain of gynaecology. It is as if all the folly of men could be explained away by, say, an archetypal fear of being injured in the balls.

It wasn't V's mask that had slipped, it was mine that had been dislodged. If an aspect of her personality contained my stereotypical harridan, that was my bad luck. I had been busily constructing my personal history of her, as if she had none of her own, wedging her into the mould fashioned for my own male prejudices, to shape the future from the past, to fix my image of her permanently so that she would always remain precisely as I wanted her – a possession, a *thing*.

I was the one who had to move.

When I spoke of it, she looked at me wide-eyed and a little wry. 'All that because of a tantrum?'

I extricated myself from the situation with whatever dignity I could salvage, feeling faintly like Oliver Hardy when it was time to pay the bill.

If you attempt to define the person you love, you deny both of you the room to change. The only reason we are so misguided is because we suffer the delusions of linearity, believing that we progress through some kind of cumulative development that will result in a desirable fixedness of being. We expend large amounts of energy trying to fix ourselves in relation to others and them in relation to us. But love is an expansive phenomenon that cannot be preserved in a selected state. Paradoxically, the constancy of love may be attainable when we cease our attempts to fix it and turn our imaginations to its possibilities.

However, I was still grovelling around in the pit of conditioning when we left the desert and V was able to shed her accidental purdah. The Great White Wonderful Western City was filled with a great many men; it was hard enough to face down the man in myself without having to contend with the rest of my sex. V's ability to light up a room now discomfited me. It was my opinion that her personality, which she shielded from my misgivings, gave ambiguous signals to men. There is a trampled border between protectiveness and possessiveness in the male. Once again the traffic was all one way: women must be restrained because men suspect they cannot trust each other not to be casual voyeurs and mental rapists. Purdah is the monument to this in the East, but the West has its own forms of it. And for the male, biology becomes a convenient premise, it being a helpless and rather endearing characteristic of his to be furtively priapic.

To set me right, V had to remind me about something I had pontificated upon endlessly: fidelity. I had decided that fidelity could be conjured into our lives *a priori* and applied with rigour. V didn't need such convoluted measures to believe in the same thing, and wasn't about to curb herself in public to mollify my rather cerebral insecurity. Ah well, it was time for me to move again. Many moves had to be made before I was sufficiently undermined to begin to remake myself. As I say, it was all in a good cause.

To be properly in love is a fine exercise in self-deconstruction, but until the process is complete men must juggle their masks like banshees. Their sexuality, what they know of each other from themselves, their consequent suspicions, must all be alloyed in impenetrable metals until there is no danger of fallout. For now, glimpses of thighs or cleavage, strapped ankles or rolling *glutei maximae* will yet unleash the poor Neanderthal. He, in turn, must be reconciled with that other pathetic figure that lurks within, the furtive aesthete, or the chap who puts women on pedestals. Roll on the day when we can put both these geezers to rest and celebrate the beauty of women! Sexuality is not circumscribed by the search for the orgasm. There were precedents for this fortunate state in old Polynesia, before the missionaries unsheathed their holy scalpels.

In old Afrika, similarly blessed, the paradigm of beauty was fertile woman, and here lay V, after a nine-month apotheosis from one paradigm to another. Some men have sunk so low in taste as to find the pregnant female form unbeautiful.

Lying on the birthing bed, massive belly hung to one side, eyes distant with waiting and hunger, hair enriched by hormones, areolae aglow, hips unlocking, V was a living archetype of beauty. What I deduced from this was that our aesthetic also must be fluid, else we could not remain in love.

That it should not be immutable, that the narrowness of the Greeks should be balanced with the sentiment of the Afrikans seemed to me to be a worthwhile notion. That way, love persists by means of change and passion itself can evolve rather than turn to nostalgia. A quest for the unification of souls must retain some driving force. I had stumbled upon an aesthetic that could sustain it.

SIX

Can predestination exist with choice? We had spoken often of a feeling that the child had been chosen for us. I could not help suspect that my revelations had been timed precisely for the few hours before its birth. Nothing could so equip us for what lay ahead as this intimation of another universe of love. There was a quickening in my discoveries of V and in larger aspects of myself that was culminating here, with the emergence of our child. We were reaching critical mass together.

V was emotionally attached to a scheme of things in which predestination did not make free will impossible. At first, I could not see this except as a tolerable paradox; I could not feel it. Her knowledge was direct and not influenced by any dominant faculty such as male logic. I myself was in a shadowland where, sensing the nature of the quantum, of parallel universes, of simultaneous time, I could no longer admit the validity of choices other than those I made consciously. V explained this away: consciousness is too narrow a territory from which to govern all choice; our being has causes and effects larger than the compass of the rational will. To me, if a thing was outside my rational comprehension it precluded choice, but there was one incident that forced me to unfix my position and throw a lot of old baggage into the void.

After almost a year trying unsuccessfully to conceive, V decided that we had created an internal barrier against the intrusion of a third person – the child. Room had to be made inside the bubble. Blow me if I knew where she cooked that one up!

Moving blindly, we signalled the Supreme Council of Anthropocosmogonic Affairs, Blastocyst Husbandry Department (or whoever!) and the barrier was henceforth removed. A few days afterwards, the child was conceived. We knew it at the time: in that particular session of lovemaking there had been a release beyond that of orgasm. Such direct, emotional knowledge rarely came to me without a filtering through my nit-picking persona. I could usually maintain my rugged masculine scepticism even in the face of a patent miracle, but that night I was booted up to the universe on the other side of the orgasm, where ecstatic knowledge exists. It is there that we make the choices we don't know we make. Great! Who needs unfeeling cogitations when we can leap through a burning portal into a state of knowing beyond all words, and a shared state at that? Who wants to miss all that fun?

V had known all along, in her wordless way. It occurred to me that if men could undo themselves sufficiently they would know as well. They would cease to be ruled by mental detritus such as logical paradoxes and the false opposition of predestination and free will. If Zen has goals, the unification of opposites is one of them, leading to a state of questionlessness. And Zen may be in the soul of women. They have no need of the discomforts of philosophy; they have transcended it. To study knowledge is to misapprehend it, and to pursue it is to assume that it is elusive.

Could it be that if there was a superior soul in our species it belonged to women? If evolution was partial in its gifts might it not have given the sustainers the key that unlocks the hidden territories of our existence? Was Adam a blue funk, passing it down to his misbegotten sons that their old lady was a harpie who had had it off with a boa constrictor, that archetype of male penis-envy, when, in truth, she had offered him the permanent way out of his limp-willed obeisance to the bearded Old Coot in the sky?

V was not given to such excesses, and put all questions of superiority down to the male compulsion for ordering things, for reductiveness, hierarchies and power. Me? I had been unlobotomized; I had no questions left, and what a relief! I wanted to shake V awake in the birthing room and tell her that all our miracles – the meeting in the desert, the quantum pact, the escape from loneliness, the penniless, precipitous existence, the dismantling of histories, the anthropocosmogonic conception, the line of fireflies, the invested spirits of the monstrous machine, had all come together to make one big miracle: my transformation.

I was casting off all definitions of myself that were limited by my sex. I was about to be born, at the same time as my own child. The iconic fertility of women made births and rebirths possible. V was giving birth to me no less than to the child. She had moved her biology with the force of direct knowledge towards the act of conceiving, and she had used something of the same force to propagate a mortal apotheosis in the person she loved.

She stirred and gazed at me for a moment. She knew something. On a cellular level she was aware of her accomplishment. Goddesses live among men, and if men were not gods it was only because they had subverted their own knowledge to mortality. Now they must know that there was a uterine wisdom, and learn again the equivalent knowledge that lay in the old deification of the phallus. If women needed no memory and no logic to create miracles, men had to recapture some literally seminal divinity. Then our oppositions would be wiped out, the nature of the undiscovered sex revealed. True men and true women leading to a greater truth. Sexuality as a generator of more than species. True love and true humanity. True myths and true rationality.

All these had lost the original power of uterus and phallus, a power of propagation, of sex, of fertility, but also the power of the undiscovered sex, which was a power within the wholeness of humanity, indivisible from the knowledge that unifies us with each other and with the universe; the Big Bang as indivisible either by time or scale from the marriage of sperm and ovum; the first second of existence indivisible from the unlocatable nanosecond of penetration of the sperm into the ovum; the quantum timelessness of existence indivisible from the ecstatic annihilation of the orgasmic moment; the quantum of sex, the quantum of love, the quantum of consciousness – all indivisible; love and consciousness as one, as the double helix of psychic DNA, as the singular and ineffable force beyond our rational perceptions, but out there and in here, generating everything, holding everything together; love and consciousness: the absolute, final and undeniable nonmaterial expression of our selves and our universe. There it was! Before my eyes, in my own body, thrusting out my child, heaving my wife's body; there it was! the quantum entity, the wholeness, the pervading force, the continuous wave. I knew it, sensed it, it was me, it was V, it is you! Finally, finally! God in heaven! Here it was! *The Unified Field!*

V's body gave a great shudder and she called out. The doctors were coming in. They gathered around. My child was arriving.

In a small café, six years before but as if it were now, in a place unseparated by time and distance, V stands before me, her eyes lifted to mine, her body brushing mine, her breath upon me.

She is saying, 'I think it would be a good idea if you and I spent the rest of our lives together.'

SEVEN

If time does not exist except as an extrapolation from the growth and movement of organisms – and we could argue that all known states are organic, the universe and matter simply inanimate organisms disappearing in and out of supposed entropy – then the substratum of events is simultaneity.

Rocks live at a pace so immeasurably slow that to them human lives are squashed into little blips of time that might as well go backwards, forwards or exist not at all for their brevity. If you are a rock, an aardvark or a chief of police you are still a blip to the bearded Old Coot, and everything that happens to you between living and dying, waking and sleeping, mating and decrepitating, happens to you all at once.

If you accept that everything that exists and happens to you doesn't exist and happen to you unless you think it does (you even have to think about the things that don't exist and don't happen), and then if you try to imagine how fast a thought is thought, you realize that thoughts, events and existents are instantaneous. They pop in and out of an indefinable measure of time and are only then captured in the linear illusions of speech or sense data. At the moment a thought is born it is preverbal. You can conjure up a thought as large as the universe in less time than you can think about. You are a simultaneous being.

The head of my child, slick and furry dome burrowing out of V, a featureless thing blindly infatuated with the idea of existing, gave me the first view of flesh propagated by my flesh. Or had I seen it before? Some months before I had had a dream that joined me with this moment of meeting my child. The dream had no sequence; it was like one complete and fleeting thought – a dream thought. In it I awoke still abed and bare-chested, to find a baby nestling on my chest. The warmth and weight of the infant, its movements and sounds of breathing and nuzzling, were sensations inseparable from the sensations of my own body. In the dream, my entire body was thinking a thought and this thought was the child and my body was the thought. Dreams interchange phenomena: the sensations of my body and the child were also a dark and liquid feeling of profound love, a sensation before analysis, the word not yet flesh. The love was not directed, it did not have as its object the child or the sensation itself: it *was* the child, me, the sensation. In the Unified Field, sensations, emotions, cognition, thought, time, sequence, are a bounding great singularity (which, come to think of it, might make a proper Unified Field, not just a post-reductionist amalgam of strong and weak forces).

Now, as a forehead and scowling brow edged from nontime into a temporal world, I felt that same sensation once again. This time, its totality was constituted of other sensations as well: if you can be in awe, in fear, in love and lucidly hallucinogenic all at once – which you can – then that is what I felt. But the connection between this moment and the moment in the dream was now clear. In fact, I realized that there were three events that I could link which had emerged from the substratum of time to proclaim themselves inseparable: the moment of my child's birth, the liberation that accompanied its conception and the appearance of the child in the dream were united. There was a precausal link between them: I could easily say that the dream had caused the orgasm had caused the conception had caused the birth, but this would be somewhat prosaic and empirical. The unified quality or sensation of the three events made it equally valid to say that any one had caused the other, backwards or forwards in linear or nonlinear time, or that they were of a piece, so phenomenally complete that they were their own cause and their own effect – singular manifestations of an underlying unified phenomenon.

If I could I would have reached out and touched the baby's head, but the doctor, a woman, it transpired, was sitting astride a metal stool heaving at forceps with dogged rigidity, her whole body leaning back at an absurd angle. Mayday! Mayday! Baron Von Richthofen hauled the rudder back as his wounded Messerschmitt boomed out of the sky.

I stood on V's right, clutching her hand and stroking her forehead, balancing the nurse's raucous cries of 'Push, darling, push!' with a litany of my own. V bawled and screamed from the effort of each push and partially, I think, from her dislike of the endearments of strangers. Leaning forward slightly I could see, peeping over V's mons veneris, the pate and brow of the child as it did a swift swivel through a hundred and eighty degrees, a quick horizontal about-turn on a precise axis, like a homuncular sergeant major. There was a furrow between the eyebrows, a scowl of effort or distress or concentration, the anonymity of the blind dome turned into a facial expression – sentience – but with the eyes still submerged, like a person about to drown. Seeing the turn, the doctor dug her flying boots into the linoleum and cursed throatily. She gave a final tug. Then, face crinkled in protest, fists clenched in a somatic reverberation of the word *no*!, shoulders springing back from the release of pressure, arms floating at the sides like a diver flippering to the surface, abdomen drawn in to squeeze vacant lungs, back arched aerodynamically, legs rigid, the child – in one eternal thrust of the human form against nothing-ness – dived into the world, hauling a crumpled, bloodied parachute behind it.

'Is that it?' asked V, trying to peer at her undercarriage.

'You've done it!' I hissed, as if she had just won a race.

The nurses and doctors converged on the flying form as it shot out into mid-air. I could see a long, smooth back as they turned it over to clear the nasal passages. I could hear a small bird coughing as they used tubes to clear the passages. There were snipping sounds, then three words, *words* from a voice that, unmistakably, has never spoken before in the history of the universe, spoken by someone who does not know they can produce sound.

Now, set your metronome at eighty-six beats per minute and say the three words on three consecutive beats, the first clearly and with a hint of surprise, the second with a tiny glottal stop midway through a roundly diphthonged first vowel, the third as if you have suddenly woken up and, not remembering where you are, realized that you are in your own bed – all in faint Donald Duck vibrato. Say the three words the child said as it was transported through the air rigid as a marble cherub; say,

'*Oh. O-oh. Oh.*'

Nobody else said a word, naturally. I peered and squinted and edged forward like a man trying to get his head over a crowd. The doctors did a sort of dance and shuffle as if they were all held up on strings. The light of the room looked like the light in an Ingres, flat and homogeneous to each surface. After the tubes gurgled clear, the paediatrician stepped forward and enclosed the child in her arms, turning it away from me, laying it on a table and hunching over it. I crept around to her shoulder.

'You have a boy,' she whispered as she counted fingers, toes and orifices.

He lay quite still, eyes almost closed, head rocking slightly, like a blind person listening for something.

'Is he all right?' I asked.

'Perfect,' she said, curtly.

I couldn't take him all in at once. I forgot to look at his face. All I could see was this whole human being. Whole but very small.

I looked back at V. She was being sewn up.

The paediatrician lifted the boy and turned back to V. 'You have a lovely boy,' she said rather formally. 'Do you want to hold him?'

I stationed myself at V's shoulder. The paediatrician deposited the boy on V's belly. V cradled him.

'Is this it?' she asked.

Under the lights, his head rocking and rolling, lids crinkled and eyeballs sliding off to the corners, he tried to pull things into focus. I was astonished. Nobody had told me that newborn babies appear to know something. What he knew was that there was something out there and he had to get his vision round it. That was the least he knew. There was a wilful effort to make sense of the swim of light and colour that confronted him, a distinct attempt to fix on something.

'Is this him?' said V narcotically.

'God!' said I, wanting some word larger than God.

We watched his eyes as they swung from corner to corner. In each swing he was picking up more information and trying to still the eyes long enough to focus. Blink, blink. Each arc of trajectory got smaller and smaller until, with the small oscillations you see when you watch someone gaze out of a moving train, he decided what it was he wanted to look at, *look* at, and the eyes were almost still.

He was looking directly and calmly and consciously into our eyes. V's, then with a little wander, mine, then back to V's, having made his first mental note of where things were, then back to mine. Very self-possessed for something fifty-two centimetres long, I thought. Someone had told him what to look for. And still he hadn't cried, just made little croaks deep in the throat. There was nothing to raise a ruckus about. He had the situation all sized up.

How astonishing it is when something is there that wasn't there before! The Big Bang is less impressive, being somewhat faded in our memories. Where had this little soul emerged from? Not from V. What had been inside V had been a part of her; this was an individual with empty space around it, occupying the volume of water that it would displace. Moreover, this was a sentient individual with eyes that surveyed, in their own erratic fashion, the space it did not occupy. Where the head lolled, the eyes reconnoitred.

I tried to imagine how those first moments felt for the boy. I could think only of the time when, falling down the dark and insulated chute of sleep, you burst out of unconsciousness, crash-land silently as the soundtrack comes in a second late, and, as it sprockets in with your startled vision, blows up the whole world.

Critical moment.

The nurse says, 'Try him on the breast, darling.'

V is abashed. Now suddenly she is asked to offer up an intimate part of her body for the sustenance of this myopic stranger. It is not unlike being asked for your wallet in a dark alley. She fumbles. The nurse, with an assurance that comes of handling other people's parts entirely outside the realm of sex, reaches over, clips two fingers on a nipple, turns it up and inserts it into the boy's mouth. The action of the fingers is that of a Hollywood mogul propping up a fat cigar for a sycophant to ignite. I remember reading somewhere that the upturning of the nipple facilitates the infant's grip, which is implemented between tongue and upper gum, the lower jaw driving the tongue up and down against the gum to form a bellows between tongue and hard palate. The adult equivalent is seen when people who fork their food into their mouths stick their tongues out prodigiously to receive it. Only the Queen of England has put this habit behind her.

The boy gags and lolls, missing the nipple, but now activating new neck muscles and optical nerves in concert to grab it on the next pass. Somewhere in his brain, trajectories, perspective, parallax and foot-pounds per square-inch are being computed billions of times a second to turn him into a suckler; a ball of incandescent flame is coursing along uncharted neural pathways, throwing off a zillion virtual baryons in its wake until, finding the chamber where all the right tunnels intersect, it booms out of existence and illuminates the whole catacomb at once. His head thrusts forward at precisely the right angle; his jaw, tongue, lips, gums, soft palate, uvula, pharynx, larynx and lungs are all galvanized into a configuration now imprinted into the catacomb – which is already a pillion times more complex, convoluted and beautiful than the caves at Lascaux – and he clamps on the nipple at the exact second that gizmopods, vacupods, and all other sucking things all over the known universe find purchase on that which sustains them. Then, brain impulses from the catacomb travel down through the shoulder and arm, brachiating into the five fingers and sweeping the interfaceable thumb in a graceful arc towards the waiting tip of the crooked index finger. Through a process of quantum nonlocation, baryons under the cup of V's breast stir up a cyclone of corresponding activity in the tiny fist and it is drawn up to the glaucous, pendant hemisphere like a planet plunging back into the sun. There it rests, a small complexity on a very large and homogeneous surface.

I can tell that V is mortified. She is confronted with the otherness of this thing. It has attached itself to her in an arbitrary fashion. She is more than the sum of the hormones which are supposed to have prepared her for this moment. They might have turned her hip joints to jelly and decanted judicious amounts of colostrum into her breasts, but they have not embroidered the sentiments of spontaneous maternity on her brain. That, after all, might be a cultural imposition. After the cataclysm of birth, it is hard to see how nature would turn into the Blessed Virgin Mary

KEN FEGRADOE

and zap the neonatal mother into a state of transcending infanto-
philia. Nevertheless, it is a matter of interpretation.

'He is not at all what I expected,' says V. 'He doesn't look
anything like I expected, though I don't know what I expected
him to look like.'

I make small talk. 'He has large eyes,' I say, 'which is what I
expected since both of us have large eyes.' An inspired retort.

We certainly didn't expect him to look like this. Like Rocky
Marciano blowing up a balloon after a bare-knuckle fight. The
marks of the forceps still on his temples. Streaks of dried blood
left by the paediatrician. The brow bruised. The lips puffy like a
wino's. The hair post-nuclear. The four-faceted steeple where I
thought there was a dome, the top of it drawing circles in space
like the prow of a sinking ship. The purplish hue of oxygen
starvation. The lolling, lolling, lolling, sucking, sucking, sucking.
A mouth with a thorax, limbs and periscopic eyes. A button nose
with pupil-sized nostrils quivering round the breast hoovering
pheromones. The weighty penis and empty scrotum draped over
the perineum like a downed zeppelin. The knees springing up to
the foetal position. Feet scattered through the air so that there
seemed not two but many. An octopod.

If love ought not to evolve into possessiveness then perhaps
possessiveness might, under benign circumstances, evolve into love.
What is pride of possession? All I felt now was that this creature
was mine. It belonged to me. I owned a living being. Never before
had I owned a living being, though not for lack of trying. I had
owned a motor bike, a drumkit, an ornamental bathtub, a bowler
hat and a set of calligraphic pens, but I had never possessed a living
soul. Nor was I comfortable with this welling up of pride in
something accomplished ostensibly by hormonal drives and chemical reactions. A motor bike is purchased through the effort of work.
A baby is created and owned through a process of decisions which
you suspect are not entirely your own. Paternal pride is corny. It
belongs to the crew-cut machismo of the fifties. Would I hand out
Havanas to celebrate a phallic accomplishment? This creature had
nothing at all to do with its origins in benign lust. Sex is the
manipulative scam of the genetic imperative. What was I feeling?
Was it pride or something discomfitingly primeval?

52

Nothing in my overcrowded mind prepared me for the sentiments I now attached to a being a few minutes old. Just as his neural pathways were being set ablaze, my own mind was being prised open and found empty but for resonances and echoes from the future. They could make no sense of this numinous thing-in-itself that wagged its legs in the air and dangled from V's veiny cup. There is no account of the point at which even emotion becomes superfluous, at which the weight of events is so overwhelming that only existence itself can be acknowledged, at which all the questions you can ask yourself rebound off an empty, black and invisible solidity that says to you simply: I am here. No account could have been written of it other than in a collection of blank pages in a book without covers, no song sung of it other than by a larynxless, lipless, whisperless being, no painting made of it other than one formed in the artist's brain and evaporated in a movement of his wrist while he lay in the deepest coma.

The first few moments of the arrival of a new human being confront you not with inevitable joy, though that is there, not with pride, though that is there, not with elation, though that is there, not with relief, though that is there, not with ecstasy, for you are tired, not with fear, for you are beyond it, not with foreboding, for that is to come, not with love, for that is not what you might feel, but with wordless, selfless nothingness. And it must be the same in every moment when you are obliged to ask yourself: From whence did this thing come?

Baron Von Richthofen washed up and left, striding out in imaginary jodhpurs, without, as they say, so much as a backward glance. To her, nothingness was a complete and everyday experience. She had no questions left, only a job to do, wresting homunculi from supine and recalcitrant women day in and night out like a plumber of the damned.

Something possessed me to run after her and hail her from down the corridor. 'Doctor!'

She turned briefly, her face expressionless.

'Thank you!' I shouted.

An eyebrow twitched, she turned again and hurried on.

V and the boy were removed to the ward, then the boy was taken to wherever it was the babies congregated. I hung around.

A large night nurse with a fearsome coiffure eyed me suspiciously. She drew herself up to what should have been her full height, but instead seemed to expand laterally. 'It's time you went home!' she bellowed.

I got the hell out.

Dusk. Or was it? The world boomed. Blue, infinite sky. Me razor-sharp from my transmogrification. I got in the car and the car drove itself to a restaurant near home.

There was nobody in the restaurant. I ordered a huge dish of something. I drank an enormous cocktail of something blue. I raised my glass to the waiter.

'Just had a son,' I announced, out of the blue.

'Congratulations, sir!' he said in a broken accent, enunciating each syllable with equal stress.

I went home and fell into bed. How do you sleep when you have split in two? There is a facet of yourself abroad in the world, a *doppelgänger*; but which of you is real? The way you feel now, you are definitely the ghoulie. A part of you has split off and now occupies a space in the universe, except that it was not a part of you – it arrived out of nowhere. Just as you once did. Just as you do now, in every moment. It is being born again, but more: being born again in every second as somebody new entirely; existing with the illusion of self, when self is really rather unnecessary and one is happiest when the ego is transcended and the self becomes multiple or oceanic.

Now I knew that to become someone else is a condition of being alive. A collection of virtual selves, with a real self emerging now and then only as a matter of illusion or consensus. But the real self rather unattractive and stifled, always a throwback to that which one tried to fix in one's character: a prejudiced ego, a jaundiced persona, and so on. How did it feel, now? Who was asking these questions? I did not know. I fell asleep. The world went out like a ship's lights over a dark horizon. An ocean of nothing was left, whispering its presence, invisible in the dark. I was afloat on it. It was taking me back. There was to be a burial at sea.

EIGHT

Now the past is a dreadful burden until you rehabilitate it. All the forms you take and the things you form have to drag your past along with them. Perhaps that is what turns us old, this increasing weight of the baggage we carry. Turn over new leaves at a whirring rate, however, unself yourself in every second and you can at least take comfort in some kind of constancy of intention, an ineffable core of yourself that is beyond time and forever forward lunging.

How to put it? V had turned me into a being continually thrust forward. My nose inhabited the future and my eyes were always at the horizon. I could no longer see any sense in being a referent for my own past except as a force for change of that past itself. The past lives on in memory, but it does not live on independently, as something fixed: it is an evolving fiction. You write it as you remember it, obliterate it as you reminisce; you tell the lie and the lie tells you; the lie becomes the truth and the truth dissolves into falsehood once more, but the dialectical relationship is an unnecessary artifice once you have become a virtual soul or a quantum being.

V recognized this instinctively, as always. She could venture into the past and rescue either of us from a retrospective false-hood. I had the uncanny sense that past follies could be redressed and the fictional characters we were absolved and defined anew, comforted, at least for the time being. By logical extension, our present selves were also being drawn into the future by the beneficence of what we were to become. To exist in love is to have the freedom to explore all possibilities of the self without the constraints of time. There is no present, only a moving point which you may observe gladly. The arrival of the boy had turned me into someone else, undefined and unreconstructed. Now it would be an interesting exercise to rehabilitate the person that I was, even as my future self was reaching back to offer an eternal means of escape from the present. Such things must occupy our days! Thus I reached back to the man who had escaped from the desert and arrived once more in the Great White Western City. I did not know then that to comfort a past persona one need only mourn for a few moments. The tears you shed now can heal the remnants of sadness that cling to you. Retrospective-self therapy. It is possible. The old selves are comforted by your mourning and your absolution and they will rest in peace or rush to join in celebration of this new metachronic freedom. This is a quantum penitence, in which all things are forgiven and all crimes recompensed. Only the illusion of time hardens us enough to be unforgiving of what we were or reticent in what we might become.

Back! Back!

Questions echoed round the catacomb. How did the boy come into being? Answer the question and you will discover who you are. Discover who you are, and you will learn, at least for the time being, who the boy might be.

Back! Back!

I should not speak for women, but I will stick my neck out for men and say that it is a condition of men to mourn their childhood. I can only surmise, though it may be unreasonably romantic of me, that the sole experience of free and unconditional love a man may have is in his childhood, and even that, God knows, is pitifully brief. Thence on he joins the stomping ranks of the walking wounded.

If you are a man you may cast your mind back to a time, however fleeting, when your universe was pervaded with a certain quality. This quality was connected with all kinds of distinct phenomena: clarity, absorption, a unity, outwardness, inwardness, timelessness, a sense of being, a sense of the goodness of others, of the goodness of yourself, of an infinity of possibilities, of the keenness of sex, of energy, of invulnerability. These might be at least some of the constituents of unconditional love. They may have been lost or perverted or beaten out of you almost at once, but if you cast your mind back there is certainly one identifiable instant in your childhood when they all come together. It is not to do with a loss of innocence; that is a relative notion. It is rather the loss of a sense of knowing – an empowerment and wholeness that is the condition of being in love.

Let me dig down further into it and see if the experience of one man can be proposed for the rest of the sex. This love, given that you were minimally fortunate in the material conditions of your childhood, encompasses many objects, and for each it reserves a distinct quality. That is what makes it rich and whole. When the object of it was your mother, it was like a remnant of the umbilicus. Here was someone, the *first* someone, with whom you could recall a seamless physical intimacy, a being who embodied your archetypal notion of trust and in whom sustenance was without limits. When it was your father, it was the miracle of a love at one remove from the physical bond, proof that love was universal and could function at a distance beyond that your mother occupied. Then, when it became love of yourself, it was the sense of a perfect balance between you and the world, a vantage point held within, from which you could observe or participate in a world constituted of benevolent things.

There is a part of me that hoots derisively at this glowing hypothesis for the past of all men, yet I cannot imagine that any of us would survive with the capacity for even the most demeaned love were it not for some vestigial memory of this ideal state. The inwardness of childhood, the terrible aloneness of being a child, would have made us all autistic but for the fact that we were enclosed in an environment in which trust was possible.

But then what happens? The tragedy of a male childhood may be that it is a prolonged term of learning the limitations of things, in the West of growing into the beautiful but sterile balance of the Greeks, who would explore only the limits of the possible. It is a thousand initiations and a thousand castrations, circumcision and circumscription, a grooming for war or a Darwinist destiny. Along the way your mother becomes a lachrymose harpie, as your perception of women is subverted, as you define them in terms of your own male power. Why? Because the power of women can never be acknowledged without betraying the fact that you have lost the ideal love and that your power for love is now acceptably circumscribed. Then you lose your father also; your initiations have made you more powerful than he, in his waning light. His bequest to you is a mantle of power, the limited power of the male. He bows out, leaving you with the knowledge that you must make a similar relinquishment one day.

And what of your love of yourself? Now you are the fully fledged self-subversive. Your self-love has become anything but itself in a thousand hard disguises, a sort of theatrical procession of maniacs and zombies, everywhere the males marching in step, everywhere the self-love of the child turned to egotism, aggression, anguish, greed, animal cunning, noble scepticism, sterile rationality, caution, false courage, bloodlust, rapacious possessiveness, suspicion, indifference, and in the final spectacular exit, the panoramic horror, the horror of Colonel Kurtz, Pol Pot, Himmler, Torquemada, of the classical model of the subverted male child, Caligula, of the phallic power of intercontinental ballistics and the glandular fantasies of nuclear fission. My Daddy can lick your Daddy any day.

This is the dreadful past of the civilized male. It is the history I am trying to dismantle for myself in order to understand where my child came from and where he is bound.

Back!

What is the primary condition of the newborn human being? If you are minimally fortunate, the very first hunger that is written in the catacomb is immediately satisfied. You reach out, all mouth and trauma, all hormonally catalysed, to find that your sustenance has not been snipped away with the umbilical cord. A close run thing! From an empirical point of view, it is unsafe to assume that this is more than merely instinct, an imprinted hunger searching for an imprinted object with which to satisfy itself. However, science is incapable of defining instinct without reductions *ad absurdum* into an evolutionary past with great gaps in it. It tumbles back into a causal vacuum. Instinct is itself an ineffable phenomenon! It is left to our emotions, those parts of ourselves that function in a precausal simultaneity, in the wordless universe, to attempt, paradoxically, some sort of definition. And then we are taken even further back.

Back!

After a few months in the womb, our senses are activated. Somebody switches on all the lights. We begin to react to external stimuli. Perhaps the first sensations we feel cannot be separated from the emotions they cause. The infant has not yet donned Sartre's mantle of the being-for-itself. If there is no evidence that prenatal humans feel emotions in any sense that adults can define, then we must assume that their reactions are wholly existential and noncognizant. This means that when the foetus sucks its thumb, it does so wholly unaware that it is giving itself pleasure; when it listens to the voices coming in from the outside it adjusts itself not out of some prototypical curiosity; when a sudden movement makes it jerk it is not out of some minuscule rejection of discomfort.

Well, we haven't yet the right to deny that what we are looking at is a being that may be sentient in its own impenetrable way, before it emerges from the birth canal. Blank slates are for boneheads.

Now: if you take this sentient being, and, the moment it emerges into the world, plug a warm nipple into its mouth and make the right sounds, its first reaction to the world is to reassure itself that everything is fine after all. God exists and is good, he or she would say, if it knew anything about God. What is more, it arrives fully equipped with information as to what to look for. Its first experience of the world, its first world, is seamlessly connected to it; it is an intimate of the universe and the first terrestrial emotion it experiences is the emotion of love. What else can it be? It began in the Unified Field of love, in the moment of orgasm; it passed down through the Unified Field of love in its utterly spontaneous and unprecedented awakening of the senses; and it emerged into a physical reduction of the Unified Field with which it discovered a seamless intimacy – which it itself *was*. It gave birth to itself. It gave birth to the world. Same thing.

We give birth, all, to angels.

Can it be true? Can it be anything but?

The huge and ostensibly superfluous neocortex began to create the world the moment it enfolded its last and indispensable convolution. When it reached critical mass it began the reciprocal dance with creation, like a dark star dances with its twin. If creation was there *a priori*, even in temporal terms, then creation fed it with the stimuli which it recognized and fed back to it: reciprocal, reflexive cognition. If creation was not an *a priori* existent then it is and was the Unified Field itself, spontaneous consciousness being born like the birth of God and bringing All That Is into existence with it, backwards and forwards in time and out of time. Who cares which comes first? In a nontemporal universe – and we have it on reliable record that that is where we live – we might as well have created the whole shebang as have been created by it. What really matters is that the process itself appears to be one in which the existence of love is inseparable from the existence of consciousness. Love is consciousness is the Unified Field, the thing that pulls everything together.

Diversion. Now, a little exercise in creating something out of nothing. Turn to page 62, and note that page 62 consists entirely of the words 'order' and 'disorder' printed in no particular order. Were we to repeat the word 'order' right through the page, it would fall into ordered columns and all you would have is a regular pattern, repeating itself in the most boring and cyclical way. This is the scientific version of history.

On the very same page, you will note that the word 'disorder' has been inserted every so often, in no particular order. The addition of the semanteme 'dis' to the order of the word 'order' brings chaos to the page. This is the chaotic version of history. A random element has been inserted into the virtual order of history by a ghostly hand belonging to no one in particular. Both ordered and disordered versions of history appear to have been ordered or disordered by no one in particular.

Now, hold the page at arm's length and scrunch your eyes up so you can barely read the words. Note that you now have a random pattern of filled and unfilled spaces. Which space is more significant, the filled or unfilled space? Can one exist without the other? Have you begun to discern the interesting internal patterns that the unfilled spaces make when enclosed by the filled spaces? *Would these patterns exist if you were incapable of creating patterns out of unfilled space?* This is not an old solipsistic argument but a plea for the recognition of our participatory and complementary role in creating the universe and therefore our-selves. You created something out of nothing, made sense of a nonsensical thing or nonsense of a sensical thing – it does not matter, you made some *thing* that did not exist before! Why on earth did you do this? My answer, which may not be the same tomorrow, is that the urge to create is the third factor that must be added to the consciousness and love of the Unified Field. And this, ultimately, is the force that I discerned or created when I began to think about my past as a child and its relevance to the emergence of my child. The meaning of both was to be my creation.

order   order   disorder   order   order   order   order
order   order   disorder   order   order   disorder   order
disorder   disorder   disorder   disorder   order   order
disorder   order   order   order   order   order
order   order   disorder   order   order   order   disorder
order   order   disorder   disorder   disorder   order
disorder   disorder   order   order   order   order   order
order   order   order   order   order   disorder
disorder   disorder   disorder   disorder   disorder
disorder   disorder   disorder   order   disorder   order
disorder   order   disorder   disorder   order   order
order   disorder   order   order   order   order   order
order   disorder   order   disorder   disorder   order
order   order   order   disorder   order   order   disorder
disorder   disorder   disorder   order   order   order
disorder   order   order   disorder   order   disorder
order   order   order   order   disorder   order   order
order   disorder   disorder   disorder   order   order
disorder   disorder   order   order   order   order   order
order   order   order   order   order   order   order
order   order   disorder   order   order   disorder
disorder   order   disorder   disorder   disorder   disorder
disorder   disorder   order   order   disorder   order
disorder   order   order   order   order   order   order
order   disorder   order   disorder   disorder   disorder
disorder   disorder   disorder   order   disorder   order
order   disorder   order   order   order   order   disorder
disorder   disorder   order   order   order   order
disorder   order   disorder   disorder   disorder   disorder
order   disorder   order   order   disorder   disorder
disorder   order   disorder   disorder   order   order
order   order   disorder   order   disorder   order
disorder   order   disorder   order   disorder   order
order   order   order   disorder   disorder   order   order
disorder   disorder   order   order   order   disorder
disorder   disorder   disorder   disorder   order   order
order   order   disorder   disorder   order   order   order
order   order   disorder   order   disorder   disorder
disorder   order   order   disorder   order   disorder
order   order   disorder   order   disorder   disorder

There is a pleasing rhythm to it if you read the page out aloud. And also the sense that all patterns exist by excluding from themselves the order or disorder of the world around them. Hence the ineffable core of the self. But it is still contingent and complementary.

Looking at the boy's oscillating, quintessentially greedy peepers, it occurred to me that he was created in order to create the thing that created him, and that he did this and it was done to him solely out of love. It could be nothing else. The reflexive urge to insert little patterns into the page of 'orders' and 'disorders' which you demonstrated to yourself is nothing less than the primary spark that is the beginning of love. It is your foothold in the Unified Field. In everyday life, it is expressed in the compulsion to make sense of things. Without that we are not human beings, and in quantum terms we are not even rocks, for even rocks have to make sense of things in their own impenetrable way, or we make sense of them. It is all the same: the urge to create, to make sense of things, to apprehend them within our own definitive universe of meaning. And furthermore, this backing and forthing of the urge, creating what it creates and what creates it, this oscillation between the thing creating the thing creating the thing creating itself is the origin of the illusion of time. The imagined lapse between an act of the imagination and the thing which that imagination imagines give us duration. But it cannot be measured, it cannot be isolated, and it cannot be distinguished from simultaneity. Yet.

This pure state of being and timelessness was what I could remember from my own childhood. We may call it innocence or describe it by what was absent from it, but it was what I discerned also in our emergent child. When we first laid eyes on it it already had a prolonged and multifarious history. In a space beyond time, it had been engaged in the work of creating itself, the world and us.

What sense could I make of my own existence? Perhaps every breath drawn is a reflexive act of psychosomatic self-creation, and of love – if only we could remain aware of it as we are in childhood. The child does not verbalize this feeling, it merely feels it; but despite the temporal and linear conditioning of words that we develop as we grow, it still does not go away; we can find those self-absorbed moments when the separation from things does not exist, and if we choose we can put it into words. I should have grabbed hold of the Baron Von Richthofen in the hospital corridor and told her not to worry: the birth of my child and her involvement in it had been an entirely psychosomatic incident. None of us existed so there was nothing to be tired and despairing of. Or all of us existed so one might as well put up a front and crack a small smile for posterity! Ah, Baron, you gaze into the cauldron of order and disorder and conclude from it that you must embrace a universe of despair and meaninglessness. But that is merely the pattern you happen to have created for yourself. You might see something else tomorrow, if you permit yourself the freedom. To be charitable, you might simply have been weary.

Back! Back!

At some point in the life of the male something happens to deprive the man of the child. This might be a tiny threshold over which one slips without noticing, or a cataclysm of pain, or the first time your mother smacks you, or your father smacks your mother. Whatever the event, your reaction is to fall into exile from your childhood. All patterns are permissible and all events open to interpretation. You also have the right to remain unaffected by events. But your reaction undermines you, perhaps because you were taken by surprise. You react to this primal adversity by deducing that your world has been corrupted, that it will never be the same again, and that since you are your world you are also corrupt. You are deprived of your inner child when for the first time you understand that it is possible not to love yourself.

I had witnessed the birth of a being inextricably connected with my own fate who was unmistakably in a state of self-love. This being sought its own sustenance and found a world – a world it had created – in which that sustenance could be taken for granted. I had been given the final proof that angels do, indeed, exist, whether or not there were gods for them to worship. I had found that there was no possible conclusion in good faith other than that the primary human state was one of beneficence, and, if you wish to make a value judgement, goodness. This was the being I had given birth to, and which, in propagating its own world, had given birth to me. This was the state that I, as the progenitor of this being, should seek to preserve for the sake of us both.

For me to make any sense of this child, I had to return from the exile of adulthood. There must be a state in which it is possible to be faithfully in love with oneself. By achieving this state one might grow large enough to extend love to all other beings and phenomena. It has something to do with the urge to create – that *act of love*. I had to preserve this and pass it on to the child. Some of us are lucky enough never to grow up.

Back! Back!

NINE

The truth was, V and I had nothing in common except the one thing that makes all things possible: we both carried our inner child around with us. For children, before the loss of self-love, the world is a place where all things are possible, so V and I could blow the conventional wisdom of seeking commonality between lovers. Two children had stumbled on each other in the dark.

The letter came out of nowhere. I caught a plane. There was a café where we would meet up again for the first time since the desert. We were old friends who had made a pact. We expected nothing of each other. Children don't give a hoot about commitments.

She was passing through the Great Western City with a sack on her back. She had apprehended the fact that life is a condition of not arriving, so travel seemed a good idea. From the Great Western City she was going to follow, with whatever diversions came up, a straight line around the world which would return to itself.

We would meet for a cup of tea, but we had nothing in common. I was a drunk from the desert, she was a nice middle-class girl who had shrugged off the labels and gone her own way. We shared no tastes except for poetry. We had grown up at opposite ends of the world, fallen foul of utterly different sorts of education, read none of the same books, could talk of nothing from our pasts that would ring bells in unison. She was indescribably beautiful to me, and I was a sort of lexicon on legs. Physically we were candidates for miscegenation, if you believe in that sort of thing.

Discomfited by crowds, I got off the train and made my way

out into a dim northern evening. I remember approaching the revolving glass door of the café from across the street. I was late. Coppery reflections slivered in and out of the door as I walked towards it. I knew that V would be inside and that she would see me entering. I was nervous as all hell, of all things wondering how I looked. It is horrible when you imagine how others will see you and you are not pleased with the image. I had fallen asleep at the barber not a week ago and emerged with a crew-cut. Not recommended for a fleshy, decadent sort of face. Did they clip Oscar at Reading? We'll make a man out of you, boy.

Getting past that revolving door I could have sworn I stumbled and fell flat on my face, but I walked through smoothly enough. We should have more poise when we go to meet a prospective lover than when we confront our Maker. Of course I had no hope that V would wish to form an association of any kind. Nor had I come with any expectations other than the extreme pleasure of setting eyes on her again – Rostand notwithstanding.

Inside the café, bleached white, gold-and-green trimmings. After the dim evening the effect was blinding. One remembers trivial embarrassments. I scanned the room myopically while the next revolving section of the door came up solidly against my behind. Someone else was trying to get in. I hadn't wanted to thrust myself into the room so completely, being timidly half in and half out. I was discomfited, nervous, excited and in pain from the revolving door. Oh, oh, oh.

The room was a split-level affair with the stylish diners on the upper level and the floor I was on for passing trade. Where was V? There seemed to be a thousand people in the café. I was scanning like an automaton, not really seeing. There she was, right in front of me on the same level, sitting alone and conspicuously attractive in a tight red blouse. She was looking right at me, smiling her bright smile. An enormous halo surrounded her.

How do you walk ten or fifteen yards without mishap when you are being watched by the one pair of eyes that makes everything inside you stop and everything about you insubstantial? You have been injected with a paralysing agent and dropped in a vat of jelly. I put one foot in front of the other but there is a lunging awkwardness to my gait that I cannot control. Suddenly I am there. Four thousand years of confusion have brought me to this point.

V wrinkles her nose in mock disgust, pulls her stunning face into a series of grimaces and beams at me. 'You're late!'

I never wear a watch but I glance at my wrist. 'So I am. How long have you been waiting?'

She looks at me, at my eyes, my hair, my clothes, my mouth, but without moving her eyes. 'Ages.'

I grope. 'I was looking right at you and I couldn't see you. Christ, you look great!'

'You look different. Where's all your lovely hair?'

(I had lovely hair and I didn't know it!)

'You don't look a bit like I remember you, but you still have your kind face. I remember your kind face,' she adds.

'You look absolutely beautiful.'

'Thank you!'

I sit down, barely conscious. 'I tried very hard to picture your face after you left, but something prevented me.' Where was all this leading? I was climbing a slope and losing footholds. 'I fell asleep at the barber.' Moments of such extreme gaucheness will undermine every good thing you ever thought about yourself.

She lifts her cup to her mouth so that half her face is hidden in the Oriental manner. 'I take it you haven't changed a bit, then?'

'You know what a self-satisfied son-of-a-bitch I've always been . . .'

She laughs and my universe folds in on itself several times, ending up pretty much as it was before so no one would notice. I had lived in a desert of sound until I heard her laugh. When women laugh the sexual overtones of sound become audible; the brighter spasms are the same as those of the orgasm.

'Good,' she says emphatically, 'neither have I, not a bit.'

We stared at each other openly for a whole half-minute. Nothing had changed.

Outside, in the great central square of the Great White Northern Western Teeming Metropolis, a crowd had gathered. It was New Year's Eve. V and I plunged through the crowd, visiting stores she had never seen before and stopping at cafés for more tea and further chances to look at each other. From the beginning we had had no problem with just looking. When we couldn't find conversation, looking was perfectly acceptable. Mostly we cracked jokes for each other. Nothing to do but laugh. Walking through the bedding department of the World-Famous, Fifty-Billion-Storey Department Store, I got a stitch in my side laughing and had to lie down on a grandiose bed, large enough to feel lonely in. V took half-a-dozen strides back, did a short run up and leapt into the bed beside me. We lay together for a moment staring at the ornate ceiling. The Sistine Chapel had nothing on this.

We took the underground train to another great and famous store. On the down escalator V stood in front of me, tiny and golden. She leaned back slightly so that her head fell lightly against my chest. I put my hands on her shoulders and brushed her hair with my chin. It seemed the perfectly natural thing to do. From then on we held hands.

Riding on the underground train, I hear a voice say, 'V! Of all people!'

It is Malcolm, the man who, once stationed in the very same desert, gave V the name of the advertising agency where we met. The three of us hit another café and Malcolm says his goodbyes and disappears into the crowds, sensing a pact. Thank you, Malcolm, we have come full circle.

Hours later, we join the crowd in the central square for the New Year celebrations. It is surging and hostile. We sit atop a pillar box, watching. The black night sky is ablaze with fireworks. Everybody is kissing. V kisses me briefly on the mouth, then kisses a row of policemen. It is three o'clock in the morning of New Year's Day. The whole world has exploded.

There is no train back for another hour. We sit on the station concourse, under fluorescent lights, like a couple of winos. A conversation unfolds that began two years ago and never really stopped. I cannot remember the words. They flow over us. We wash and stroke each other. The station floor is cold, the lights are harsh. There are sinister elements abroad in the station concourse in the Great Teeming Hostile Metropolis, mecca of alienation. But V and I have stepped into the bubble.

The first available train appears to be bound for V's temporary abode in The Leafy Suburb of the Great Teeming Metropolis. We take it and are almost two hours in the journey for having caught the wrong train. This is how we shall proceed, I think to myself, while V finally succumbs to sleep on my knee – a couple of nontemporal beings forever off in the wrong direction because it does not really matter where we are going.

While we keep up the appearance of travel and the pretence of destinations, the truth is that we have already arrived. Inside the bubble, there is stillness and no direction. The world has exploded and then it has stopped. Like the masters of Zen and the shamans of South America, we have succeeded in stopping the world. We are like those tribals who, given a first taste of locomotion, were convinced that it was the world that was moving outside their train windows and they who were standing still. Of course, they were right. All kinds of illusions attend the feeling of unification, of being in love and as unseparated from the world as a so-called primitive. Your self-love is rehabilitated. The world moves or it does not move. You look out of the window at the convoluted parallax of moving things and then at the stillness of a kindred spirit asleep on your knee, and you realize that the greater energy, the more momentous movement, at least to your delightfully addled senses, is in the still figure reclining upon you. The way you feel, nothing has ever moved or will move again. For a fine brief moment you know that this is your true state and the true state of all things. You have found a moment of that old absorption, a fleeting repose in simultaneity.

The universe sweeps by and by.

Leafy Suburb not far from where V was schooled as a child. It has drawn her back. She knows no one here. A few schoolfriends have become distant acquaintances. She finds a shoebox in which to deposit her sack, and wedge a bed. I adore the nonmaterialism of some young women, nobler Spartans than Spartan men and much more graceful at having nothing. V adorns the tiny room in the suburban boarding-house like a queen in a great hall. We brew coffee and light cigarettes, settling on the floor in front of the small fire. The windows are steamy. Outside it is cold. V has slept

for an hour or so on the train. I have not slept at all but feel
revitalized by the discovery of this first territory of hers. I cannot
pin down why it is so appropriate that I find her in this tiny room,
unadorned, anonymous and nondescript. I surmise that it is
because such a place is itself nontemporal and 'in transit'. There
is nothing on the mantelpiece. The carpet is threadbare. The
kitchen shelf boasts a solitary can of tomato soup and a jug
stained with orange juice. There is a tiny pair of walking boots
under the bed. The window is high and cell-like, looking out on a
small patch of grey winter sky. The ceiling is a hundred feet high.
She has brought me to a rooming house in heaven.

I was tired and elated in the same way as I was during the birth.
In retrospect, the two events connect. All events connect; they all
happen at once or do not happen at all in locatable times. Only
we, as spectators or participants, force them into a temporal
framework in order to build fictions that will be accessible to the
linearity of words.

We talk for the entire day. That night we make love for the first
time. My memory is gone. It blocks out the traumas as well as the
moments of apotheosis. Conversely, perhaps, events have, within
their own allotted time, an integrity that shields them from our
memories. Why is it impossible to reconstruct properly a loved
one's face? Of our lovemaking I remember only a fleeting awkwardness and an exchange of reassurances. Certain colours. A
warmth that can be tasted. Gazing out of the high window at a
few lonely winter stars while V sleeps in the crook of my arm.
Outside the cold, inside the heat. Hell is not made of consuming
fires, for consuming fires are comforting things. Hell may be only
endless distances that the heart cannot leap. This is the rooming
house in heaven. This figure asleep beside me has only just now
been joined to me. We have welded the core of the bubble. In the
moment of sex there is no sex, no separation of the man and the
woman; instead there is the reunification of the self with the self,
and the self with another self that has reunified. Convolutions.
There is the undiscovered sex which lies deeper than our definitions and shows itself only when our love is oceanic. It is at the
same time the neuter of childhood and the complete sexual being
of the internal godhood. Begone, Lawrence! V's body is a land-

scape in the moonlight beside me. She has buried her head in my armpit and made two small fists with which to prop her chin. This is the fiction, this is the fiction. I cannot reconcile her white and undulating and beautiful materiality with what I feel. Only the third person inside me, the unified sexual being, encompasses this body which is not my body. I cannot find my other, fragmented self. I conclude that I have been destroyed. In my place is a benign mutant, a collocation of V and me. I have given up the ghost. My ego is a small retreating figure. Oh God, this is grand!

For three days we do not emerge. I have just enough cash left to have a taxi deliver groceries. I have always just enough cash to accomplish one thing at a time. This is the state of my being. It is so for the same reason I catch the wrong trains. I am not bothered by it. For three days we talk and talk, and in between we make love, testing our appetites. This is a prolonged and evolving consecration. You go to the priest and the priest waves his hands and dismisses you. With your loved one for the first time you are awash with blessings. You test your appetite for love without holding back, emptying yourselves into each other until you are each transformed. The crowd of selves that has afflicted you and delighted you is banished; you are distilled into something rare and fine and thin and crystalline. The tips of your fingers disappear.

Lying in bed in the dark, we improvise.

'Let's assume,' I tell V, 'that we are not really here.'

'I'll tell you what it feels like,' she says. 'It feels as if we are deep inside a cave. The walls of the cave are bluish-cold. We are rolling rocks back and forth.'

'Absolutely, we are hiding from reality.'

'Not because we are afraid.'

'Because it doesn't exist!' (And now I cannot remember who said what.)

'And the rocks are ideas, new things to play with.'

'I am making them up for you and you are making them up for me. We are exchanging ideas.'

'Yes, yes. They are delightful. You are rolling a rock in and it is unbelievably funny. I crack up.'

'And guess what, this whole scenario, this reality we are creating – it's just another rock.'

'Exactly! We are making up this story about making up this story!'

'Perfect! That was another rock you just brought in!'

'And so was that!'

'Are we in the cave or are we really here?'

'Aha! A question rock. It's got holes in it where the dew pours out! Shall I roll in an answer rock?'

'Yes please!'

'We are in neither place. We are inside each other looking out at each other looking out from inside each other!'

'Fuck me! That's a huge and convoluted rock!'

'Here comes another question rock: just now when you said "Fuck me!" – did you really mean it?'

'Tell you something else about the rocks . . . '

'Yep.'

'They glow in the dark!'

And on the night of the third day we emerged from the rooming house in heaven, and I swear we were each of us no more than eight years old, abroad in the wild twilight of suburbia, adrift in a virtual state. We had successfully detached ourselves from reality, whatever the hell that was. Our original pact had been prophetic. We knew where we were bound from those first few moments together.

There are ways and ways to find your child or someone else's. The point is to get them together so that they can *play*!

TEN

They say real life impinges, but hey ho! that's another story. When all things are happily a matter of interpretation one is at liberty to expose only those facts which seem apt at the time. When one no longer accepts the immutability of facts themselves, one may launch into a suitable fiction and then discover that the lies are more apposite than the truth, that the dialectic is a false one, that, in quantum terms, the virtual particles, the parallel lives, the metaphors of existence, the ghosts of our intent, the past and future selves are just as valid and often far more interesting than this inert and self-conscious condition that we oblige ourselves to accept as reality.

What else curtails our freedoms?

I hadn't been to a doctor for thirteen years, except once to get checked over so that I could satisfy a mortgage company that I was a good risk. Ha! You pay them to lend you money which you increase on their behalf and you're the risk! The doctor, at any rate, was an old colonial type of Englishman, bluff, congenial and phlegmatic, I believe the words are, who pronounced me fit, and, escorting me to the door, slandered his profession, muttering, 'Keep away from doctors, old boy; they'll ruin your health!'

So I went to a homoeopath instead, being assured that what they dispensed was mysteriously therapeutic, or at worst, harmless. Gervase, his name was, a well-groomed man of about forty with gleaming white cuticles which he inspected often. He wore his hair from back in the seventies, like a rug but not a rug. It clung to his head no matter which way he inclined it.

Gervase the homoeopath consulted an ancient book while

sucking in the corners of his mouth noisily. 'Let's see,' he said. 'Do your extremities feel chilled in the mornings?'

Stone the crows, I said in my head, and then volubly. 'Absolutely! Spot on! I wake up shivering, tuck my pants into a pair of socks and make sure my wrists are covered.'

'And you say you take no exercise.' He looked at me with an indolent glint in his eye. I liked Gervase. 'Why not?'

'I burn up calories in my head,' I explained. 'Never could bring myself to rush anywhere, make any effort that wasn't strictly a matter of life and death. Sort of innate belief that if you're making an effort something is wrong. Mind you, do a bit of yoga once or twice a month. Did I ever tell you I have a diploma in yoga?' (I do not.) 'They do not recommend effort as part of the search for mental or physical well-being. I intend to live at least till 2047 AD.' He was making mental calculations. You couldn't talk to a doctor like this. I suppose homoeopaths are trained to look for types. I liked being a type, or, if appropriate, several types.

He slumped back in his chair and laughed, half-disappearing behind his large and ancient book. 'A cerebral type, huh? Nothing wrong with that. You will probably outlive a lot of uptight perfectionists.'

If this guy was a shrink I would gladly have consigned myself to certification as a lunatic. 'Blow me down,' I said, recalling Popeye with my inner child, who was getting very shifty in his chair.

He peered at the book again and flipped the pages to cross-refer.

'Yes. Oxygenation, certainly. A metabolism that does not take kindly to stirring. An altogether self-assured person, would you say? Perhaps overly so, despite your tendency to what you describe as self-effacement.'

I like a man who conditions his clauses. 'It's a rather irksome duality,' said I. 'You see, I try to give equal rein to all my conflicting inner characters. A sort of internal democracy. You have to start somewhere, do you not? Why not with yourself? V finds my self-assurance and self-effacement both my most irritating traits.'

75

'I'm not surprised. It's the sort of thing that can be misinterpreted.'

'She feels that those two characters in particular are obstructing my ability to understand her problems.'

'You do not understand your wife's problems,' he said flatly, making a mental note aloud.

'Ha, ha!' I fumbled. 'A slight variation on the traditional plaint! It's a bit complicated, actually. Let's see, she cannot understand why I cannot understand why she cannot understand why I cannot understand that she cannot understand my point of view, which is that her problems are not really problems if only she would understand that if she changed her perception of them they might not be problems at all. Do you follow me?'

Gervase was unperturbed. 'Ah,' he said, as if he had just detected the common cold, 'the relativity of relationships, so to speak.'

'Precisely.'

He flipped through the book. He was reading and talking at the same time. I did not know this was possible. 'But do you not think that this might come across as somewhat presumptuous on your part, I mean, attempting to convince her that her problems do not exist?'

I drew myself back to the customary politeness between male strangers. 'I have not implied to her that I think her problems do not exist. I have said that problems will always exist, but that one is better off in many instances for ignoring them – particularly if they're the sort of problems we have – you know, domestic trials, the grind.' Inexplicably, in my head, the word 'grind' had typoed itself into *gringo*. Gervase had the tenderness of a gringo. A porcelain persona.

He licked his finger in slow motion and turned a page. 'But if you have this attitude yourself, what is the source of this stress you suffer from?'

Time to dig up the Freudian. 'I have a short temper. Always did. I think it was a self-defence mechanism I was obliged to construct as a child. My mother and father always sent messages to each other through me, even when they were in the same room. I had to learn to be a diplomat at a very early age in order that these messages were not misconstrued and all merry hell broke loose. I had to learn to use words in such a way that life itself would not be threatened. But when I had half a chance I'd get my own back by losing my temper over something or other. Show them that I was capable of creating a hell equivalent to theirs. This was a form of showing off as well, but the temper stuck.'

'Let me see, if you carried the message wrongly, your parents would end up fighting. Is that correct?'

'Ha! It wasn't that simple. Between receiving and delivering a message I had to reconstruct it, keeping it close enough to the original so as to seem likely, but not so close as to cause offence and uproar. This often when they were in earshot of each other. The indignity of it! I had to invent the relationship between my warring parents, I had to invent palatable versions of each for the other. Soon we all pretended to believe the lies I told, but I developed a pathological fear of being misunderstood. You can see why.'

'You developed a singular talent.' This guy knew his stuff. 'Have you carried this fear into your adult life?'

Bells were ringing in Calabria. 'I hate the old child-is-father-of-the-man claptrap.'

'And would you say,' he continued, 'that the root of the stress you have been feeling is your suppressed rage when V misunderstands you — that is to say, when she refuses to accept your interpretation of events, of problems and so on?'

I sat back in my chair and pondered this for a moment. There are times when you are thrown down a sort of chute of self-realization. You plummet down blindfolds of it and tumble out into a dimly illuminated landscape. Dim but illumined enough for you to detect that you are being threatened by a putative fact.

I said nothing. Gervase nodded with his eyes fixed in their sockets as if watching a yoyo. Dammit, V was right again!

Gervase made a pronouncement from a great height. 'There is a tendency in many men to construct controlling mechanisms for themselves. Emotionally, I am afraid, you are still falling into the old traps.'

I looked at him as if he had accused me of necrophilia. Was his accent faintly Nazi?

He went on, gently remorseless. 'It is evident to me that you are acutely aware of the need to unite your mental and emotional personae. You have a theory and a controlling mechanism that points you always in that direction. But I am afraid you are falling down in practice. This is the result of the stress and the cause of it, if you like. Don't get me wrong. I am not making a diagnosis here. I am trying to help you to identify a particular fiction that you have concocted for yourself, in the way that you concocted fictions for your parents. Do you think I am on the right track?'

A necrophiliac. So be it. 'It's all fiction,' I said. 'You must be getting warm.'

He reached inside a battered black bag and produced a bottle of small white tablets. He dangled a fist in front of my nose. 'Open wide. Suck, don't chew.'

I sucked on two sugary pills. To hell with doctors, I thought.

'Now you may feel a mite queer over the next week or two. Call me if there's anything you can't handle.'

'Is that it?' I asked.

'That's it,' he said.

'What were they?' I asked, still sucking the tablets.

He rose and ushered me to the door, embracing me on the way out. 'Nux vomica,' he said.

Nil desperandum, I thought.

So we are all innocents abroad. Every thought we think about ourselves is suspect. The children come out to play and what happens? You create the world and the world creates you back. You have the quantum choice, which is that you may or may not create the world you wish for, or are capable of wishing for. It is all in your ability to imagine and all in whether or not your imagination has been freed well enough for you to make up a world in which your progress is pleasurable.

If you understand this, as V and I did, then the process of creation becomes the thrill; though dangers might seem to over-come you, your liberated imagination can at all times remove you to a distance sufficient for you to appraise your situation and say, Blow me down! I have landed myself in a right mess here – or just laugh. Laugh and laugh! When the vulpine forces have been unleashed, when the cryptofascists and nonentities and drudges and speculum-laden women in white coats are all after you, when the middleman finally pummels your portals, you can leap out of some back door in your mind and remember that the worst thing that can happen to you is still not happening to you.

V and I had exercised a quantum choice in getting hitched up together. There was no conceivable reason to do it or not to do it. Reasons don't suffice, at any rate; only decisions interrupt the space between you and dead circumstance. If you love somebody, that is enough. You can take all your reservations about being tied down or about the economies of cohabitation (as if such things exist!), or about how fabulously well you both play a chukka of polo and hurl them out the nearest heaving porthole. None of them will do. Only love. Only love is the reason that goes beyond reason. That is what it is for, to urge us beyond the illusions of what is possible.

Our quantum choice consisted of this: Let's do it. Yep. Let's do it. Got any reasons why we shouldn't? Nope. Got any reasons why we should? Yep. What are they? Who cares, let's do it! Got any reasons why one does anything at all? Nope, reasons are only part of the story. Maybe we shouldn't trust ourselves to do anything at all unless there is a large area of unreason about it. We shall embrace the ineffable, darling, and dance always on the edge of the precipice. Like poetry, says V: you don't write a poem for a reason, you simply create. Same with life, marriage, birth, death and all the big words, says I. Yep. You just do it. Time to die? So long! Goodbye! *Wiedersehen!*

Those first days in the rooming house in heaven were the beginning of one long run up to the precipice. When V and I decided that we would never again be without each other it wasn't a leap into the proverbial unknown, it was a flying run followed by a joint vault into shattering oblivion. But then, says I, every goddamn moment of your life is exactly like that! If you no longer perceive this salty fact, friend, you are probably a member of the walking dead. Having perceived it, however, you owe it to yourself and to those around you to learn how to dance. The only honourable approach to the edge of the precipice is the dance. The only poised momentum in a life in which every second leads to the unknown is the momentum of a hefty rhythm. Jig. Jitterbug. Lurch. Thrust your pelvis in every available direction – you might make contact with someone else who is having as much fun as you. Your parts might briefly touch. You see, fun is not a contingent phenomenon. You do not have to clear a path in order to arrive at the point at which you have fun. You do not have to get a degree, build a home, have kids, mend your car, mow the lawn, entertain your bank manager or buy a yacht to have fun. You just do it. On the day you die you won't tot up your bank balance, you'll grab every last croak you can muster to recount the fun you created. In fact, if you go out in style, you might just devise a way to die laughing. With or without God, who is far too serious for His own good, what else is there to do? When your grandchildren remember you, do you want them to:

shiver ☐
weep ☐
run home and do their homework ☐
swear posthumous revenge ☐
psychoanalyse what you did to
their parents to make them such
schmucks ☐
come over all queer ☐
roll around on the lawn
all day laughing? ☐

Tick as appropriate and mail to yourself, first class.

V and I pushed the boat out. This is how we were. Nothing could destroy the bubble except death. And even death would not destroy the meaning of what we had created. This was meaning larger than reason alone could comprehend. You can call this meaning God, the Universe, The Quantum Gutbucket, but whatever your proclivities, if you are in love you are simply connected with meaning. You just do it. You just live your life without allowing preconditions, calculations or partial considerations to cock it up. You discover that there is nothing at all that merits your misgivings. Otherwise the events around you concatenate unnoticed and the marvellous patterns of order and disorder flow straight over your head and the one pair of eyes that will stop your heart dead as a stone turns up and *what are you doing*?

You are having lunch with your bank manager.

Besides, if you live life on the edge, there is a certain authenticity to your problems which is not to be laughed at. Or rather, the only appropriate response is to laugh! Fun is not contingent, remember? On the edge you are continually confronted with that Department of Eternal Verities which dispenses the hard stuff, oh yea! Drink diss down, boy, and prepare to meet yore Maker! Then when you look around and realize that the majority of Great White Urban Conurbation Commuters is still cribbing about the dogshit on the kerb and the price of the laundry you feel like a Samurai. Follow me down this alleyway, San, and I will show you the glint on the face of death and with any luck you will not trip on a lump of Chihuahua dropping as you exit hastily stage left.

And yet you realize still further that the face of death is just a mask drawn over the meaning of what you are. The mask drops and you are free. For V and me the meaning infused everything. We called it 'the 98 per cent', the substance of everything that held us together, the Unified Field, the quantum, love, consciousness, immortality. The remaining 2 per cent was the darkness through which we would hurl our particulate selves, the alleyway crowded with vulpine forces that one must acquire the imagination to uncreate.

Follow me down the alleyway, San!

Sartre had hell down as other people. There is the unity of solitude, the megalomania of it. Alone you become a grub or a dictator. You fall to pieces, become a pellicular being, or depose your internal democracy and let havoc rule for a while. It is therapeutic and fun. It is dancing with the old decrepit reprobate that lurks inside you. You are a particulate being, whole, as far as you can determine for yourself, and perfectly autonomous. Sartre's hell was the impenetrable ontology of other people; the way they can deprive you of the unity and stillness of yourself. Fair enough. But other people also force you out of yourself and into an ontological relationship with yourself. Circumstances and events then become a matter of dual perspective, until you discover that the dual perspective is insufficient – that there are more than four dimensions visible when more than one pair of eyes is doing the looking, and that what you attempt to fix between you inevitably betrays you.

Consider the farcical situation that arises when more than one pair of eyes examines a particular event or object. We are separated by the material world. Even in our closest embrace there is a displacement of vision between you and me: the surface we inspect will show you more of one angle than is available to me, and my aspect of the same surface will provide a different area of extra vision. Then, when we attempt to describe the object to each other, the edges become blurred, and at this point a magical effect is required – we have to cross over into an ineffable region, using our imaginations to arrive at a consensus about what we observe. But this is still, for each of us, an approximation. You will never see, in the same time, with the same eyes, in the same light, from the same angle, with the same personal history, what I am attempting to describe to you. In the interim, you will have changed imperceptibly. The moment is lost. Only imagination can possibly breach the gap, and then with an approximation. And this is further compounded by the fact that what I describe, the words, gestures and inflection I use, will be heard by you from your angle of hearing, from your light and with your personal history intervening to filter what I say, to give you an approxima-tion of an approximation. What are we left with? A third-hand interpretation of a reality which cannot truthfully be said to exist except perhaps for an instant under unique and unrepeatable conditions by a single person. Then there is also the possibility that if we turn back to reappraise the object, it will have changed.

This example began with two people in the closest embrace, but we are more often than not separated from each other by much greater spaces. When V and I shared the Parable of the Cave in the rooming house in heaven, our brief unity was generated entirely by the imagination, by images produced in an ecstatic state. In exile from that state we are all separated by an impermeable vacuum. If we cannot reach our consensus without resorting to mutual fictions and interposing a kind of 'unreality' between ourselves, what chance have we to isolate the truth from the multitude of peaks and traumas we have to negotiate together?

Stone the crows! Suddenly the very nexus of humanity and reality is dispatched to oblivion. Everything from politics to sex, everything that takes place outside of a certain enclosed space within the individual, is consigned to a wordless and intractably undecipherable zone of unreality. The particle vanishes; the wave is activated. The principle of indeterminacy applies to every single thing about which you or I may have something to say. Then, if you accept that events are concatenating things, that they have no beginning and no end and no discrete existence, that somebody's grandmother dropping a handkerchief can lead to a particular orgasm in the obscurity of a suburban night – and *then* if you attempt to isolate one event or instance of personal or common history and agree on what, when, how or if it was – you realize the whole thing's a vast goddamn shadow-show.

The trouble with Sartre was that in his prequantum *fin de siècle* way he got thoroughly nauseous about the whole business. He had little schooling in how to have fun, by his own account. His uncle Albert Schweitzer should have come back from the jungle and taken the boy in hand, teaching him a few things he might have learnt from shamans and witch doctors before he cured them of the white man's ills.

The real complications set in not when you try to share the mere phenomenology of an event, but when, in the company of someone you love, you try to agree on its value, to wit, whether it was good or bad. Hence the old and tremulous query, 'How was it for you?'

How indeed was it for you? Do tell!

And that is how, fresh out of the rooming house in heaven, drunk on the suburban twilight, packs on our backs, pinkies intertwined, V and I began our trip down the alleyway. To traverse the distances of heaven you must first rattle around in the confines of hell. Do not prejudge the situation by saying that everything has its price. It is your heaven and your hell. It is your laughter that makes it all blissfully meaningless.

ELEVEN

I remember. V is lunging at me. I am lying supine on a pile of cushions. That is most of the furniture we have. It is good furniture for a cave. V is lunging at me. Her small fists are clenched; despite my teaching she has, like most women, never learnt to make a proper fist. If she strikes me with any force, with those fingernails tucked into the mound of Venus and those thumbs stuck up like antennae, she will more than likely break a finger or two and scratch my eyes out into the bargain. Later I show her again how to make a fist.

V is lunging at me. How did all this start? I am lying supine on a pile of cushions. I am so stressed, my temper is so far gone beyond mere breaking point that it has turned into a ball of flame and lodged in my chest where, undoubtedly, it is growing carcinomatous. I am thinking: Good! I will fold up with my malignancy just out of revenge. In our future history she will have to come to terms with having caused my eventual destruction by all manner of organ-eating gribblies. My rage has imploded with such force that I have to assume a submissive position. If I stand up and alter my centre of gravity some tantric wave might rise up from the middle of the earth and, coursing through my thorax, reaching my extremities, cause me to detonate. I want to disappear, to dematerialize. I would be grateful to all the forces that be if, at the end of her lunge, V were not to make contact with me but with a small pile of cinders. That is all I want to leave her with right now.

Her beautiful face is contorted with rage, but not contorted to ugliness. Shay! lisps an internal Humphrey, youse ain't all that bad looking when yer blowing yer top, Lady! It is falling towards me. I am not stretching this event cinematically. There are no time-expanding edits here.

This is how it happened. It took several thousand years for V to progress from the first application of force to the terminal impact of her lunge. In fact, what is coming at me is not V but some primeval mask: the features have the painted and artificial rage that fails to convince on the theatrical masks of Venice and ancient Malabar. Aha! think I, she is aware of the underlying unreality of this moment! She tripped herself up in the very first instant of the lunge, realizing that she and her rage had become separated. This makes her even more angry, especially because she has sensed that I know it. She is now acting out two sets or levels of rage. She will certainly make contact with me in a few millennia.

Her beautiful face is contorted with rage. How did all this start? I am lying supine on a pile of cushions. I am having to reorientate myself constantly. What am I in each moment? Frightened? Yes! No! Reeling with resentment? Yes! No! I have adjusted myself to the fact that I am about to be struck. I will suffer some pain, though V is small, and even with all her weight behind those fists, that small body flying towards me, it is unlikely that I will bear great damage. A bruise, perhaps. A momentary stinging. Perfect miniatures cannot harm each other. Her terminal velocity cannot be so great that it will do more than jar her body against mine. It will be the same contact we make in love, in comforting each other or dancing cheek to cheek. I am in love with V's fleeting hatred of me. The twins inside the bubble – inside the womb – have adjusted their positions. There is a small, inconsequential war over personal space. No one is hurt. I am in love with this moment. This hatred is theatrical; it is drama. There is drama in our lives, thank God! Afterwards we will not remember the plot, only the high points. V is falling towards me. I have lifted my forearms to guard myself in the manner of a boxer. My knees are drawn together to protect my balls from the crush. She is frozen at an angle of forty-five degrees. A line extended through her centre of gravity is now piercing my midriff. It extends far down into the earth and moves forward along her falling frame until it will reach, say, the top of my head. Then she will be on top of me.

How did all this start? In the small cave on the edge of town in the Great White Western Suburbia the sun had risen normally.

The vast bow window where we sat for morning tea formed a backdrop of brilliant light. I was blinded. Something in the morning light had obliterated me. V and I were discussing some matter of – of what? I cannot remember. Finances? No! *Attitude*! Either she or I had suggested to the other that he or she needed to make an adjustment in their attitude. Of course, this is the most dangerous territory. To suggest that someone needs a change of attitude is to imply that they have misjudged their situation in a fundamental way. Who was it that required the adjustment, or was alleged by the other one to have required the adjustment? I do not know. V and I are interchangeable beings, after all.

No, perhaps it was like this: perhaps one had suggested to the other that a change of attitude was required, and then perhaps the other had either retaliated or genuinely responded that the reason why the first had come to this offensive conclusion was because *they* required the said change. In this situation, the imagination is not free to interpose itself and blur reality enough to undermine respective positions. But wait! This goes further. The response of the first person to this inversion of the argument is to allege that his or her antagonist's response is, in turn, incontrovertible proof that he or she is the one requiring the adjustment! Consequently we have arrived at the point where we have a proliferation of antagonists and perspectives. Now it is hard, cold armour against armour and the clash of sword and shield. The room for interpretation has been removed. There may be a verbal assault in which painful truths, that is, truths of the moment and as held by one party, are hurled at burning ears. This is often followed by the only logical recourse: a physical attack. If we are lucky this is merely a ritualized or dramatic hostility; hence, I think, the impossibility, at the moment of hitting somebody, of taking oneself seriously. The theatricality of life is exposed; we realize that someone else, who is nevertheless ourselves, is in charge of the script. Hand-to-hand combat is the final democracy.

V is falling towards me. Her fists, inefficiently clenched, have begun a drumming action as she falls through the forty-five degrees and approaches the point of impact. Her face hovers above mine for a few hundred years, and I cannot say that the look of hatred in her eyes is not the hatred she feels because she loves me. Because she loves me she is licensed: she has permitted herself to hate me in this fundamental way. This is a fine drama. As much as it hurts and I want to be somewhere else, I am, if I had the time to contemplate it, enjoying this drama very much. I feel a dull, thudding pain on my left cheekbone. The length of her body slams against the length of mine. Clefts and valleys and dips and curves commingle.

We are winded, but we do not feel the same any more. We are not the same people we were a moment ago. Something has lifted and passed on. Here is a small connection between love and death: to love or to be loved is to practise, benevolently if you are lucky, the continual killing off of the other. We are not linear beings, we are simultaneous. We are not organic solidities, we are events. We come and go. We help each other to come and go. Sometimes with violence or sometimes with an embrace. Or with an embrace that is a little death!

The relativity of relationships, Gervase had pointed out. What is it in the emotional universe of women that constitutes an area utterly uncharted and inexplicable by men? If some of my earlier conclusions (which you must not hold me by – we are, after all, exercising quantum choices throughout this mutual confession) are correct, then I must suppose that it is inexplicable through a deficiency in men. A thing is not made culpable by obscurity and I cannot summon any corresponding deficiency in women. I have never heard a woman say that she does not understand men, only that she understands them too well. If she is a younger woman, this might be said with some resignation, but matriarchs say it with disdain. What women might understand is the deficiency itself: the absence in the male of the emotional dimensions that they themselves possess.

Discomfited by this inequality, men compensate themselves with rationalist poses. If you can define a feeling, you need not understand it. Twentieth-century psychology is a convenient tool for the classification of emotions, and provided they are correctly named, feelings may be brought under control (for what good I do not know) in the face of overwhelming odds, in wars or in bereavement. Categorization is the method by which phenomena are fixed so that when it is politic to do so they may be deprived of their meaning and validity altogether. Empiricism is the death of wholeness.

If we rid ourselves of this mentality – and it may simply be a matter of undefining our history, starting with the history of the sexes – we might the sooner become reacquainted with the ineffable side of ourselves, the mysteries and symbols in our consciousness that persist even as we try to deny them, and, incidentally, with that large area of the cortex which is supposed yet to lie fallow. The essence of the quantum mentality is that it removes the restrictions on internal and external choices which are the result of falling in with a particular cast of mind. There is no conceivable reason for making up one's mind in any given situation. Whatever you do, do not make up your mind. The nature of life is such that you will inevitably be forced to reconsider your position. Life expresses all possibilities; an unconditioned mentality helps us to participate in this expression, each in our own way. Even in Darwinist terms, it is the adaptable who survive, but let us not disinter old corpses. Reason is only one tool in the process of navigating through life. The urge to control (illusively, for control is always one-sided and life is not) the things that affect us only puts us in opposition to those things; by becoming static even for a short while in one's mental cast one becomes an antagonist of life.

It seems to me that this is the state of men and the cause of their deficiency. I cannot locate the same deficiency in women except that they have given up some part of themselves to live in a world conditioned by the weird dreams of men, in which men's illusions of control are pervasively unsettling. For men who fear the relinquishment of their hoarded power, let me ask this: What do we now control of the world and of our lives? Less and less, it seems; all we do now is narrow our lives down to predetermined sets of choices, aspire to fixed states, equip ourselves with limited freedoms and think it is noble and altruistic to do so. That isn't life; it is merely what we believe. It is the way we have hitched our imaginations to every wayside post and donned our harnesses before limping off into the wild blue yonder. Harnesses are instruments of control for both master and beast. It is man who invented burdens.

We all require an adjustment in attitude, but one that will give us the ability to function without a fixed attitude at all. Moving targets. Dancers. Only the dancer occupies all spaces and angles at once – the fluid and improvisatory being who manages now and then to interrupt the light in such a way as to cast beautiful shadows.

And to this extent, V was the fluid being and I was not.

It is more difficult to discern a truth in total darkness. Picture the end of twilight, when the dark hemisphere of night shades over each half of the world in turn. This is the region where the spirits play and truth loses its solidity, where, between dreams and sleep, men and women lie together.

In the darkness, your voice becomes material. Close your eyes when you speak and your voice becomes internal, resounding in you and in your loved one beside you, a sensual thing more than in the day when it is merely noise or music. In this zone of darkness, voices constitute the world. On a planet devoid of light there will be a population of sounds and caresses; the senses of hearing and touch will define the universe and matter. On earth, when we are in the zone of darkness, we migrate to this planet. Men and women travel together, their truths unfixed from the concreteness of vision. They have no need to believe their eyes and cannot find refuge in the ambiguity of frowns, smiles, gestures. Words become the world.

V and I are lying together. There is our Georgian window, against whose insufficient light I can discern the line of her shoulder. Her back is turned to me. She is using the silence.

I am making a mental catalogue of all the things I hate in women. All my prejudices. Women use silence as a weapon. It is detestable. Men sulk, which is a different thing, but women use silence premeditatedly, creating a vacuum around the man and choking him for want of air. Air is the vibrating medium of sound; women turn it to shards of ice.

Why, it is an execrable tactic and shows the insensitivity of the female sex. If you love someone, you do not use the love as a tool for bargaining and manipulation, withholding it by being silent. Women play upon the emotions of men, which are the more vulnerable for being hidden. Gangrene. Hidden wounds hurt more for your consciousness of them, for having to keep them hidden. Women know this and use their knowledge for their own ends. It is detestable. For all the wars of men, I am thinking, there is none of the subliminated malice that women seem to possess. I hate women. I hate to love women. I love to hate women. I detest the opposition in the natures of men and women and no longer put it down wholly as the fault of men. Men are no more deficient than women. In choosing their weapons, women have no concept of honour. They will hit you with what hurts the most in your tenderest spot. Silence is a detestable weapon.

The line of her shoulder dissolves and I hear a sigh. Now she is making sure that I know she is awake. She has closed off her thoughts from me and makes sure I know it by sighing. She has compounded the silence by indicating that what is going on in her head is no silence at all but a bloody and vituperative battle between mythological monsters in which I am the child-eating Saturn. In this silence are the distant screams of war. I know it well, Gervase, it is the silence our parents use to disembowel each other.

I am running through my catalogue of prejudices, arming myself for when the silence is broken. Who will speak first? I shall take the initiative with a preemptive attack upon the silence, but I shall have to say something inordinately canny, something that stings but at the same time could be taken as an olive branch. This will gauge her mood. I am ready for peace or war. I do not know what this silence is about. That is the other reason why the silence of women is such a vicious weapon. They keep silent: they do not tell you why. They are manipulators, emotional bandits. Love is unconditional; they should not withhold it when it pleases them to do so. Like taking candy from a baby and then using it as a bribe. Twice the crime. And to withhold affection is to judge when someone is deserving of it. Women are judgemental. From the unknown dimensions of emotion they inhabit come all kinds of alien instruments of torture. Perhaps the first initiation of boys is the ordeal of surrendering to the silence of their mothers. And so on.

I am not thinking well or clearly. I am being emotional, but I am not as good at being emotional as women can be. Then I realize: women use silence to deprive men of their loud and insistent voices, to send them back in silence to their sparse territories of emotion. Forty days and forty nights. Silence the weapon of women, words the weapon of men. But against silence, words are defenceless, and men are driven to physical force. Women who are silent must become slaves for their silence. They must be forcibly denied every other category of power. If they will be silent then men must create a world for them in which nothing they ever say or do will emerge from silence.

I can find nothing inordinately clever to say. V undermines my subtlety. It is her fault we cannot have this altercation in a civilized fashion. Words are civilization. Silence is barbarism.

I, the undermined, shall hereby speak. Why is it up to me? I must break the silence. Nature abhors a vacuum. I mean to say, in a neutral voice, as one might enquire of a stranger the condition of their health upon perceiving them to be suddenly lame or however afflicted – I mean to say, with perhaps a tinge of something solicitous but not too familiar in my voice – I do love you, after all – I mean to say, to ask quietly and soberly, What is the matter?

This comes out as, 'What is the matter with you?' The appending of the last two words changes the tone of the question. It is now more personal than I intended as well as slightly accusatory and impatient, implying that there is something the matter with her. Screw that! I might as well have said, Are you hysterical again, woman? Once again a slave to your damnable emotions? Or am I imagining all this? I am on the run, I am frightened. Her silence is making me retreat even as I advance.

She does not reply. I have to rummage around in our mutual history in order to answer my own question. The words came out wrong, but I am not going to backtrack. I cannot say, No, excuse me! That is not the way I meant to ask the question. What I intended was a nonspecific question in a diplomatic and neutral mode, enquiring generally as to the state of your health and, if you would permit it, eliciting a reason, if indeed there is one, for your unaccustomed silence. Well, normally we are at song and dance in the bed; this darkness is our common territory, is it not? So you see why I am a little discomfited – no, concerned – at your remoteness . . . don't you? Of course, since you have not indicated that something is wrong I must assume that your silence is entirely a personal affair, having nothing to do with me at all. I hope you will not think my concern misplaced.

No, I think; you know perfectly well that she is silent because she is upset with you. You can hear the internal war being fought. Your words trip over into the truth, in the darkness where your face cannot put the lie to them, and you make the preemptive attack that your impulses demand.

She turns over again, this time to face me. I do not know if I should let her see that in the darkness I am trying to find her eyes, or something in the attitude of her body that will speak to me. Momentarily, a swift beam of light from a passing car is refracted through the window and I glimpse her eyes. She is looking directly at me. She does not blink, or if she does it is not visible in the half-light. The intensity of the light is too low to allow visibility of so brief a movement as a blink, I muse. Or was I seeing things? Was a trick of the light imprinting a wounded stare on closed eyelids? I peer at her again, taking a risk. How absurd if in this situation she should find me eyeballing her! It was a trick. Her eyes are closed. I untense my neck and shoulders and relax into my pillow. Perhaps sleep is the answer. I close my eyes and am at least partially returned to myself. Sometimes, I think, intimacy is the brother and sister of paranoia. If the imagination were free to wander without having to commit itself to a position on this, that and the other, perhaps we would avoid the paranoia of doubt, of relative positions, of having to assess one's own situation in the light of another. Chimera.

A hundred years have passed. She has slipped away to Antarctica and returned without my noticing. She answers, 'Nothing.'

The answer has been so long in coming that I have to recall the question. I have the eerie feeling that a single word has risen to the surface of her mind and been jettisoned out of her vocal cords – Nothing. I have known her for seven or eight years and until now she has not spoken a single word, and then the single word emerges in the darkness when I have almost forgotten what question prompted it, and it is – Nothing. Now I have lost the momentum of even this inept interrogation; I cannot find what to say in reply to – Nothing. There are conventional rules to apply in such cases and I invoke them; however, to do so is to risk the beginnings of an argument. Never mind. Anything is better than – Nothing.

'Then why are you so quiet?' I ask. I did not mean this to sound challenging. I did not mean to imply, Well, if there is nothing the matter then why are you burying yourself in silence? But that is what comes out and that is what will be heard. In the end, I suppose, that is what I meant. Is this why women fall silent?

'I'm just quiet, that's all. I'm just *feeling* quiet.'

Aha, the emotional excuse. Despite myself, I become oversolicitous. 'Are you sure nothing's the matter? Has something upset you?'

'Yes. You have.'

'Aha. So it's not just that you're feeling quiet?' Pointless ramifications.

'It's that as well. One from the other.'

I withdraw to regroup. I do not want to beg an answer. She has come clean. I have upset her, it's up to her to tell me why, to make sense of the hundred-year silence. But she is being manipulative. It serves her purpose to keep me in suspense. I am being provoked – or softened up.

But this is not me, not the way I think of V; this is Gervase's relativity of relationships, destabilized by paranoia – or some such thing. I must be dignified but loving. I have no pride to protect. I must find out. After all, she is the wounded one.

'What on earth have I done?' Wrong again! No need for the 'on earth', old boy! Implies unlikelihood. You will really drive her up the wall if before you even know what you have done you imply there is nothing to it. The words are snakes that swallow themselves.

This time I can see that her eyes are looking at me in the darkness. They are wide and full of hate. I cannot hold her gaze. I sigh.

She replies, 'Nothing.'

I begin to use the logic that I know will infuriate her. My resolve to be conciliatory is slipping away. I could be kinder, but such things are not always possible. 'Now, let me see: I have upset you, but I haven't actually done anything. Have I got that right?'

'Yes.'

'Well . . .'

'Well, what?'

'Is that it?'

'Whatever you say.'

I get it. She is attempting to collapse my logic by fielding only a few noncommittal words that will allow me no purchase on the argument. Whatever I say is fine with her. It will not get me anywhere or help her to feel any better. That is worse than silence. Now we have the fierce Cold War. Now the words are double-agents. I move to a conciliatory position once more. There is a chance the tactic will confuse her. Either way, I am covered. 'Tell me about it,' I say. 'I'll just listen. I won't interrupt.' We have a working truce for some situations: the one must listen to the other. It is a polite arrangement. Release the pigeons, old boy.

'It won't do any good,' she replies.

'At least let me know. Maybe I can do something about it. If you are going to treat me this way I have a right to know what I've done.'

'I'm not treating you in any way. I'm just quiet. And it isn't anything you've done,' she hisses.

'Well, what is it, then, for Christ's sake!'

'It's no good trying to talk about it. You'll just take what I say and turn the words around to suit yourself. Sometimes I can't get through to you, that's all.'

'That's the problem?' Things are speeding up. Downhill locomotion.

'Part of it.'

I jump in. 'I promise I'll listen.' How pathetic that sounds! Bribery and bargaining.

'I don't have to tell you what the matter is just because you promise to listen when it suits you to do so. You have to listen all the time. You miss too much of what I am.'

Mutual history time. 'Are you saying that I don't listen to you properly *most* of the time?'

'Did I say that?'

'Look, if that's the problem we can come to an arrangement. Consensus, remember?' We do nothing unless we reach a consensus; consequently we do nothing, which suits us fine most of the time. The bubble is intact. I need the reassurance.

'That's a part of the problem.'

'So you've said. What's the other part, then?'

'It doesn't matter.'

I am beating back the silence. 'It matters to me. I can't bear the silences. I can't bear it when we're like this. It achieves nothing.' I can't bear it when *you* are like this, I should say. There is always the space between what we say and what we think where the virtual intervenes, where the original thought generates a crowd of imitators. She senses this in me, and this is the problem. No, wait a minute. That is not what she said. Hear what she says. She said I do not listen; nothing to do with my concern for the ramifications of Heisenberg in the transmission of meaning. (Ha!) The problem is that while listening to her I am really always listening to myself. Nothing new there: same with everybody. D. H. Lawrence said we are all alone. Filters for data coming in from existentially removed person, event or circumstance. Maybe just me. Perhaps other people really do listen. No end to human talent for overthrowing logical impossibility postulated by poncy nit-picking intellect. I beseech you in the bowels of Christ, consider the possibility that you might be wrong. It must be possible to form an empty shell that merely receives incoming signal. You had constructed your own imaginary filters, old boy, and had begun to believe in them! Go back to the beginning, back to the Cave of Rocks and listen with something other than implanted prosthetic.

But . . .

Maybe that's not the problem either. I cannot know for she will not tell me. Perhaps she has already told me and I have not heard. I have drowned her in my internal monologue. Consider yourself honoured, old thing.

She draws in a long breath and holds it for an instant. Suddenly she concedes. 'It's the way men are.'

Zounds! The tactic has worked! I have moved her beyond the particular. We can now cover things up in philosophy and generalizations. This is comforting; a successful manipulation of the virtual possibilities of meaning, accomplished impromptu by yours truly! Often we turn our differences into stimulating discussions and end up in complete agreement. Cancel the Cold War!

There is a flat, measured quality in her voice. 'Women have to fight to be heard because men have never learnt how to listen,' she says.

Now I will use a disarming tactic. I am not ashamed of using tactics, even though I know V would never be so conspiratorial. 'You are absolutely right,' I tell her. 'I don't know what it is in men's – in my – make-up that – that . . . ' I trail off; I do not know what I am trying to say.

She comforts me. 'You aren't so bad. It just triggers something in me when I can see that I am not being listened to. I need you to listen without thinking how you are going to respond even as I am telling you something. It's really disconcerting. It makes me want to shut up. That's why I retreat into silence. You are doing it now, I can tell: I can feel you thinking about how you are going to cope with the next thing I say or the last thing I said. Why can't you just listen?'

I keep silent. There is no answer other than a listening silence. She takes the cue.

'It's like being constantly interrupted without the other person saying even a single word. It's impossible to talk to a person when you can see that all the time their thoughts are getting in the way, like having a third person in the room who refuses to say a word but still manages to disrupt the proceedings just by being there.'

I am getting a little indignant. Damn the tactics. I am thinking that there is more to it than she admits. She is transferring her frustration with something else on to this, well, rather trivial matter. She is worried about something else. No, I must listen to her and believe her when she says something is just so. Or perhaps she does not realize what is *really* bothering her.

'And you have this incredibly annoying habit of taking what I say and turning it into something else. As if I don't know my own mind. I hate being patronized. I don't want to be protected even from my own analyses of things. If a thing is so, I wish just for once you would agree it is so. Just say, That is so. Don't go putting all sorts of other constructions on it. A thing can be just what one thinks it is, it doesn't have to have hidden layers or nuances and subtleties that are only visible to you – so you can patronize other people by telling them what you think they do not see. How do you know what they cannot see? You yourself are capable of missing the most obvious things. I know! It's your ego, isn't it? It's the male always crying out for some kind of recognition. Listen to me! Listen to me! the little boy cries. The little boy in you, but not the endearing little boy, just the bully who has to clamour for attention. See what a clever boy I am!'

So what! I am thinking. So what, so what, so what, so what! Isn't that the whole point? That we exchange what we have of the world, your version and my version? I never implied that there were things only I could see. It's not my fault that you don't have the same mental language as I do. I cannot be expected to speak your language, and if a thing isn't just so how can I agree? It's your word against mine.

But I swallow and shut up. I shall never be able to run to you enthusiastically when I discover something. You have slapped down the child in me. You are destroying my spontaneity with your inane and envious feminism. There are little things we cannot forgive in each other. They become the mutual history, quadrascopic vision, the twilight zone. A netherworld where neither you nor I exist but where our embittered ghosts are always abroad, waiting to suck the blood out of our passions. You are sending us there.

You have silenced me, as you say I have silenced you.

She twists the knife. 'Now I can tell you are going to be a martyr about this. I hate the way men can't stand criticism. You live your lives as if you are never wrong and nothing is ever your fault. I can't stand it!'

I hate being accused of resorting to martyrdom. There are triggers that will detonate my reasonableness. I won't listen if you push this too far. You have no right to prejudge my reactions. It would appear that I am not the only one who puts up internal barricades when we have an exchange. You function from your preconceptions as well, just like anybody else. You happen to think you cannot talk to me because you have erected your own barriers to being heard. It's your problem, not mine.

I keep silent, but she hears my thoughts. 'And I know that somewhere in your head you are turning everything around so that it isn't your fault.'

'It isn't anyone's fault, just a problem with communicating. At any rate, I shall try to listen to you the way you think I should. I guess I have something to learn.'

'Damn right you have something to learn! And it is your fault. Just for once, accept the responsibility for what you are.'

What am I? 'I don't see it the same way, but I shall try.'

'Thank you. Good-night.'

Damn the tactics, they never work! Nothing works but the truth. It is hard to discern the truth in total darkness. When only the voice makes contact, masks are ineffective. If she could see my face, she would see I am hurt; that is no mask. Perhaps then she would relent a little and understand that our positions are relative. Still, it is my interpretation of the way we are. There are tears in my eyes, but I do not know if that is because I have just yawned.

TWELVE

At the beginning and end of nature is chaos, or that which we interpret as chaos because we have flung ourselves into the shallow dualism of order and disorder. The smallest detectable components of matter describe no order that we can define except in uncertain terms – contingent terms which allow the duality to unite. Things are all yes and no, maybe and also, absolutely and somewhat. We may be otherwise enlightened at any moment, but it appears that there are no longer grounds for the pursuit of certainties, and, by implication, perfection. The way the universe is fashioned shows us that certainty might be only a matter of human values, or, as it may turn out, misguidedness. We can no longer assume benevolence from an order that might be contingent; the benevolence is our own creation – the important thing is to recognize this and celebrate it as our gift to this implacable void.

For us to have meaning in this universe is not a matter of whether it will accede to our definitions. We find our meaning for ourselves and may then proceed to impose it on the universe, which becomes, according to the integrity of our fabricated meanings, in turn benevolent, beautiful, blind, ordered, disordered, unknowing or uncaring, or somehow welded to us in our significance as individuals, or even emanating from our very souls, which we may postulate as *a priori* existents if we choose. It is a quantum choice; who will stop us? The universe is who we are; there, we may say it!

Now, because of our diversion into scientific and mechanistic paradigms, indeed, because we believe in paradigms at all, we have imposed an order on the universe which does not surrender to change unless there is a struggle between oppositions – with a victor and a vanquished.

One theory of the universe must topple another: the progress of our knowledge is harnessed to successive phases of (paradoxically) contingent certainties; at each stage we attempt to fix the universe in our own image while dispensing with its other possibilities. The problem is that we attempt to fix it at all. And we even fix, circumscribe, delineate the processes of change we observe in it, inventing such disillusioned concepts as entropy.

Entropy, like all temporarily fixed and successive theories of the universe, conveniently ignores the fact that we know little about the nature of time, outside of our own present ability to assimilate it. It is a linear and temporal affair, but time itself is fluid, relativistic, virtual – hardly the premise for a fixed perception of our destiny. Perhaps quantum physics may create its own unwarranted limitations for the same reason. In the theory of Schrödinger's cat, a moment of observation is postulated as being the decisive factor in the death or survival of the cat, but by its own assumptions, quantum physics ought not to be able to locate this moment in time or deduce a causal relationship between the cat and the observer. To accept a causal relationship is to accept that time has a linear dimension, but empirical evidence, and, if you will pardon the rude interpolation, the evidence of our hearts, makes this less and less tenable. The cat and the observer bear only a contingent relationship with each other until further notice; any other relationship is imposed by assumptions.

And similarly, if the evidence of our hearts is to figure in our new set of contingent relationships between all phenomena, the widely accepted barrier of the speed of light must bear further scrutiny. The evidence for it can be gathered only in the realm of infinite possibilities, when we are no longer limited by our empirical tools and by the illusion that we are separate from the phenomena we observe. Instead, it may prove worthwhile to interpret it as a cultural imposition: as such, it is an implied end to our development as a species; the scientists are at pains to tell us that there is already a point past which we shall not go. If we are not going to get past a certain destination, why bother to travel at all? Why not settle down and fix ourselves at whichever point is recommended by whomsoever's interest it is in to recommend it? Yet, if we begin to understand that we are simultaneous beings, our nature might itself change sufficiently to make the speed of light passable, or at least irrelevant. These are the possibilities.

The duality of scientific paradigms is easily detected in certain inconsistencies. No amount of caring noises that scientists have made in the face of protest has yet to disestablish the basic premise of scientific progress, which is that the object of understanding nature, of knowledge itself, is to grant us control over it. This rules out the constructive relationship that may be possible if we were somewhat more democratic about the universe.

It is our constant scuffling to fix ourselves and the universe that makes it all slip from our grasp. It is the business of making up our minds, then inevitably encountering the thing that will change them, and then failing to make the adjustment that propels us towards Sartre's version of bad faith.

In my prequantum years, I had unknowingly fixed myself in relation to V and her in relation to me. I was unable to cope with the multitude of personalities that comprise the relationship of two people: they themselves, the crowd that is their respective perceptions of each other, and the procession following that makes up their perceptions of their perceptions of themselves and of each other. They were nothing more than a succession of fixed points, the pools of stasis in which we drown each other. Versions, histories, interpretations.

If we cease to relegate such aspects of ourselves as love and emotion to the dark zone between understanding and knowledge, science and intuition, and begin to experiment with them as real components of our natures we might get beyond the point where we can define unimaginably small and mysterious particles of matter but fail to arrive at an accommodation of love and pain and grief and ecstasy.

What understanding of ourselves, of the universe and of others can we possibly embrace which will not itself be subject to change? If the universe dances, why should we stand still?

The internal democracy, the crowd within, the impulses, the love, are all there to be danced with, not merely to be controlled. If in your personal and God-given pursuit of happiness you believe that there is some fixed path to perfection, you are implying that your path is better than someone else's. If you happen to love that someone else, you become one of the walking wounded. Make no mistake. The first flush vanishes. The solution is a multiple, simultaneous and quantum being, a quantum society and quantum romance. And if you think I am laying down definitions I will submit that quantum is only a working word we have for states in which perpetual uncertainty, contingency and the beautiful order and disorder of the universe become identifiable. Not definable, take note; just identifiable. Just something that offers a rich counterpoint to the tune we can't get out of our heads. Just a rhythm you can dance to.

If there is an irresistible impulse in human nature it is towards anarchy, which is not the same as entropy, no matter what the scientists would have us think. Anarchy is really the state in which all possibilities exist. If that frightens us now it is because we have hoodwinked ourselves into the belief that there is security in a fixed order. But take a look at your newspapers each morning!

Possibilities are much more interesting than static perfection. Virtual events are just as interesting as the wave-collapsed paths of real events. In a quantum mind and in quantum love, the duality is lost and the two merge to produce a new richness of life in which everything may occur, where probability or fear need not condition our view of the future. All things are virtual and all things are real; belief is not obligatory. You have merely to be open to the enjoyment and increase of knowledge and perception.

Thus, what you imagine may be more important than what you believe, for your beliefs will always fix you and your imagination always liberate you. Imagination is the faculty that makes us, in that ironic term, *homo sapiens*. The interplay of the imagination with the universe of possibility is the process that constitutes the real acquisition of knowledge. When our imaginations fail there is only the dead learning which enslaves us and the endless repetition of mistakes. Our fear of the advance of machines is partly a fear that there may be nothing to us that cannot be replicated in a soulless device. Well, if machines succeed in reproducing imagination, if they can conjure the processes of virtual realization that are a habit with us, then we have nothing to fear. They will be as frail and fickle as we are. What we have really to fear are the pseudo-mechanoids in ourselves whom we have elevated to sanctity in the foolish belief that we must aspire to mechanical order and fixedness. No doubts, no questions, no growth, no love, no impulses, no imagination: just one long internment in the bowels of nothingness.

We must experiment with living this quantum state as individuals. Fortuitously, we all have the chance to practise at human relationships; they provide a personal and easily accessible theatre in which the quantum conditions of relativity, contingency, uncertainty, complementarity and stubborn impenetrability are all freely at play! Shakespeare propagated a certain nostalgia about our all being players, but you have to ask yourself, since it is you who writes sizeable chunks of the play, whether you might ever climb down off the stage and discover a life without masks, costumes and ludicrously tragic behaviour. How ironic that we spend our lives in search of perfection and endanger our enjoyment of life in the process! If the value of perfection is not wholly abstract and indefinable, and there is a reason for pursuing it, it must surely be to make us happy. So we give up great opportunities for happiness in pursuit of something we imagine will bring us happiness. It doesn't even make sense as a sentence!

Deferred gratification, as the sociologists sensually termed it, is the fetish of the twentieth century. It began somewhere in those dark nights of Victorian Britain, from whence our Western ethic had its last great emanation – the culture that devised anti-masturbatory alarms to fasten on their infant sons so they could burst in on them in the dead of night and administer a good thrashing to discourage the child's discovery of himself. Self-love is a prerequisite of self-knowledge, but nothing in excess, you understand!

Until we begin to act and think in the quantum mode, we will continue to pay a price for the past. In personal terms, we fix ourselves in relation to others, referring constantly to a past definition of ourselves. It is crazily two-dimensional. Abandoning our fixed positions helps us to accept the validity of the other person and of the persons we may have denied in ourselves. This is the democratic soul of the quantum being, in which the depth, understanding, tolerance, natural compassion and *noblesse oblige* of the human condition have a chance to reemerge. We all know that they are there somewhere.

This is why V and I first saw ourselves instinctively as parallel beings. In the first flush, all lovers traverse the quantum state naturally, and it is only one example of the way our instincts may operate within the realm of infinite adaptability and the infinite freedoms that are our birthright, that are *love*.

I fail to understand people who won't give in to their infatuations and impulses unless they have certain prior assurances. You don't often get a chance or reason to test the limits; you may get a chance to visit the moon or to buy a Van Gogh for the price of a loaf of bread, but rarely does that wide window open that gives you a long look into the face of your own destiny and says, Jump Through Me And I Promise You This: You May Not Be Sad, You May Not Be Happy, But You Will Never Be The Same Again. How can one resist the opportunity of becoming someone else!

If you begin to perceive that there are such things as concatenating events and change in every second, you open yourself to the challenge of your destiny. Then if you realize that the challenge of your destiny also changes in every second – that that is the *fun* of it, that the fun is doubled when you can share it, that dying alone is a pain in one's eternal ass – you leap through the window laughing out as loudly as you can. And isn't the universe magnanimous! For there is usually at least one occasion in the life of each of us when we are given the opportunity to make this leap, and that too in the company of someone for whom we feel the overwhelming thing called love. Fan my brow!

The truth is, V and I were lucky. We were so overwhelmed by the glittering abyss the window presented that there was no question of saying yes or no to it. We were simply swallowed whole.

Naturally I see the paradoxes in all this. Wasn't it V who accused me of being overperceptive? But the paradoxes are superficial. By unfixing yourself you become locked into a condition of being that makes you permanently susceptible to change. The paradox is that you become something that is relatively continuous, and this is not congruent with being unfixed. Nevertheless, I am talking here of states of being, not of rationally definable states which can be captured without damage. Paradoxes arise only when we insist that all things must be accessible to certain criteria, that is, fixed points which are even temporarily more significant than other fixed points. Once the undefinable encroaches on one's existence it is time to go off and have some fun. That is probably why it does so in the first place: in order to unhook us from the illusion that everything will submit to the right question.

V and I had preserved enough of our childhood personae to float away quite happily into oblivion. The encounter with Malcolm, who had been the collapsing force in the concatenation of events that had brought us together, showed there was a pattern in things. This pattern is not to be mistaken for a manifestation of order or determinism. Events concatenate because they express all possibilities. In a quantum universe there are thousands of versions of V and me who met and didn't meet, hitched up and didn't hitch up. Outside the boundaries of linear time all of these virtual characters exist now and are V and me. They include the V and me with whom you are now acquainted; that is the fiction of truth, so to speak. This realization of simultaneity and of infinite possibility enabled us to validate what we were; a democracy of selves permits you your own value, and then you need no reasons for love other than love itself.

With all the millions of years of evolution behind us, with the astonishingly mysterious perfection of the human organism, with the infinitely complex possibilities of the human mind, with love and joy and grief and ecstasy, with the quantum freedom of a universe of possibility, with the cry of a billion orgasms beating back the dumb mechanoid, with the gifts of poetry and science, with the laughter on the faces of children ever able to renew itself, with the earthly paradise of sensual or psychological intimacies – with all of this, in our infancy on this sceptred orb, we have built a world in which our future, destiny, power, capacity to love and reprieve from solitude are finite.

Until V and I had acquired conscious intimations of our quantum freedom we were thrashed. The world pressed its weight against the fragile surface of the bubble. Everything conspired to tell us that we had no right to exist. The problem is that without the quantum mentality you are drawn into believing that you must put up a fight. The delusion is that there are forces arraigned against you. This is their way of making you docile; the tactic is to propel you towards fixing your beliefs, and this is what makes you manipulable. The imagined conflict may trip you into being expedient rather than protective of your rights. It may fool you into giving up the choices and possibilities of your life in exchange for their false security. Whoever they are, they want us to forget this final freedom: that the human condition does not allow us to survive when the quality of our lives becomes degraded. We clamber ashore and die of asphyxiation like our cetacean cousins. Forfend, sweet children! Beware! You are being initiated into the ranks of the walking wounded!

THIRTEEN

The wave and the particle are dual yet identical manifestations of a unified phenomenon. The virtual and the real are contingently linked in their existence so as to make them inseparable, or to make the boundary between them invisible. Time is simultaneous, but is converted through a felicity of the human imagination into something perceived as linear. The masculine and feminine might prove to be, in analogous terms, wave and particle of an omnisexual unity, though complementarity frees each sex from being only wave or particle. Events disappear into nothingness at each end of their existence, so that all causes and effects become contingent and collapse in nonlinear time – theoretically, that is; in practice we are too often unable to discern the causes of things and seem reluctant to accept their effects.

If determinism exists it must apply equally backwards and forwards in time. Our present mental equipment leads us to the inescapable conclusion that even God cannot exist without creation. In simultaneous, noncausal time, the meeting of sperm and ovum might be a focal point in the progress backwards and forwards of each person's history (which deconstructs history as a whole); or it might not! As the child reaches for its mother's breast, the action may be caused by love or instinct, but now we cannot wholly assert that it took place as the result of a linearly *preceding* set of events: it may have occurred because the love and instinct were retroactive, booming in from the future. Let us loop the loop in time!

Everywhere we look we perceive the unity of all phenomena. Then, if we are sharp-sighted enough, we perceive that this unity does not exist separately from ourselves. Skin, in the words of mad old Nietzsche, is an illusion.

Let us go step by step. Now let us trot out some of the basic assumptions of our age: all things have a price; there is no reward without effort; only the strong survive; war is in the nature of humanity; human nature exists *de facto*, and is immutable, and its primary characteristic is self-interest; survival is all; evolution has ceased to operate; our race is an old race now.

In all of these assumptions there is the underlying sentiment of the human being as an antagonist of life. No wonder the Buddha cracks himself up in a few thousand statues all over the dying world of South Asia! No wonder the Afrikans have never been able to respond to the Great Western Ethic without laughing themselves silly then going off to have some fun!

Whether or not the universe happens to be benign, your capacity to enjoy it is a function of your imagination. Conflict is a wasteful way of achieving things because it postulates a false opposition between phenomena: it fixes them into only two positions, from either of which a relativistic assessment is imposs-ible. The unity of all things, even if it is only imaginary, gives us a participatory birthright in this universe, rather than an antagon-istic role; we feel more at home.

The acceptance that there is an essential unity between the sexes or between reason and emotion – that they are relativisti-cally equal because they are expressions of a unified phenomenon – allows us room to function outside the boundaries of reason; it acquaints us with love and mysteries in ways we might otherwise miss, and from which we may learn something.

The personal quantum mentality, with its wide-open mental spaces, with its sharp and shifting focus, with its inoculation against bigotry, might bring us the immensities of personal freedom that do not depend on freedoms handed down to us by consensus; they might, in fact, reconstitute our collective freedoms and make us internally incapable of denying them to each other.

Despite being thrashed – and I am not claiming heroism here, only a requisite looseness of character – V and I clung to our hopes. We were propelled into the quantum state by the wild looping of events, by hormones and psychic implosions, but we had not the practice or any means other than our own compulsions with which to operate the quantum choice and to effect our liberation.

What a way to go!

From the rooming house in heaven we took the bubble back to the desert and then back again to the Great Western Suburb, where I had the appalling lack of good sense to experiment with the ownership of property. By our natures we would have kept ourselves free to move along, catching a train at the drop of a banknote, but what were our natures? We had begun to succeed in undefining ourselves. Embryonic quantum freaks begin by going against their own natures, realizing that to have a nature is a mistake in the first place! Or maybe not! You rebel against your instincts or better judgements from a sense of perversity, because you no longer accept that there can be one sensible course to follow, or that being sensible has any validity of its own. Then we took a step further and abandoned all of those successive positions, deciding that owning a suburban hideyhole would be an act of rebellion against our perception of ourselves. This is not so overweening as it sounds, only a detailed way of describing the process of rebellion and counter-rebellion that occurs when you have removed your grounds for a particular course of action. A sensible act may be reconstituted as an act of rebellion; the important thing is that you have made a small step in freeing yourself from your past personae. While we were still mostly antagonists of life, suffering from the delusion that we had to put up a fight, rebellion was the only way to initiate in our characters the ability to change in every second, even if that meant settling down for a spell.

When you meet a rebel, ask them if they are capable of the final act of rebellion, the act which allows them to graduate to that transcendent state of rebellion that is the quantum state: ask them if they can rebel against themselves and activate that crackling interface between imagination and the universe. Oh aye.

We were right, of course, inasmuch as being right is a thing that will sustain you until you decide that you were wrong after all. Time unheals the slightest wounds! What the hideyhole did was provide us with some moments of respite. It was an experiment in finding out if there was any value in routine and the opportunity of a fixed abode, mental and geographical, from which to sally forth into the unfixed world. Naturally, events congregated like mourners at a funeral to witness the demise of two impulsive beings. You cannot sustain a mortgage on the basis of a daily bash at a typewriter; not to begin with, at any rate. Then you must go forth and beg sustenance, unless you are willing to fix yourself and become a sensible working member of society. Neither of us was fit for careers as, say, actuaries. You cannot have a career unless you have defined yourself or have consented to be defined. Witness the number of us who fall ungracefully apart when the definition is withdrawn! How astonishing that we live in a world where people are defined by what they work at! I shall not know ye unless I know whether ye are in astronautics or stevedoring! Define thyself, man, and define thy woman forthwith!

The vultures lumbered down from the cruel sky. An enormous complex of tax gatherers, corporate phantoms, mainframe computers, credit retrievers, debt piranhas and postmen from hell began to afflict us. We did what we could to retain a few hours of peace each day. The answer, naturally, would have been for one of us to have got a job. Life is simple when you are under threat. But neither of us could pin ourselves down sufficiently for this to emerge as a solution.

There was, after all, our grandiose lifestyle to preserve: not grand materially, you understand, but in its opportunities for leisure, contemplation and talk – those fires of human creativity! For all of history men and women had had to rise with the dawn and do God's good work on this swivelling globe. Technology hasn't changed that. V and I were the only people in history aside from the rich and the damned who could rise exactly when they pleased! Have you ever experienced the extreme mellowness of being on a permanent holiday? Your mind undergoes subtle changes and your clock is redundant unless it also makes tea. Ah! rise at 11 a.m., breakfast at lunch, lunch at dusk and dine at midnight. In between, lounge or lurch about or go for long walks – they being all you can afford – and, talk, talk, talk! When your mind is not forced into compartmentalized time you begin to feel your natural rhythms surfacing. What have we lost! The enormous collection of faculties that you have clapped in irons while you pursue definitions of yourself and stretch yourself thin in linear time comes alive and takes you over. It reactivates your imagination, which you had forgotten was such a source of delight. Your body becomes poised because it has unlearnt the rush and the illusion of somewhere to go. Your emotions, being free from the interruptions of your mechanoid voice, recapture their continuity. Your inspirations become frequent and prolonged. Your appreciation of the finer things in life – food, sex, the occasional altercation – becomes sharp and focused. You are having fun!

V and I behaved as if this state was our birthright, and so it was. While the fanged wolves of decent society were moulting at our door we had locked ourselves in the bubble and were experiencing life to the brim. The whole purpose of this excursion into permanence suddenly became clear. We had given ourselves a chance to feel entirely unencumbered by the mundane and we trusted our luck to survive against the odds.

Now you may wonder how it is possible to abandon all missions and traverse the distances of heaven when you are on the run from all the responsibilities heaped on you for the fact of being born. The sensible among you might argue against courting death to find out about life. But what is life except a process of mucking through? And with no linear mission to fulfil, no static definition of who you are, you realize that the fun is in the mucking through, the thrill in starting out at some point and ending up at another with no idea how the way was constituted: the mingling of events and your fine perceptions of them deliver you, and you can say, God in Heaven! I now see how it was! I have learnt something about the purity of an existence unconditioned by rules and definitions; I have found that an essential destination of my life is internal; I have reawakened forgotten gifts and participated in my own evolution. Now there's a mission!

V and I put all this together in our refusal to live as if we were going somewhere or had a job to do. But we were thrashed all the same. Perhaps in the future the task of undefining oneself will not be fraught with perils, but when you have just invented the task for yourself, you do not know enough whether it is a sane or brave undertaking. No one else appears to think it worthwhile; it must be madness to imagine survival without any means of support; you are lonely and conflicted; you worry about where your next meal is coming from even as you rejoice in the fact that you do not have to catch a subterranean monster-machine and join a crowd of aimless, hurting people who are scratching around for theirs.

And then something in you unfixes even further and you realize that worrying doesn't make a damn bit of difference: the challenge is the same challenge that humanity has always faced and now there is some authenticity to your experience. The Samurai emerges. You understand what it feels like to meet each day with no guarantee of survival; then it occurs to you that whatever you happen to be doing, whether you are a clerk or a mountaineer, this condition still applies! There are no guarantees! In attempting the quantum state, however, you are not wasting your risks on blind chance, you are taking them as a warrior does, with full responsibility and the freedom of yourself. You have fashioned a small wagon that rolls in the path of your very own destiny. A minor adjustment of vision is all that is needed to convince you that your luck is now your own. The experience you have accumulated makes you feel rich enough to forget the trivial oppressions of fiscal woe.

V and I now moved from state to state faster than the decisions we made. We were able to see how an act of the imagination can create present and future, as well as rehabilitating the past. We could journey without encumbrance.

The quantum idea that our participation in the universe actually creates it suggests that if there is an 'essence' we are it; but no matter, if there is an indissoluble reality out there somewhere then it must be God, and if that old critter cannot change He can't be good for much. Where's the fun of it, M. Sartre? Where's the love and the lust, old crock? Give us this day our share of sex and revelry! If we cannot yet dance to the music of the spheres, let human laughter ring out defiantly and from its resonances some distant galaxy take form. If consciousness is the Unified Field and the Unified Field is inseparable from love, let's all get on with the astonishing opportunity that being truly conscious provides. That, in my view, is the next step in our evolution, speaking in strictly linear terms. We will have cast off our defined selves and become multidimensional beings without a single anchor in linear time and space; we will traverse the distances of heaven; we will exceed the speed of light because it does not exist other than we have created it; we will create our own sustaining energy if it turns out that God has dumped us in an entropic universe; we will *become* the ineffable. Perhaps our descendants will wonder what took us so long, and why we wasted so much time.

You can only waste time if you believe it exists.

If you free your imagination, you can reinvent the world.

If everyone does this, we will have a vast richness of worlds.

Get out into the night and look long and hard at the stars: this is where we belong.

Then cancel your appointment with the slobbering pinstripe who tells you you cannot have any of it unless you pay his price. He wants to turn your consciousness into a commodity, in case you invent a world in which he can't call the shots. He'll tell you you can have it back if you pay in convenient instalments, but by the time you get it back, assuming it's the same thing you gave away, it'll be too damn late to enjoy the worlds you invent.

You might as well retire from life right now.

As for V and me, they never did find us. We were so far away from anything they could understand we could walk right by them and they wouldn't know it. We could mosey along right up to them and take what we needed and they wouldn't know who in hell we were. As far as they could tell we were beings so alien, from so far out in the galaxy, that they never could figure out if we were alive or not. We had slipped into another dimension.

We were moving targets.

Or V was.

I had forgotten to reinvent certain aspects of myself. The quantum mentality hadn't wholly emerged. V is lunging at me. Gervase is smoothing his hair back unnecessarily. Rostand is spilling whisky over his cheeks. Malcolm is straphanging in the Underground. I haven't stopped wandering in and out of work. We have decided that V should take the first plunge and give up all pastimes other than making the internal trip to find who, severally, she is. It is difficult for her. She was bred an active and vivacious person, wholly immersed in a predefined world. There is no way back, even if she wanted it. Sometimes she does.

I stray in and out of paid or half-paid half-employment until I can muster the courage to throw further caution windward. V urges me to do it. She speaks for the faltering rebel in my own tremulous overmale nature. I hear her voice because she holds me to my words. I cannot take the stress of being fixed and unfixed at once. I begin to fall apart. V is lunging at me. I started the row. We finish the row, unable to remember what it is about. We never do. It is merely theatre.

Find help, says V, you are becoming a pain. I hate doctors, says I. I see it as my inalienable right to hate at least one genus in our species so long as my hate is not based on colour, creed and such. Profession, yes. I hate the prescriptive types. Quacks. Cold-hearted quacks.

You are talking nonsense, says V. It's my right, I reply. Here, says she, handing me a slip of paper with a number on it: Go and see this homoeopath.

There is nothing the matter with me I cannot handle myself, I say.

Never said there was, says V. Go and see this homoeopath for fun; rebel against the old dada inside you who says there is nothing wrong.

So I went and saw Gervase and took the Nux vomica and went wholeheartedly and blissfully mad.

FOURTEEN

I am putting the key in the keyhole of the hideyhole in suburbia. Gervase said if there was anything I couldn't handle from feeling a bit queer I should give him a call. I am one suggestible person. Already, I am not quite feeling myself. Literally. I have always been convinced in quantum fashion that we are not the same people any of us were a second ago. I get on the train and somebody else gets off. He or she is me; I am not me. When I think about who I am I get this feeling of not being – not not being here or there, simply not being. When I wake up in the morning I am definitely not the person who went to sleep the night before. Therefore, I never seem to get any real sleep.

I am beginning to find my quantum personality, I think, as I put the key in the keyhole, but first I shall explore the boundaries of not being myself. Everyone a winner! Interesting stuff, this Nux vomica; it cures you of your precious phthisis by turning you into somebody else and then somebody else again. Along the way you may forget that whoever you were had anything wrong with them. Interesting.

Who the hell am I?

There is no one at home. It is mid-morning. I look in the mirror. The person in the mirror is thinking thoughts about someone looking into the mirror who is not me. Who are we? As events concatenate, so does matter. Matter has concatenated to form these features of mine which are not mine. Historically I am there. The nose has been coarsened by a well-aimed punch; it was a punch I delivered to myself when having a lonely tantrum as a child – fed up with my parents' wars. Damage myself to damage them; no more their sweetface. This is a fine suburban hideyhole. I want to shit on the carpet, in the middle of the living-room. It is the only room in the house; the rest is a cabin of a kitchen and a hole in the wall for a bedroom. If I shit on the floor in the middle of the carpet, I shall change for ever the nature of this abode. This shall become the abode in which once, irreversibly, I deposited a living turd on the carpet. I look again in the mirror. Who is this person who wants to shit on the floor? He has gone, poor wretch. But something has to be done. Some statement of personal transformation has to be made. The line of the jaw has disappeared under burgeoning jowls. It runs in the family. Past thirty, we all subside in the face. Moon-faced people. Moon people.

Naturally, I haven't forgotten who I am. I am the man who is married to V and who shares this home with her. But this is an historical 'fact'. I have created myself and V and this home in retrospect. I have imagined it all into being. I wish, accordingly, to create one solid moment and produce a phenomenon that will not slip away into my imagination, something external of which I cannot say, This does not exist. I want an external consensus with another person who can say, Yes, this does exist and is not contingent or affected by the relativism of our positions in the world. I want to deposit a lump of turd on the carpet. Better it is left there for a few hours before V comes home, so that it solidifies and becomes more itself.

Now I am regressing into analism. My being is inverting itself so that its primary point of focus is not the objectified mental process – the internal chatter of thought – but the action and delivery of the anal sphincter. My arse is my mouth. My mouth is my arse. My neocortex is my large bowel. The soft flesh between my brow and the bridge of my nose is my perineum. My tongue is my penis. My penis is now possessed of a sense of taste. Different portions of it are molecularly keyed to respond to saltiness, bitterness, sweetness. I shall go into the kitchen and stick my penis into a wedge of chocolate fudge cake. There is no chocolate fudge cake in the kitchen. Such is life. Only chocolate, the dark, sensual emanations of the cacao seed, will do to satisfy my penis's longing for uncontingency.

But I can do nothing. I cannot stick my penis into a cake or deposit a lump of turd on the carpet. I can make not even the smallest plan or intention to be or do anything. That will be a transgression of my existencehood. That is the only word for it: Existencehood. The moment I realize a thought in the outer world I become fixed and myself. The man who shits on the carpet will be identifiable as myself. Until then, I am no one: I am free.

At last! Now I have unbecome myself. Rejoice! Because I have unbecome myself I am suddenly free to create a multitude of realities, each of which will belong to whomever I am at the moment I create them. I am God. This final freedom to do or be whatever I wish means that I need do and be nothing. There is no need. While the effects of this Nux vomica last – I assume for a few weeks – I have only to be an observer of my own mental process. I have gone mad in order to observe the internal landscapes of madness.

Now I subside, and, in truth, know that I have become finally and irrevocably sane. My consciousness has linked, through this process of unbecoming, with the essence of being. I have become essence. Soon even the words will stop and I shall be only a pair of internal eyes. Then the eyes will close and I shall be only a sense of hearing. Then all that will go to darkness, thought will cease, and I shall become a one-pointed consciousness. I shall defy and go beyond God for even He has to exist. I do not: I will obliterate myself and thus the universe as well, having created it, and since I will be nonbecome I shall have no memory and in nontime I shall discover that the universe never existed because I cannot remember it. However, not being there to discover or remember will wipe out even that nonevent. Not existing will then not exist. Not not existing will not exist. Not not not existing will not exist exist exist. Not not not. Exist exit exist exit sexist sexist shit. The final state of not existing will be no more or less an essence than a lump of sexist shit. What is a lump of sexist shit? How can a faecal fragment possess an abstract quality such as sexism? Quite easily! In a nonphenomenal world anything can be called anything. You may have sexist shit, or democratic piss. I laugh. There is some scope for humour here. Let me invent and therefore bring concretely, phenomenologically, into being a complete new category of existents that are incongruous in their very essence!

Sexist shit, democratic piss. What else? What else? Nervous

thoraxes! No! Let's get beyond the physiological. Voracious
pianolas; tall, rather angular envy; subversive damask antimacassars; numinous biscuits; applauding alveoli. Yes, let's go to action
– have action instead of attributes. Let's see – I can't get away
from the physiological! – cogitating smegma! Ah! Disgust! Disgust
is a conditioning aspect of awareness; it touches the boundaries,
moving ahead like an Indian scout to tell us where not to tread!
How long before I become a serial murderer for the sake of
observing it? No, no. Let us continue; you cannot be or do
anything; you have progressed into a state of benign observer-
hood. On with the action! A congregation of replicating guitars.
Ah, replicating! The molecular equivalent of lust! Let's see:
copulating . . . copulating what? What can we predicate as
copulating? Something utterly sexless and without material existence . . . copulating acronyms . . . how's that! Or copulating
syllogisms! Ha! Cop that, Aristotle! I have reduced your scheme
of things to . . . to what? Aha! Copulating nonentities! Ha and
double ha! Explain that you old Greek fart! I have scented the
remains of your fart, a fart you farted one lonely night in some
hovel on maybe Naxos while you were dreaming of young boys,
and I have turned your fart into an analogy for the interdepen-
dency of order and chaos! Ha, copulating nonentities! Nietzsche
had nothing on me! It is a privilege to go mad. It is the greatest
privilege known to mankind to go mad and to be able to observe
the process. Not even God can do this.

I hear a key in the door. I scuttle into the living-room and sit
down, pretending to read a book. It is a book about nothing. The
words stare at me from the page. They say nothing. They cannot
be heard.

V is home. She breezes in.

Who in hell is this woman I have married? Her hair is in tight
blonde curls around her tiny head. Her cheekbones glisten. She
has had a perm. Women have perms. I detest the whole concept
of perms. I deplore the ornamentation of women. Women should
be what they are, under the whale extract and vaporized antelope
glands; they should be the soft, weak, doughy flesh and the body
odours and the vaginal discharges; flawed, ill-designed creatures
on God's earth; creatures of pain controlled by their oestrogen

levels, by blind molecular interactions; creatures of faulty spatial perception and lachrymose fragility; glandular creatures altogether; the worst kind of creatures – creatures who need looking after and who cover themselves in glandular secretions; walking repositories of musk and semen, of semiotics and sema- phore and pheromones. Semaphore whores. Who needs them?

She looks at me. I am hunched and scowling, but I am not the person who is hunched and scowling. I have gone on ahead. We made a promise to each other once that if one of us goes on ahead the other would gracefully relinquish all claim to the marriage.

'Oh-oh,' she says. It is not like the person I am not not to smile a welcome. 'Shall I come back later?'

I shall pretend that everything is fine, for everything is fine. But I must tell her that I have gone on ahead as soon as possible. We are so good at communicating with each other that there is no need of prevarication. I look at her squarely.

'I have gone on ahead.'

She smiles broadly. 'Good for you!' She breezes into a chair. 'Want to tell me about it?'

I decide to take a different tack. 'I am seriously thinking about shaving my head.'

She says nothing. I can tell from her eyes that she knows the jig is up. A curtain falls behind her eyes: it is the usual prelude to tears. I have hit her hard.

'While you were out,' I announce calmly, 'I finally got around to cleaning the video – you know, the recording head.'

She looks at me, biting her lip.

'And I replaced the broken bit on the guitar – you know, the machine head.'

She rises abruptly. 'Would you like some tea?'

'Once, when we were in Sri Lanka, I saw a man pouring tea in a long stream from cup to cup in order to cool it; wonderful tea – tasted better for the pouring, which, incidentally, gave it a head.'

She goes into the kitchen. She does not know whether to take me seriously. I must have one more crack at ending a sentence with the word 'head'. Head is what it is all about. I raise my voice so she can hear.

'You'll never guess what they call the lavatory on a boat . . . ' I say.

'Tell me about it.'

'The head.'

She pops her head round the kitchen door. 'OK, what's all this "head" business?'

'I saw Gervase.'

'I know you saw Gervase.'

'And since I saw Gervase, queer things have been happening in my head.'

'It'll wear off. It's part of the cure.'

'Gervase didn't say this would happen.'

'Apparently it affects different people in different ways.'

'But I think I know what has happened. Gervase has freed me, only he has freed me too much and I have gone on ahead.'

'Does that mean what I think it means?'

'Yes. That.'

'You want to leave me?'

'I have left already.'

'Will you be back?'

'No promises, no conditions. Remember?'

She brings in the tray of tea. 'Very well, if you feel the same way after a suitable period of time, we'll make the necessary arrangements.' Then she adds, sweetly, 'But I shan't give you up without a fight.'

I am touched. She pours the tea. Even God wishes to be loved. She is such a fine, small specimen of womanhood – not a glandular repository, really. God can hate as well as love. I can change. I can think one thing in one moment and completely the opposite in the next moment. I am truly free. I cannot even be conditioned by my own thoughts. They cannot find me. She has such compact and graceful movements. I have always admired the way her knees dance in unison when she shifts in her chair. If her skirt is short enough, tiny little arcs of forbidden flesh twinkle in the dance. So what if I have gone on ahead! I can choose to be wherever I want to be because, in truth, I am nowhere. I can be everywhere. Hurrah!

I say, 'Perhaps the very state of being ahead makes me free to choose who I wish to be with. Therefore I choose to be with you.'

She draws herself up and does her capable-woman act. 'Good. That's that, then. I'm very glad you went to see Gervase. I think if you feel different already, you are going to feel amazing in a couple of weeks. That's all it should take. Then things will be back to normal, but you'll still feel free.'

'How the hell do you know all this?'

'I just sense it. What you imagine is more important than what you believe. Remember?'

'My God! Hoist with mine own puerile petard!'

She knows more. 'Gervase has freed you to exercise that power. Let your imagination out of the cage you've kept it in. You of all people! Now you know why I disapproved.'

The elation disappears. I am demoralized at being so neatly defined. The whingeing boy emerges. 'But what am I to do?'

She rises and comes over to me, taking hold of my hands. She looks into my eyes. She is in love with me. That is the meaning of everything. There is somebody who I am. I am the person whom V loves. I exist gratuitously. I have an existence separate from the nonexistence I made for myself.

'Why do you have to *do* anything?' she asks gently.

'We have to live.'

'You stay at home. I'll go to work.'

'That's out of the question unless it is what you specifically want. It was decided that you should not work.'

'So what?'

'We'll be destroying what we've been trying to do. The point is not to have to work.'

'But we haven't managed it, have we? You've been in and out of work. It's locking up your imagination.'

'So what's the answer? What can I do?'

'Precisely nothing. Stop working. Stop everything. Do nothing.'

'How will we survive?'

'Who cares?'

'Is that it? Who cares?'

'You need to stop working, so stop working. One thing at a

time. We won't starve – not yet. We'll borrow a bit more – whatever. One day it'll all be the same, anyway. One risk is as good as another.'

There is hot tea warming my insides, and V is nourishing me. 'If I stop working I can internalize completely. What a holiday that will be!'

'It's time you had a holiday,' she says.

'Do you know which part of me needs the most rest?'

She prods me in the crotch.

'Not this?'

'My head,' I say. 'My head.'

I am sitting alone trying to be analytical about why work has driven me mad. V is having an afternoon nap. She sleeps a lot. She has decided to devote a portion of her life to the exploration of dreams. She uses a pendulum to analyse her dreams and is making an astonishing record of dreams interpreted by an instrument of chance. She has already begun to explore the interaction of chance and destiny, using her instincts, emotions and whatever else comes to hand as tools of divination. I am exploring the interaction of chance and destiny by allowing myself to go spasmodically insane.

We can't be such bad people after all.

Ah. Work. How can you work when you perceive that your true state is without anchorage? In social situations, V and I are confronted with The Question: *What do you do?* We spend all our days and some nights as well exploring the interaction between chance and destiny. Really? How *do* you get by? On a wing and a prayer! What do they think of us? Who the hell cares! They have one thing right: they have guessed I am insane.

I take the holiday and render myself incognito. V is out spending the last of the money we have on things we don't need. We can always borrow more, paying off the debts years from now when the pain and doubt will be a small memory. My bank manager is investing in a mission to explore the interaction between chance and destiny, only he doesn't know it. He thinks he is tiding me over until I revive my business, which is something to do with advertising.

V has no sense of caution. She is the more highly developed quantum creature of the two of us. Her lack of prudence and thrift and all those Victorian values that are still furtively part of my conditioning often frightens me. She challenges me, urging me to do the things one mostly shouldn't do. Do not merely abandon caution but when you come to the precipice, leap! Leap, leap, leap!

I have leapt. Gervase the homoeopath has given me the push. To what end must one unfix and uncondition oneself? From this detached and mild insanity I can see that it is possible to be unconditioned enough to go smiling and forgetful to your own execution. There must be an immediacy of being, a way of distilling yourself completely into the present so you become sufficiently 'in the now' to eat, drink and be merry till the very instant of your disembowelment.

It is surely madness, an abandonment of the will, a betrayal of human nature. But I have undefined human nature, and the will is only one shuffle in the dance with which you create yourself.

So I took the holiday. Madness mingled with the remnants of panic I felt at abandoning our one last source of daily bread. Soon, in a month or two, the credit would run dry. V didn't care. I was terrified of having to go out and pick up a shovel in order to feed us. But after a few days of the madness, the terror subsided. I began to run off with my imagination, consoled by the joys of the utterly civilized debate progressing within my internal democracy.

In the meantime the debt mounted, thousands upon thousands, as V and I dismantled our caution. In some parts of the world people queued for a loaf; we weren't going to wait in line for ever while here, in our prodigal world, the tasks of life were dictated to us by those who controlled the commodities.

V's answer was to exist wholly in the present. She had sharpened her talent for that. We would do what was needed, but only when it was needed, leaning not one millimetre into the future. Debt was merely a dimly lit tunnel to some brighter place. Every bill for utilities acquired – for the few moments we worried over them – the import of a death sentence. Each

123

computerized threat, with its appalling mechanoid language, was bitter medicine until your system had digested it.

I was challenging myself, not only in the experiments in madness, but also in my male conditioning. If V was brave enough to go through this, I could at least be braver, for I was the one on whom the axes would fall first. That part of myself that was still frightened was the fixed and conditioned part; if I were to get rid of it by living dangerously, then so be it. We knew no better way. We were following a path blazed by some ironic destiny. In the end we had no consistent opinions about what we were or where we were going; we were engaged only in the present: one meal at a time, one impulse leading to another.

However, my cautious self, the staid little pedestal wimp, had begun, insidiously, to develop a hatred of V. He was never much inclined to surrender to the Goddess. He hated mysteries, hated abandoning his mincing little will, the only tool with which, heretofore, he had been able to carve up the world. The parts of myself I had begun to kill off were festering.

V had an internal democracy, too, and I hated the person in her that saw life as a collection of problems. It always maintained a certain correctness that betrayed the courageous dream diviner and dancer with chance. I could not reconcile these conflicting aspects, in the end putting them down to feminine neurosis. This was just a step away from an hysterical hypothesis. I saw the oppositions in V because I continued to view the world, despite myself, in the old dialectical way. V did not have a theory of opposites to apply to herself or to others; for her, the human condition was a flux of organic and spiritual aspects that absolved her from consistency. Her natural way of being and her success in keeping her courage were precisely what I was looking for in my quantum journey. I was the theorist but she practised these things naturally, in full awareness and as a living compulsion to be exactly what she was at any given point. I hated her unfixedness even as I tried to unfix myself. I still wanted to be the first man in history who had tried, really tried, to uncover the undiscovered sex, to experience the nature of women and find the unity behind both sexes – outside of love or our sentiments or the mysticism of anima and animus. What sharpness in my spirit had to be quelled if I were to be, in the old sense of the word, *inspired* by this other being?

At the interface of chance and destiny many inexplicable things happen. I had learnt that if you go with the flow you learn something, and in a magical way you come through. Now, to become V I had to explore the possibility of hating her. The homoeopathic madness gave me the freedom not to be myself, precipitating this. Back from Gervase, the first thing I had said to V was that I had gone ahead. I felt free to hate her, abandoning our love if an impulse large enough took me over. I did not know then that I was shedding the last traces of a fixed love. The death of romance is complete and irrevocable unless we understand that love cannot be stilled or defined. For me to accomplish this – as a natural process in the self-transformation I had undertaken – through the homoeopathic and other madnesses – I had to detach myself from my old feeling for V and experience something else. What would it feel like *not* to love V? I knew that I was bringing pain upon myself. Such is the dedication of the self-subversive.

Now it wasn't just V's generic womanhood that I hated. I deplored all kinds of things in women. It is precisely the unfixed-ness of the female that the male detests and finds intimidating. That may be why it is the male who does the courting, to use an old-world notion. Women have to be netted because they are capable of being free.

The free and unfixed person is many people at once: the part of me that was still incapable of following my theories of quantum choice and freedom could not abide this in V. I expected her to be consistent and to believe in the male Utopia where, every day, through the exercise of an infallible will, things get better and better. On days when she was worn thin by our existence or our numerous frictions I found her intolerable. Where was the old courage I had romanticized into being and bestowed upon her? I had defined her and she was failing to live up to the standards.

I hated her neuroses, but they were not more acute than those of any dweller in penury. A woman's biology precludes the stiff upper lip, I thought. But what I ignored was that V's emotionalism gave her the release to transcend the shit we were raining down on ourselves. It was a facet of her awareness, which was encompassing. She experienced a wholeness of being in whatever state her circumstances obliged, with her emotions given unrestricted space to react. This seemed to me to be the only appropriate response to life and events. It is no use meeting God with half one's faculties put away. And in the quantum sense I also saw that just as chance and destiny intermingle, emotions and events must reflect each other across the barriers of perception, as waves and particles of a unified phenomenon. Only the full play of emotions allows us to react properly to the events of our lives. Only the state of unfixity allows the full play of emotions. There is a hypothesis that says that all that can be achieved will be striven for; but without the release of emotion and the rehabilitation of our unified selves, men will continue to scurry like rats, hoarding filth and striving for voracious powers.

V would come home and weep. I would check the time of the month. I could theorize endlessly on the metaphysical absurdity of pain, with Camus as my noble predecessor, but I had shielded myself from the *emotions* of pain and could no longer feel them except in unguarded moments. I had not cried since I was a teenager, but to hell with that! I wasn't on a mission to become the lachrymose man and still am not. I knew, though, that there were large territories of emotion from which I had excluded myself, and that here was this woman whose ability to feel I despised. Like most of the men I had known, my emotions had mutated into the casual psychoses of our age: depression, inexplicable rage, mundane madnesses, drunkenness, nameless fears, the rootless obsession with work – all this a dour manipulation of what I was really feeling in order that I would not, at any cost, admit it to myself. For this I hated V. Women showed no control, no mettle when the going got rough, even though it was they who survived when the coronaries, cancers and anti-personnel mines had decimated the rest of us. They have freed themselves enough from ideology that they can pick up and carry on when men's lunar periodicity unleashes the occasional holocaust.

The softnesses were merely signs of weakness; the pheromones inadvertent betrayals of biochemical slavery; the tears stupid – a surrender to circumstance: I hated V for the personal slight of her being a woman. I could not see the strength of tears, thinking that to weep is to relinquish one's will when all it is is a regrouping of emotions that can deal better with the affliction. If crying has a meaning, that must be it: the catharsis that delivers us from where we were a moment ago.

And after emotion, there was the question of the female intellect. I began to imagine that under V's fine form and style, under the physiognomical appeal and warm wit, there was no substance. For a man, intellect is most often the ability to define a great many things, a quantitative faculty in the great traditions of the reductionist. Knowledge is defined as something to acquire: the more of it one acquires, the greater one's intelligence. The unspoken war between males is the Cold War that involves intelligence gathering. It accounts for the hoarding and protection-ism among academics and scientists. But at the palaeolithic root of it is men's belief that this is how they equip themselves for survival. Knowledge is power, but they cannot fathom what this power is for or how it can be deployed without fatalities. By definition, to acquire knowledge is to fix it.

In the relationship between the sexes, the illusive power that knowledge bestows gives men very loud voices. The large hoard must be volubly proclaimed, and in an altercation the strategic deployment of munitions will win − that is to say, silence − any argument. The marshalling of a great many facts, most of them useless, gives men the power to shout louder and longer than many women care to; and if one happens on a woman who has herself a stockpile of sharp axioms, she can still be outshouted. God must undoubtedly have been a man.

The facts that men acquire, at any rate, are highly questionable as facts or fallacies; their ultimate use is censorial, so while men are loath to betray emotion they will undermine free speech without a second thought. The ensuing silence of the woman, or her disinclination to treat knowledge as a shallow commodity, is interpreted as a failure of the intellect. V's passive resistance to my verbal assaults, her silence in the face of The Great Historic Theory, her instinctive refusal to resolve an issue solely by assembling corroborative fact − these I began to mistake for signs of an 'inferior' intelligence. After all, I was learning to hate her.

The notion of there being a hierarchy of the intellect is in any case indefensible. There is no consensus on this planet and no position about which I can imply, in the fanciest and most Latinate garble, an inherent inferiority. Not even the lowest scavenger of human ordure rummaging through the darkest heaps in the darkest continents of the world can be said categorically and before God to have been endowed with less natural intellect than you or me. It simply isn't possible. It is a racism of the mind which, with many of the other fond traits I catalogue here, will surely be dumped into the past when we have woken up and learnt to be ourselves. It ignores all evidence of intellect other than it can define for itself. I make the rules.

As long as I was able to romanticize V, fixing and defining our love, I saw her intellect as instinctive and womanly. When the madness unleashed for its last foray the quasi-Darwinist male fascist, I was able to hate her. Until I had perceived the undivided being, the unity of love and consciousness, I could not know that love subsists only in fluidity, with the freedom to die or to achieve its own apotheosis.

I had begun to hate my own creation, a ghastly rancid wraith of V that I had taken for myself; the final toothless ghoul of the Pygmalion complex who mouths your own words back at you because that is all you hear. It was not I, experimenting with reality, who had gone 'ahead'. V had been obliged to leave without me.

At the appropriate impasse, one may obliterate oneself. I had a whole lot of theories about what was on the other side but had failed to dissolve my old solidity well enough to slip across. A quantum choice was necessary. You may view a critical transformation as an emetic process, throw up all the poison, cauterize your brain, have your stomach pumped and your genitals zapped all at the same time; or you may simply choose to *forget* the whole damn thing.

I was fortunate: I had unfixed myself sufficiently to heave all the old baggage out of the big bow window. I didn't have to shit on the carpet. I was capable of changing in every living second. There!

What was left? A being for whom all things were interchangeable, but whose last faint desire was for a persistent love.

Welcome home, old bean.

*

In the bedroom V snored gently. In the birthing room she made one last lunge at nothingness and stole from the void, from the Unified Field, from the echo of the orgasm, from the puckered orifice of eternity, the tender evidence that we had not been travelling alone: the boy, Will.

FIFTEEN

In the beginning are the sperm and the ovum, two particulate entities called to each other by a causality we do not understand. At least, not in scientific terms. Where were you at that precise point: when your father's sperm and your mother's ovum were about to get on the bus together? Were you having lunch with your bank manager?

No.

At that point you did not exist. At least, not in the terms of our linear time-frame.

So the question arises, as it must over, let us say, breakfast or while you cogitate in the bathroom: When exactly did you begin to be?

You began in the nanosecond of first contact between your father's sperm and your mother's ovum. That will do for now.

But how is that nanosecond to be measured? When does it start and when does it end?

Congregate, friends! This is where we disappear into simultaneity. Packets of time – that is, any conceivable duration – can be broken down like the quanta of matter into smaller and smaller phenomena. A billionth of a billionth of a millimetre might loom like the dome of St Peter's to certain nameless *genii incogniti* who live below the wavelength of light, in the caressing darkness, for all we know, of another dimension. Likewise, the moment in time may be pursued through finer and finer measurements, down and down into durations so infinitesimal as to make the enunciation of the word 'infinitesimal' an incomprehensible groan fifteen billion years long. These durations are so short that they have no detectable beginning and end. Within one of them, which to your preexistent self – the little warp in the texture of nothing that

130

once you were – might have lasted for eternity, you were born. *Velkommen ombord*!

The beginning and end of any event can only be named, they cannot be isolated in time as we know it, and events, at any rate, appear to fade in and out of each other with something akin to quantum indeterminacy. That is why Schrödinger's cat might just as well have been a sewing machine. Now get Einstein in on the act with his relativity and curvature of spacetime and you are reduced to wondering whether you began in time at all and whether you are here *wondering whether you began in time at all and whether you are here.* In such predicaments, of course, language disappears up its own epiglottis. And the sensation propagated by this existential doubt is uncanny, particularly if it assails you when you are engaged in some universally inconsequential activity like having lunch with your bank manager.

However, if you are engaged in a momentous orgasm or witnessing the precipitate emergence of your first child, the sensation is altogether different. If you were once benignly mad, your dishevelled brain cells might tart up the experience for you, allowing an inkling of the essential unity of all things. You might develop a few half-lit thoughts on the indivisibility of love and consciousness or on the extra-scientific significance of the Unified Field, in between clutching your wife's trembling brow and guiding your startled gaze over the skydiving form swooping out of her undercarriage.

So entered Will, the Skydiver, fifty-two centimetres long, dolphin-sleek, gory and with all digital extremities manifest and perfect except for a kink in each last toe from ramming his feet against his mother's sternum.

I am having breakfast with Will, who chomps like a puppy, rejecting any comestible not white or brown in colour and glutinous in consistency. Somewhere in his cerebrum is written a program detailing the precise viscosity of acceptable nutrition. The effort of working this viscous mixture between gums and palate and finally down through the pharynx makes his eyes stand out in their sockets, and, with a ring of oatmeal around his lips, renders him into a dwarf-mute version of the Jazz Singer.

He cannot say 'Mammy' yet, but has two partially formed semantemes with which he manipulates the universe. The first is a voiced bilabial plosive generated from the diaphragm, a lip-trill demi-semiquavered after the downbeat: Bbpp. This serves as a basic binary for controlling the world and his gods: Bbpp for 'yes' and with greater force and disdain, Bbpp for 'no'.

Bbpp.

The other semanteme is wholly specific and, in the language of computers, dedicated. It is his first attempt at descriptive prose. Being somewhat taken aback at the sound of his own cough he has adapted the glottal plosive onomatopaeically to invent the word 'cough'. This he delivers as 'Kfff' and he is at pains, whenever he coughs, to inform us that he has coughed. 'Or 'Kfffd'.

This is the sum total and *raison d'être* of the character with whom I am sharing my breakfast table; nevertheless, he has caused me to ponder one of the momentous questions of the universe. Throughout our Judaeo-Christian history we have been told that humans are divine in form yet must strive for perfection. We are made in the image of God but along the way and through our own fault have fallen out with Him. Therefore it is our stated mission to refashion ourselves as nearly as possible into The Real Thing. Another futile promise of some illusive perfection. Now I am watching the Canine Skydiver at repast and thinking: Look what I have made! He would be no less remarkable if he were, indeed, Mr Schultz's Snoopy, for I will have made him no less in the flesh and blood.

Hold it in mind that I am just twelve months recovered from the homoeopathic heebie-jeebies and only seven months rejuvenated by the crackling currents of the Unified Field. I am now reconstituted into a quantum being for whom speculation is the stuff of life, and embarked upon recreating my life and the universe in every second, with great relish and with great fervour for the numerous trivial (or momentous, as I like!) tasks this generates.

So here we are recreating the history and destiny of the human species and the question that Will provokes is this: If we ain't so divine, how come we have the one basic ability that is the only known qualification for Godhood: We create *beings*?

How come?

Have we been bamboozled by the chaps in pointy hats for so long that we have forgotten our fundamental talent for the miraculous? If it were Snoopy sitting in this high-chair slurping oatmeal and coughing it would still be a freaking, fucking, neuron-shattering miracle. No less.

A being's a being.

I say this aloud and bang the table to make the point. Will is watching me with his orbital eyes. He will agree with almost anything I say.

I leap into the bedroom where V is putting her feet up in the belief that after seven months she still deserves a rest.

She looks up from her manuscript of divinated dreams when I tell her about it. 'Absolutely,' she agrees. 'There's nothing more to say about that is there?'

You bet your sweet pouting fanny, I think, lumbering back to the breakfast table feeling distinctly like the chimp who discovered the club in Clarke and Kubrick's *2001*. I have thrown a newly minted implement into the pool of human ingenuity.

You see, you may insist that the universe burst out of the bowels of some demented machine or that none of it exists, but you cannot deny, no matter how many times you invert your reasoning, that for us organic critters to be here there has to be your basic Father and Mother, i.e., God the Father and His Mrs, God the Mother.

Now, this does not make me a religionist. For all I know, Mr and Mrs Deity might have plugged it a long time ago and left us all adrift in tarnation. I don't particularly care. What I do care about is this: in their infinite kindness and wisdom, they left us with the one talent that made them rather unusual – the ability to create beings. Not hamburgers, not radial tyres, chandeliers or coat-hangers, but *beings*. And ponder the significance of this: we are able to create something that will exceed us in every way, acquiring its own will, its own freedoms and its own preference in breakfast cereals. Combine that with the fact that it is impossible to tell at which point in time you began and that likewise, the same applies to your offspring and you realize that you and he or she and I all inhabit a vast simultaneity which we propagate through a series of quantum acts: the act of creating beings, of creating the universe through our perceptions and of killing cats shut up in cardboard boxes for indeterminate lengths of time.

Will has just managed to get a spoon to traverse the distances of heaven. He has moved it unerringly from the oatmeal bowl to the gaping port of his mouth. This act has subverted all his perceptions about the world he lives in. He has made a quantum leap, constructed an archetype and acquired a manipulative talent all in one step. Nothing will ever be the same for him again because he has discovered how silly it is to assume that the world is a place where the distance between an oatmeal bowl and a mouth can only be negotiated by exceeding some arbitrary barrier such as the speed of light.

Even he cannot tell when precisely this event began or when it ended, but there is a depth in his eyes that shows he is thinking about it.

Kfff.

If we are all possessed of the one talent that qualifies us for Godhood, all that remains is for us to start behaving like it. This may be achieved if we allow ourselves to understand that love is the generator of all things.

Will, whose internal debate on the nature of distances is fading – he has only a short-term memory yet, but the program has been wired – is looking at me as if I am God. And so I am. The child's first perception of the world, in those very early moments of cognition, is of one or two pairs of eyes. Eyes that float in a precausal void, materializing at the first instant of your own vision, are quite rightly assumed to be those of Mr and Mrs God. They got there first: this is a consideration above omniscience, a talent for plagues or the gift of turning complex and intelligent molecular assemblies into pillars of salt.

The child's entire world is constituted of these two (if he is lucky) divinities, from which all things emanate and to which all things return. This venerable couple are there and waiting even when the child returns from sleep and they are capable of all kinds of manipulative, organic, and technological feats that bring the universe into being. I speculate, eyeing the remains of Will's

oatmeal, that the archetype of God is the Parent. The bearded
coot with the radioactive hairdo is merely someone we insert into
a universe already ruled by two all-encompassing beings. Devoid
of the linearity of speech, we might in the first instance call them
Bbpp.

All hail, Bbpp!

The way in which we design the bearded coot will depend very
much on the internal archetypes that have been set up for us by
the behaviour, demeanour and general sobriety of the Bbpps. If
we are unfortunate and they turn out to be a couple of lice we
shall design an old coot with the salient characteristics of a louse
and fashion the world and our opinion of our sibling lice
according to the universal criteria of lousehood.

It is practically inevitable.

If we are fortunate and the Bbpps are all-round decent types,
we shall construct a God as someone who gives us a fair chance
to enjoy our oatmeal and, subsequently, the discovery of such
phenomena as caviar, pudenda, erogenous zones, orchestral per-
cussion, stride piano, stargazing, Havana cigars, Scotch whisky,
Polish vodka, William Shakespeare and taking all the time you
need to move your bowels.

Therefore is the world and the universe capable of reconstitu-
tion as a benign, creative and wholly enjoyable place. The
historical mistake we have made is to have passed the buck
upwards, thinking God responsible for putting this mess together
and for eventually sorting it out. As we now know, however, the
hirsute geezer is only a gargoyle made from the old, smooth stone
of our childhood memories: memories of that worthy couple the
Bbpps.

So hold on to the buck.

The moral universe of the human being begins with your
archetypal perception of who your parents are. Having passed the
point at which, in your stoned-out, short-term infant memory,
they were deities, you have extrapolated that original view of
them and formed your world and ethics from it. Watching the
Skydiver emerge, I saw, unmistakably, a being inherently predis-
posed to love. If a child is among the diminishing numbers of the
fortunate, its primal experience is of its own benign and reciprocal

gods, and of a place where all things are to the good. This much we control. The descent into an exclusively linear existence, particularly in cultures that have lost the magical influence and validity of the unknown, fools us into believing that we cannot choose what we become; the bribes are accepted; we acquiesce in the diabolical processes of initiation and conditioning – by nasty Bbpps, men in pointy hats, bank managers, mechanoids and various subgeneric mutants of our empirical past.

But we can forget the whole damn thing.

Every breakfast with Snoopy presents us with this astonishing opportunity. The universe of quantum choices grants us a continual, latent freedom. The ability to change in every second gives us the power to ignore history and to choose for the good. This is the way we form our future. Having chosen to forget our fixed moral archetypes or precedents we can begin to play with an infinite range of fluid and dynamic criteria with which to judge the way we might proceed. One such criterion is fun. As a measure of dos and don'ts it should prove much more effective than anything your local bishop can prescribe.

Does it *feel* good?

In this context I hereby declare the science of biomysticism open. Biomysticism is the formulation of metaphysics through the simple criterion of whether a thing feels good in one's biology. As infants we spit out lumps of oatmeal because we know instinctively that they will choke us to death. This is biomysticism: the wisdom of the body, of our biochemistry and its transdimensional indivisibility from emotions, and also from the operative freedoms of quantum existence. If you observe an infant you will see all three alive and well. As adults we are convinced of the necessity of doing things and swallowing lumpy objects that we do not enjoy. We spell out the virtues of harsh medicine and sanctify error or suffering. Then we look at the world we have formed and conclude that our species must surely be conceived of the devil.

And then we thrust this view on our children.

We bequeath them our stale, dead, and damaging morals, our fixedness, our stupid, unchanging beliefs, our mistrust of our bodies and of our imaginations. We turn their biomystical talents into potent carcinogens. We reduce them to one person when we should encourage them to be the many they are.

We fix them good. Kfff!

When Will, in the first moments of his birth, searched out and found our eyes, I knew that we must be born with an innate capacity for love: that we are born *from* love. Perhaps in quantum terms it all goes back and forth in a sea of simultaneity, love creating us, we creating love; no matter, for it appears that in our ineffable state we are indivisible from a benign universe. If you ask yourself what causes the first movement of a tiny fist to cup a breast, only a mystical cause will do, only love is a sufficient explanation of the phenomenon. A whole complex of neonatal talents as well as subsequent developments in language or physical dexterity are dismissed by our culture because we have been persuaded to define them as 'instinct'. But where does instinct begin?

Will eats his breakfast as if he has temporarily reassembled himself into a bowl of oatmeal. It strikes me that the thing-in-itself, despite the plaints of Sartre, is constantly accessible to us, if only we let our guard down. It is a state which is natural to us, a focus in the present and an unconditioned openness of mind into which we fall every time we remove the cultural and ethical restrictions that forbid it. After a certain age, the child is banned.

Will gazes at his empty oatmeal bowl for a moment, then at me, then back at the bowl. Being intractably focused in the present he cannot conceive of a thing's ending. He lolls back in his chair, entirely befuddled.

The self-absorbed or thing-absorbed child emerges at every opportunity, even in the adult. We are like creatures whose eyes are permanently fixed to the horizon; what afflicts us is not our lack of absorption but our failure to recognize when we are absorbed, to enjoy it, to revel in it and trust it rather than attempt to defer or move ahead of it. Idleness, when not disaffected, can be a creative force, a refuge in stillness and in the elusive present.

Watching Will loll back from his bowl and disperse himself in his own presence, I see that he has nowhere to go, nothing calling him to the future. If as adults we relinquish our right to idleness for the sake of achievement we throw away numerous opportunities for inspiration. We also discard the balancing force, the lightness and humour of the soul that saves us from ideological madnesses. If science is to be believed, we may even threaten the mental well-being that requires an equitable exercise of the right and left hemispheres of the brain, though I suspect this might be a reductionist simplification. At any rate, we kill off the poet, the daydreamer, the charismatic, the impulsive one, the imaginer, speculator, deducer, the grasper of things-in-themselves. The crowd that makes up at least half our inspiration and without which our enjoyment of life becomes dulled, premeditated, purposeless.

Where's the fun?

And consider this: our pursuit of the future is not for the good things that we might create; it is like an illusion that inverts itself to our perceptions – in truth, it is an obsession with the past. Our past conditioning, our ideologies, make us pursue the future at the cost of self-absorption and the daydream – at the cost of the present. We are taught to be concerned with doing rather than being. Doing is future directed; being is a state unconditioned by backward or forward thrust. My contention, revealed to me by an oatmeal-slurping seven month old, is that, no matter how obsessive we become, we constantly fall back into an unconditioned state. We cannot survive otherwise, but we do not recognize it; our consciences won't allow us the persistence of focus or the 'idleness' to appreciate it. We believe that we shall not do the good work of God unless we propel ourselves forward, but, of course, this is monodirectional – one fixed trajectory that turns too much of passing life into a blur. We lose our focus, ignore the present, proceed only with assumptions from the past, forget our simultaneity, devalue our idleness, defer our inspirations, become slaves to an idiotically simplified notion of time and then lull each other to complacency with the vacuous lunging forth that characterizes most of our enterprise.

But we do not truly move except in the present. We are not linear beings no matter how we try to fool ourselves. Our loss of focus makes us blind to the active intermeshing of present and future, and deprives us of a primal knowledge: that we use quantum choices to *create* the future. The child knows this and practises it naturally, but we cannot accept the magical creation of the future except in the contingent and limited terms of the past; ideologically blinded, we cannot abandon ourselves to the present except in unguarded moments. These moments save us from the pressure of a world in which only one direction and one focus are permissible; in personal terms, they give the internal crowd that makes up each of us the room to change and perfect its reticent product.

Watching Will, I can see that there is no difference between his natural absorption in the present and my own. Mine is usually reluctant, however: the admittance of a clamouring mob to the ordered and guarded delusions of my mentality. But there are many fine and beautiful voices raised up amidst the clamour telling me secrets I would seldom find in my conditioned states. If I run my internal democracy wisely, these voices will have their chance to undermine me with their benign songs and protect me from fixed ways that make me dead while I am alive.

We all need the protection. The child is allowed to focus in the present until a certain age. Its transition from a nonlinear to a linear and timed state of being is helped along by our conditioning of it and would be no bad thing except that we tend to view the nonlinear state as undeveloped. It is the state in which the child is delivered into our world; if we had any faith at all in the workings of nature we would find ways to preserve it and discover how it can work alongside any developments we see fit to make in the child. Instead, the child is often pared down; the loss of its delightful spontaneity is something we then mourn, even while instilling it with a sense of limits and preparing it for the docility we abhor in ourselves. When it grows a little and rediscovers, ineptly, some of its old impulses, we are reduced to bribery and threat.

If you observe a child for any length of time (assuming you have permitted yourself the time for such a wayward occupation), you must come to the conclusion that it is greatly talented at existing, and with its immediate and clear focus, greatly equipped to learn. Then you know that if you are to assist its progress and leave it the better, you can only do so with inspiration and love.

No theory or ideology is ever flexible enough. That this seems an impossible task may only indicate how much we have forgotten our own talents for the miraculous. If you think this is balderdash, then I must again point out the state of our world, of the male sex, particularly – because it is the one on which the more stringent conditioning is imposed – and of children in general al over this planet. Infanticide is widespread; whether we kill our own children or those of populations that we victimize, whether we do it with neglect, or heartless profiteering, or war, it is the final, massive evidence of what we lose when we forget who we are and reconstruct ourselves with empty, moribund ideologies. And it is always a personal as well as cultural failure.

We have thrown away our talents for the miraculous. By seeing off the daydreamer and ignoring the internal democracy we jettison most of the essential equipment we need to understand our children. It is impossible for us to remember how they *feel* because we have executed our own inner child; nothing can compensate the loss of emotional identification with the child that we discard so casually. But if you try hard enough and watch the child with unconditioned attention, you may remember.

The way we deal with very young children, in particular, demonstrates our lack of nonlinear understanding – an emotional lack. A few exercises in the nanometrics of meaning, language and events might help. Observe a two year old scribbling on a piece of paper and you will soon realize that the paper is a four-dimensional phenomenon for it; try to teach it a geometric shape and it fails to understand. Is this because it lacks your tutored knowledge or because it has a wonderful, open perception of space and time which it has not yet learnt to reduce to ordered shapes and events? For the child, things *happen* on the paper; for you it is only the means to an end.

Our half-baked, blank-slate theories betray how much we have forgotten of nature and what intimacy we have lost with the workings of our own minds. In quantum terms each one of us remains for ever a blank slate: if we are free and unconditioned we are able to 'write' ourselves into being in every moment, and the process is inherently delightful. But because we have limited ourselves to the view of cumulative knowledge and existence, the blank slate is undesirable and the child as blank slate is barely elevated from the moronic. We teach our children how to live without understanding how underqualified we are to do so. To obtain the minimal qualifications we must relearn the nonlinear language and mentation of the child inside us; personal experience of the emotions involved is essential. Then we see that the child is anything but ignorant. The way in which it grasps things is minutely interesting. The free association it makes between phenomena, events, language and so forth is infinitely imaginative and powerful, with all the complexity and creative energy of chaos itself. This enormity of awareness, free association and absorption is what gives the child its prodigious ability to learn. Because it does not yet condition and define every perceived phenomenon, it can connect it at random with any other phenomenon, event, symbol or activity; in fact it is free to define and redefine constantly, experiencing not only the thing-in-itself, but deploying, with its playful impulses, its own power to create and enjoy the world around it. It interprets the world according to an unfixed point of view. It is a quantum being.

We may not be obligated either to curtail or prolong this beneficent state. What we must consider is that the state itself, especially since the child arrived in it, must be a part of its development towards a larger state in which all human faculties, the willed and the unwilled, remain operative. It is certainly a betrayal of love, of our natures, of whatever genetic imperatives might exist, if we continue to view it as ignorance or infantilism. Remember that the child's own perceptions of its first world are bound up with you. You are the God. The interplay of power, or emergent God and ruling God, of the non-rational and the rational, or chaos and order, are wondrous. We can no longer close our eyes to wonder.

There is the possibility that every child is a prodigy and every human being naturally prodigious in its own talents – talents which are exclusive to it just as its physiognomy is uniquely its own. To attempt to mould and condition those talents by digging a spur into the nonlinear infant is only a small step from trying to breed humans who are all alike in appearance. Hitler's Aryan lurks in every obsessive parent: the blond, blue-eyed, straight-nosed, smooth-kneed oick who has exterminated the daydreamer and who has less appreciation of our true ability to create miraculous beings than your average fungus.

Will's nonlinear focus in the present demonstrates how humans exist at the very edge of meaning, at the interface of chance and destiny. He is the daydreamer who is unutterably surprised to discover that he has certain abilities, for instance, of hand and eye co-ordination. He is an awakening soul in an awakening body, and because of the quantum freedoms invested in him by the universe, if he keeps his focus in the present he will continue to awaken till the day he dies. (And beyond, for all we know!) I hope he will stand always poised on the unfolding edge of destiny.

I read somewhere that the prenatal child spends most of its time in dreams. I hope that Will is not obliged to abandon the dreams he brought with him. I hope that he may be among the first to merge them with his dream of earthly life.

Putting Will to bed at night, I see the dreamer. V and I have come to the conclusion that throughout the history of the human tribe children must have been coddled to sleep alongside their parents. In our world, before packing them off to be institutionalized, we wean them of the tactile comforts of night. None of us as adults is prepared to admit any joy in sleeping alone. For a new human, night may turn out to be the archetype of hell, the time and the place where the gods disappear into darkness.

We try to strike a balance, giving Will enough of our nights to make him feel that he is not alone. I ponder the loneliness of the new human: like the loneliness of Adam. Nothing between you and your gods but darkness; floating in an undiscovered space without the language to comprehend it, without the comfort of illusory control; only the comfort of dreams of the land whence you came.

Decent Bbpps can be a great help.

This night, when it is my turn to persuade him that darkness and sleep are future friends, I lie with him. Stories are told and songs sung; then I pretend to sleep and peek out of the corner of my eye to see if he has taken the bait. He lies perfectly still, his body relaxed, his eyes open and unmoving. I watch him for five minutes, perhaps more. He sees nothing in the material world. His consciousness has moved back halfway to his dream-world, and there, with his eyes wide, he is spectating on some grandiose pageant of nameless forms and symbols. I open my eyes full to see if he will react. He does not. He is treading the sweet path between his world and ours. He is parachuting through a warm swell of perfect nonreality. I am looking at the quantum being, indeterminate, nonlocative, real, virtual, dual, single, multiple, free . . .

For the child it is second nature to make these excursions into a quantum state. As adults we resist, but it waits for us to dream or drop our guards then creeps back in to save us from ourselves. Despite ourselves, we leap in and out of time, sneak out in the dead of night to hold court with minstrels, visionaries, magicians, revellers – all who have not forgotten that to be alive is to play.

Will's eyelids flutter down like a moon setting in a night pond, and he is gone. For a good quarter of our lives there is not time at all, except by the testimony of others or of mute signs. For all we know we open our eyes as soon as we close them. Half the planet slips into oblivion, a hemisphere at a time, like a snoozing dolphin, and we cannot tell when an event begins and ends in time, cannot draw a dateline precisely, down to the last nanometre, to tell us which half is asleep and which awake. The two states are unified manifestations of an overall state, the state of the quantum dreamer, of the marriage of matter and nonmatter, of event and nonevent. We cannot tell. We do not need to know, in the sense of an acquisitive knowledge. We can only draw a spectral line up and down the flattened globe and talk as if it will exist without us. But it will not.

Somebody ought to tell the children not to take it too seriously. Somebody ought to tell them that their dreamworld is just as good as this divided world, or better; that, if they can preserve their world it might help them to recreate this one without falling back into the past at every step.

There is hope. The idle soul survives in every moment we trust ourselves to be unguarded, and when we sleep we are on the precipice itself, on the edge of meaning, unhinged from the single pursuit. We are at play in a place we can never name, but somewhere in the embrace of chaos.

In a quantum world all things are interchangeable. A thing is not what it is, but it may also, if we choose, be named, and be as we call it. It is virtual and real. In a world of nondiscrete events and phenomena it may also be all things beside itself.

This is not new, or a discovery of physics, it is the reinterpretation of magic, alchemy and the transmutation of matter. In delirium or narcosis, these states impinge on our moral awareness – as they do in what is called schizophrenia. We judge them as delusional, admitting the primacy of our conventional reality, but even psychoses are relative states. Our conventional reality is proving its own obsolescence; the fixed state is patently moribund, and the psychotic state might just turn out to be the affliction that arises when we cannot balance our definitions of what is real or unreal in our selves.

Conventional reality must therefore be seen only as a component in a larger awareness, and it, also, is interchangeable. In the indeterminate world of the dreamer, reason, cognition and linear ways of thought or being are interwoven and interchanged: they are no more important than we would choose to make them. To give them primacy is to let ourselves be arbitrarily ruled.

There are certain waking states in which we fall back towards the dream. Reflection, concentration, ecstasy, absorption, the orgasm, the daydream, all make us larger than the monodirectional being we force ourselves to be. They allow us the free space in which to recollect ourselves, and, paradoxically, to constitute a world in which action becomes possible. In this world we are able to follow a course of action or even an impulse with the assurance that it originated in the wholeness of our nature. We become poised, acquire the unconditioned balance of the benign warrior and unite our oppositions. We also know that if mistakes are made they are part of a process that moves forward in a real sense, rather than one in which our momentum comes from only a partial use of faculties. Then, we are fully equipped to understand how our mistakes were made. If they do not curtail someone else's freedoms, we can laugh them off.

In our smaller, less expansive selves there is only the mentality of opposition. As individuals or societies it obstructs any action we may wish to take and we suffer the fate of the unfree. As quantum beings – dreamers with a grasp of the material world – we can approach action with all our faculties engaged, with all the characters of the internal democracy entitled to a minimal justice. This can extend to all of society from within the individual. It is an extrapolation of each person's quantum connectedness into the multitude; through it humans might *evolve* to conditions of peace.

Does it sound difficult and unattainable, an abstracted Utopia?

It is with us all the time, in our unguarded moments, when we sleep, on the dark side of the planet, in half of the sleeping dolphin's brain, in the divinity of procreation, in the unity of the sexes, in the orgasm, song, poem, revelation – and all around us, from the beginning of time till now, in the child. Each time, the child renews our species' chance of freedom.

And if evolution exists, this is very probably the next step: the abandonment of fixed positions and the liberation of imaginative powers of an order that, perhaps, we have not allowed ourselves to imagine. These things are not called quantum leaps for nothing.

Goddamn and hurrah. Let's take care till something wonderful happens.

And if evolution exists, it is an absurd notion that each forward step must run the duration of millennia. New awareness is like the event: it leaps out of nonexistence without announcing itself. Some of the monumental ideas that have changed our lives must have been, for all purposes, instantaneous. All that was needed was a change of mind. All revolutions are revolutions of consciousness. Things must have happened overnight.

Stand by. Stand by. Listen carefully, you may hear a distant humming. Don't forget to dream, you may wake up in another place. Don't forget to be in love, you may discover whence you came. Don't forget to watch the child even if the only one you can find is inside yourself – and revive it for the purpose. Don't forget to be bone idle so that you may cultivate idleness effortlessly. Don't forget to be human. Don't forget to be God.

SIXTEEN

Now Will is asleep, I give him the once-over to make sure he won't fall out of the dreamworld. Later, V and I may join him in this large bed or extricate him gently and lay him in his own.

We live in a tower now. Two floors above two floors, draughty in winter, bright as a greenhouse in summer, with the sun sweeping over from bedroom to living-room and setting fire to the Great White Western City at dusk, a conflagration V and I watch each evening after Will has been fed, watered and bedded down. Often in winter I place my rattan chair at a vantage point before the living-room window and wait until, in the south-west, when the twilight has died, Jupiter wheels round – magnitude 2.6, hanging in the sky like molten metal.

Jupiter has invisible moons. I do not know if it is more enjoyable to imagine them or to see them for real with an optical device. What difference?

V, between cursory glances at the television news and writing up her dream book, makes small-talk. The wolves are temporarily absent from my doorstep; through luck or daring or obliviousness to danger we have a small reprieve. What difference?

V likes to keep things short and sweet. I cannot hear her above the news. They are showing something horrible. I leap for the remote control. Years ago I had the misfortune to see a documentary in which a man was hunted down by a group of men and felled with a single bullet. He thrashed in bushes by the side of a road, then lay still. In the few moments of his twitching I saw a struggle not against death but against the confiscation of an ultimate freedom. Most of all, he must have been lonely. There was not one to see him off except his killers. An eternal indignity.

I hit the button on the remote that mutes the sound and change to a French film: beautiful long still shots and a slow unfolding of some morality tale.

V is looking at me. She is impatient when I do not answer. We have a range of subvocal signals with which we inform each other that we are present and correct.

'Verdict,' she says.

'On what?'

'How you feel.'

'Me? Not bad. Not bad at all.'

'Not *good*?'

'Oh no, good. Definitely good.'

'Then why don't you say so?' V is in her granny mode.

In the film a man is crouched on his haunches, muscles tensed, head craned, watching a woman bathe through a crack in a door. The woman is almost too thin, but her bones are covered alluringly here and there. I can feel the weight of my balls between my legs and the first pulse of an erection at the base of my penis. My imagination leaps forward to the prospect of a full erection, half luxury, half pain. I hold my breath.

V notices my involvement. 'Too thin,' she says, 'but a lovely, pert face.'

'I like thin women, you know. Always did.'

'I can't imagine why, old boy. Sublimated homoeroticism – a taste for the androgyne.'

'Nothing so decadent. Hormonal aesthetics, actually – that is, simple lechery. Everything about a thin woman points straight at the fanny, where I always imagine a prodigious pubic mound, cushioning a tight, er, hot orifice.'

'You'll get me going if you talk like that.'

'Yippee.'

'She doesn't have a prodigious anything.'

I examine the girl, who is now standing in the bath, and in hiking her legs up to towel her toes gives us flashes of a very refined little fanny.

'Too young yet,' I say.

'Age has nothing to do with it. Why did you hitch up with me if you're so keen on bagpipes?'

'You're fishing.'

'Maybe.'

'Well, you had just the right degree of slimness, combined with one or two rather spectacular overstatements of sexual semiotics. The best of both types really.'

'How fortunate for you that I qualified as a physical specimen.' She says this with eyes shut tight, nose wrinkled and her lower jaw stuck out rudely. A chimp signal.

'Heap big bonus,' say I.

The man crouched at the door, eyes watering. All through his body there is a liquefaction of hitherto dormant substances. His engine is turned on; his heart beats faster, enraptured by adrenalin. He rises, stands for a moment in the darkness, lit only by a hair's breadth of light from the crack in the door. The lighting cameraman has waited for this from the beginning of the film. Starting in mid-shot – where the voyeur's tense upper torso reveals his unease and a slight forward inclination his looming intentions – the camera moves in imperceptibly to frame his face in tight close-up; a perfect profile, backlit softly, and with the light from the door-crack exaggerated to illumine his face from below. This flares his nostrils and throws a crude brow into relief, with the dark shadow of his cheekbone engulfing his visible eye. Then he throws his head back to look heavenwards and the shadow slips down his face like an executioner's hood. Being a French peasant, I assume he is saying a silent prayer. He tugs at his waistcoat with gauche decorousness. This is a typical gesture, of course, and the cameraman has implied it out of shot, holding the close-up. The acting is internal and the close-up is held so we can read the man's mind; but this is a quiet joke of the director's for the man's mind could never be more obvious. His intention of approaching the girl is made clear by the trivial act of tidying his appearance, and his absurdity as a man is depicted by contrasting this petty decorum with his intended mayhem.

The camera now moves slowly round to the back of the man, outlining his dark head against the glimmering texture of the door. He kicks it open and the frame floods with tranquil, feminine light.

V looks up from the dream book. 'I wanted to ask you if the holiday has been worth it.'

'You know it has.' I am watching the girl. She has whisked a towel about her and stands frozen.

'Yes, but you haven't told me why and how.'

V pursues literal detail, but this only from others. She herself will account for most things with a nod or a half-sentence. I am having to extricate myself from the film, from wading around in my own thoughts. But it will be worth it. This is the way we like to play, with plenty of channels going at once: sex, cinematography and a few universal questions thrown in.

It was now almost eighteen months since I had taken V's advice and given up all pretence of work. This reprieve might be as short-lived as a day. No doubt the wolves were regrouping, trying to mobilize the lumbering machines it would take for them to eventually nail me. A hundred dumb computers all over the country were rearing up to spit out the next round of reminders and threats. I dealt with these by sending begging letters to the authorities concerned, usually imploring them for more time. If appropriate, I would also dispatch subtly worded missives, which, once fed into a computer, were likely to confuse it for eternity.

What was the time for? For the cultivation of idleness, until, having refocused myself completely, I might be superbly equipped for some constructive activity in the world. In this small-minded, madly driven world, I knew that this was insane and irresponsible. I knew that I might pay a heavy price for it. But in a universal sense, I felt as if I was experimenting with something no one had thought to do. Drunks and scoundrels might seek to retire from the world and live in grazing contemplation – they have the excuses of pathology; I had nothing except a conviction that I was capable of making some internal, evolutionary change in myself – in vain moments, of making it for all people. The chimp with the club.

Somehow I knew that if I trusted this hybrid and phantom luck of mine I would get away with it. Old societies had the shaman and the storyteller and the people who carried eternity in their dreams. Now we had the riches of technology and the great superstitions of science, couldn't we bring back the old faculties to complete ourselves?

In the space of a day, at V's urging, I had taken a simple

decision: I had decided to do nothing. I had retired from life. I had extricated myself from the need to do and consigned myself to the privilege of being. I wanted to *be*. I wanted to sit back and let all the conditioning, the pointless motivation, the futile pursuits, the unplayful thoughts, the desperation, the striving, the forward orientation, the loneliness, the ticking of clocks, the primacy of sex, the past, the future, all leak out of me and disappear down some unmarked crevice. I wanted the distractions removed that would obscure my focus in an unconditioned present. For a year or two or more I wanted to experience my existence unfolding, without the intrusion of any external factor to steal its integrity. This wasn't to be a meditation or a Buddhist retreat in the depths of suburbia; it was wholly playful, a skipping from moment to moment. The only continuous experience any of us have of this state is in early childhood, when nothing trespasses on our consciences, but I wanted the adult version, the knowing sensation with equal privileges as observer and participant. The holiday.

Take a holiday – in the comfort of your own mind.

V understood that while I was in this state I could not be obliged to prepare for any unforeseen circumstances. The future was not to be a factor in any of my considerations, unless in the course of my playing the game it merited a certain playful attention. I had no conditions set for myself. The only decision I had taken was to do nothing; its only objective at the start, and completely provisional, too, was that I refocus myself into someone less likely to cause me grief. But the need of objectives or anything that would condition the experience was soon discarded. You don't check your parachute after you jump.

Fortunately, Will arrived while I was still on holiday. This gave me the time to find out what he was about. What a stroke of providence that I had stolen for myself the freedom to be a tribal parent! We sold the cave just about the time Will was born and used the profits to pull ourselves back to the surface of a heap of debt. No profit left, you understand, just another reprieve of six months or a year while we worked our way back to the bottom of the heap, but time enough to get close to Will, make love to V in the afternoons, and launch myself in leisurely style on a series of adventures in idleness.

150

Through it all, V and I never had the bad taste to let on that we were treading the edge of perdition. We amassed another huge debt without batting an eyelid, inveigling enough out of the unwary mechanoids to fit up the tower and keep ourselves fed and watered for a few months yet. I couldn't look at the furniture without thinking of the repo man, but after a while he became a sort of friendly bogy, and, wrapped in the comforts of my wife, my child, and my own enormous and pulsating quantum ego, I soon forgot about him. Some ogre will always dog your footsteps, so you might as well let them lead where they will. Or, if you are like me, you might just put your feet up and let your progress dissolve into an entirely mental adventure. Nobody can get in your mind unless you leave everything unlocked. Let the bastards whine and drool while you cultivate your higher self or whatever self you think you have neglected thus far. So be it.

V and I had moments of panic and times when we were bamboozled by rich acquaintances, but we had to be content with being exiles. There was nothing we could do that would not involve sacrificing ourselves to the future. This was more than conviction, it was in our blood. No ideology or rebellion would have driven us that far. We had forgotten everything so we could enjoy each other at play.

And Will would be privileged to join us.

The French peasant had cornered the girl. Feigning compassion, he was trying to talk her down on to the towel, which he had wrested from her rather unceremoniously and spread on the floor. I sensed great flights of idiom and metaphor in his French, but the subtitles were minimalist. 'You have nothing to fear,' it was written. 'I wish only to express my love for you. I will do you no harm; simply lie down and leave the rest to me.' The girl had the lineaments of the upper classes and kept her eyes from the peasant as much out of revulsion for his station in life as because they were the last of herself she could hide. The peasant stooped like a crane, seeking out the eyes. If he could fix on them it would be his licence for rape.

V was demanding an account of how the holiday had *felt*. The man moved over to the girl, trangressing a forbidden space, and

KEN FEGRADOE

ushered her to the towel as if he were showing her to a pew in church.

'I feel extremely mellow,' I said to V. 'And all my pleasures are acute, as if I'm feeling them with more of myself than was present before.'

'You feel more like you do now than you did when you got here.'

'An old saw.' I laughed.

'And were you frightened?' Her granny solicitude made her look as if she were darning socks.

'It's a question of choosing which scary things in life you want to face. Once you make the choice, they ain't so scary.'

'We'll survive. I know it.'

'Yup. Me too.'

'I feel like saying "I told you so".'

'Say it and I'll jump on your bones.'

I poured myself a substantial vodka, chilled to a syrup.

'The mentality of the walking wounded is hard to shed. We're conditioned to view life by weighing up the negatives like living inside a condom, a prophylactic way of life with all feelings at one remove. Now I've begun to feel as if all of that is behind me. No fear, at least. No fear that I cannot turn into some sort of internal plaything.'

She makes marks in her manuscript and looks at me sagely, 'The internal plaything's the thing. And the quantum thingy, too. The willie, too.'

'The willie is a major determinant of the quantum mentality,' I say. The frigid vodka is calibrating my throat. 'The sex drive is the only drive we haven't been able to organize – yet.'

She has given up the granny and started to freewheel. 'Men think with their whammies. Maybe that isn't such a bad thing.'

'A penile philosophy, a vaginal ethic – what's the difference, Ladymissus? In biomystical terms a unification of opposites, you and I just a couple of warm currents in a cold neutrino soup with incorporeal potencies such as the sex drive to keep us warm, to defy entropy.'

'Entropy. I've always thought that a distinctly anal word. An anal concept. All things must pass.'

152

I agree. 'The whole universe as potential excrement. Yuk. Like the word "ethics" has always reminded me of some sharp instrument. "Ethics, please, nurse!" Or like the word "morals" has always suggested to me things that crawl up beaches *en masse*!'

'Very picturesque, darling.'

'Hence,' I wax, 'the moral majority: a featureless cluster of half-witted molluscs or eyeless protozoans; a mouth, an anus, a gut and a couple of primitive proto-digits adrift in their own sperm. Aye! the fundamentalists of slime, the bourgeoisie of creation – all endoplasm and indignation, all peristalsis and tight-lipped, clench-buttocked righteousness, the officers of mediocrity, the orifices of entropy . . . '

'Tell me more about how there's more of you now, especially the bits I am interested in.'

'Nyet and double nyet. This is leading somewhere. You see, I've emerged from the entropic personality into the quantum personality, living without fixed or conditioned knowledge. Death may be a fact, but one fact is as good as another.'

'What took you so long?'

'Fuck off!'

I was three vodkas gone by now. The girl had turned her back on the man, who was, quietly and in a very civilized way, disrobing himself. 'Proceed in the joy of things and learn that with no fixed point of view you drop all your baggage and enjoy being adrift. Then, when you learn to *play* with the rip and ebb and surge and flow you acquire the benign power to influence your own future or even to change the past, but without losing your grip on the present, and oh, the fun of it!'

I was breathless. V had laid her manuscript down and was supine on the sofa with her eyes closed, grinning to herself. The girl had finally looked up at the peasant. Seeing him presenting himself bollock-naked, she reaches down into the depths of herself and brings out a sharp, disdainful violence: she slaps him plumb across the chops and he is suddenly deflated. The man might have expected clawing, spitting and screaming, but the girl's class has triumphed over him. Such a dignified slap, delivered with choreo-graphed poise, as if she were swatting a fly.

She turns on her heel and strides out of the room. I note that she has a slight overhang in an otherwise perfect backside, now rolling out of shot. The man collects his clothes, gazing after the girl, fumbles in his waistcoat for his watch, checks it and winds it. Cut to close-up in profile as the man winds his watch and begin voice-over in French. The director has refrained until this moment from crossing the line of action. Since the man entered the bathroom, the camera has kept him at screen-right. Now it tracks around the back of the man's head in close-up, crossing the line as his internal monologue begins in the voice-over. He is talking to himself about the price of various items of farm machinery. The director cuts to mid-shot, then to long-shot abruptly. The man, sunburnt and hairy, stands all alone in the middle of the pink and floral bathroom, all undressed and no one to fuck.

V is idling away, one leg jutting over the arm of the sofa, the other curled under her so that her hips are slightly thrust out and her torso stretched languidly. The sight of the girl's backside has put me in mind of sex again, right in the middle of my diatribe. The vodka has sharpened my emotions. My loins, in Lawrentian fashion, are weighty and hot, and my mind is crackling with this fine, incendiary talk that V brings out in me.

I love these evenings with V. Much conversation between men and women is a transcendent version of some old courtship dance; humans are blessed to be able to add an abstract and symbolic faculty to the strutting and preening. Everything worthwhile is done in love and everything in love can, if you are lucky, have its resonances in sex. Thus sex is more than an act; why, it is practically a sort of parallel entity in each of us, one of the characters in the internal democracy – or several. Again it is a matter of being enough in the present to grasp the moment and feel it fully; then, with all your senses alight the future disappears, you are immortal, simultaneous. What chances are missed for men and women being too much about their business! What work of art is more worthwhile than this art of fabulation, when every word exchanged has as much power of arousal as our invisible friend, the pheromone. In a quantum scheme of things, of course, words and pheromones are interchangeable.

V tucks her hands behind her head and her breasts jut out. 'It's obvious how much more relaxed you are,' she says. 'You had me worried for a while back there, railing on about the walking wounded while you were one yourself. Welcome back.'

'Fabulation,' I say. 'That's what it's about. *Inventing* life, getting away from all this gratuitous organizing of it.'

'Daft to try and plan things. Much more fun to feel the flow and swim a few strokes now and then – see if you can adjust your course without fear of drowning.'

'What is there to be afraid of? Life is grand, life is hell, it's a dream, it's a harsh reality. Life's a bitch and then you get used to it. It's one thing and another. I prefer to look at it in biomystical terms. Somehow I'm going to arrange a huge celebration, one to last forever, with an open door to any passer-by who feels the need of some forgotten sanity.'

'And how are you going to accomplish that?'

I tap myself on the noggin. 'Up here,' I say. 'The party's up here.'

'Like I said, welcome back!'

'How did you know?' I ask. I have arrived in the territory of chaos and there she is in the flesh and blood, waiting for me.

'I was able to detect that the only thing holding you back was your male conditioning.'

'Explain yourself, woman.'

'Men are fools – endearing fools for the most part, but fools nevertheless. They need everything planned and structured, like trying to turn the whole world into a sort of security blanket. It's the end of men: they've made such a mess of things that their own silly logic will force them to acknowledge their failure. But the sensitive ones can free themselves if they are lucky, get back to being human beings.'

'Ain't too many of them about,' I say.

'It will come. Men have low expectations of each other, that's why they compete.'

'They think the competition is some sort of biological imperative.'

'The half of their natures that they have suppressed will surface constantly and make them miserable until they change.' She lights a cigarette, takes a puff, grimaces and passes it to me. 'What I'd like to know is how they got that way. And, by the way, I'd like to know what made women their accomplices.'

'They got that way because they were bribed. The history of capitalism is a history of bribery. But forget all the isms; the point is that once we got beyond the scale of the tribe, man abstracted himself into the mob. As soon as the human race became an abstraction, we needed fixed beliefs and hoarded knowledge – secreted powers, Brahminism gone global. Men sharpened their first appetites for demagogy on women; they just happened to be at hand; after the animal husbandry, the wife husbandry, so to speak.'

'Ha! You can count me out if you think the answer is back to the jungle!'

'The jungle is here. If you look at the surviving tribes on this planet, you see that the ills that killed them off were always imported . . . '

'Yes, but that is the argument used by those who say that might is right. If the tribes had been strong they would have survived the onslaughts of so-called civilization. Not that I agree, mind you.'

'There will always be something or someone stronger than you. You cannot construct a society or an individual ethic on the basis of invincible power because it simply doesn't exist. Tomorrow some alien fleet could blow us all to house-dust with weapons we may not even see, or the planet itself will decide it has had enough and vomit us back into oblivion in an equivalent second of geological time. Who will miss us? Once there were tribes that honoured their disabled and sanctified their Down's children. Now we have commercial forces and desperate conformity, the death of cultures, the suppression of languages – all for abstractions whose meaning and objectives have been forgotten. We have one half of the world plundering the other half; international bribery and hidden corruption practised by people who never need to show their faces. A tribe will never tolerate the likes of them.'

Full steam now. Four vodkas down and ten thousand three hundred to go. The French peasant dressed and then undressed again, all the while reeling off lists and prices of farm implements.

He fingers each of the girl's expensive potions. Then he runs the bath. It is wonderful to play; to blow out long streams of smoke and fabulation. I ain't fooling anyone, least of all V, but the play's the thing.

'A new tribe?' says V. 'It will all happen naturally when men have found the other half of themselves.'

'After all the fine illusions we have created for ourselves! Perhaps we will be remembered as a tribe that excelled in the art of constructing illusions.'

'Most of us are basically kind, no matter how else it might appear.' V is so kind. She will leap up gracefully on my bandwagon and strut her stuff. Mind you, it goes both ways.

'I always think that if some galactic authority came down and asked us to account for ourselves or be exterminated, that is what I should say: that at heart we are kind animals. I suppose in purely quantitative terms we might claim success for ourselves. More people live in peace now; our numbers have increased. We have gone forth and accomplished the multiplification – multiplication, I mean.'

'A bit simplistic, I'd say.' She screws up her mouth.

The French peasant climbed gingerly into the bath and lay back in the steaming water, which he had saturated with all of the potions he could find. In close-up again, he winces from the heat, opens his eyes and gazes heavenwards. The camera pulls back to a slow, tracking mid-shot down the side of the bathtub and settles on the man's hands. He is clutching a small, glinting fruit knife. Moving back to close-up, the frame is now a composition of two disembodied hands, with the knife a sinister counterpoint to the soft flesh and warm water. I am reminded of an astonishing van der Weyden in the Prado, in which he juxtaposed two limp hands, one of the dead Christ being taken from the cross, the other of the reeling Mary. It seemed to me that van der Weyden must have painted the whole picture so that he could make that study of the meaning of those two hands. Likewise, the director had constructed the whole sequence so he could move to this denouement: the hands swirling the water around, caressing each other, then suddenly turning palms up and with sharp decisiveness the one hand attacking the other, inserting the knife neatly below a pallid vein and lifting it out of the wrist; then, the wounded hand-held fist clenched in a small gesture of triumph, blood melting slowly into the pale greens and whites of the composed frame; and then – an interminable fade to black.

Out of this darkness voices and footsteps materialize and the scene reconstructs itself around a group of men. A mid-shot from the rear of the men, at hip-level, shows them stooping over the bathtub and jostling each other to get a view of the dead peasant. The focus has been pulled on the peasant's heaven-turned head, so that the foreground is at first all black shapes; then the focus is resolved gently into the foreground and we see, in the exact order the director intends, the hands of the men in the group, each holding scythes, clubs, axes, picks: farm implements. Cut to a side-on view of the men's craning heads screen-right, with a top-angle on the peasant, head and shoulders afloat in a bath of pale blood. Cut to a head-on shot of two of the men in the group. One is peering at the corpse impassively. Then he turns to his fellow and says, 'Curses, the bastard's escaped.'

V and I got roundly drunk that night. It was the night of the Pact of the Seventeen Martinis all over again. Nothing much had changed. Every single thing in the whole world had changed. Who gives a shit about being consistent?

SEVENTEEN

Men and women are kind creatures, born kind. If you need evidence of this, of the existence of angels and of the possibilities of human nature, you have only to look at children. Why didn't anybody tell me this? Why didn't my church let me into this secret, instead of treating me, even when I was very young, as some kind of tarnished and wayward being? The existence of evil is a prerequisite of institutionalized religion. There's an example of the worst kind of fixity in belief: that one must have the lowest expectation of one's fellow beings.

If ever someone says 'I am here to save you', run like hell. Run like a banshee. They believe something you don't, so you have one less belief than they. Which should keep you light enough to outrun them by a long, safe distance.

Will, at one year of age, is the angel. I am the God. He is totally dependent on me. I have never been totally depended on before. His life is totally in my hands. I have created it. But in a quantum world the linearity of causation collapses. I ponder whether it is I who have created Will or vice versa. Why is the reversal of causation so repugnant to our reason? In purely sentimental terms there is a very real sense in which Will is creating me. He is changing my life and the way I look at things so profoundly that he is adding an entire throng to my internal democracy.

Funny thing is, contrary to what one is told about the tribulations of spawning, he is doing me a good turn. He is so demanding that he is teaching me to focus very acutely. I am getting to practise what I preach. He exists wholly in the present and so must I – to be with him. I have to disconnect the consequential part of my awareness, participating in utterly inconsequential acts on his behalf. I have to be prepared to do seven hundred things at once, and give up the idea of organizing any of them into a manageable sequence.

Babies are the enemy of routine. I have to have the ultimately adaptable character not merely to impose myself on Will, trying to get him to do things my way. That wouldn't work at any rate, even if one believed in the discipline of such methods, for Will has no notion that there is a *way* of doing things. He is hardly aware of doing and only vaguely aware of things. He is wholly in the present.

I am so glad I took the holiday when I did. I begin to understand the work of women. It needs a radical adaptability, for, to start with at least, there is no slight chance of being in control. Children challenge us to deconstruct our worlds. Whatever men do, the assumption is that control will somehow be achieved; but as is proven too often, this is not an attitude that succeeds with the newly arrived human being. What we have here is the quantum personality intact; you have to speak its language and breathe its air; it has not yet diminished itself sufficiently to be able to breathe yours. We have to learn it again, like learning to swim.

It was born full of love, already a part of the quantum connectedness and subject of the unwritten constitution. A little time given to this being reveals that it spends all its waking hours in search of the one thing – love. Expressions of love might take different forms, but it is the base sustenance in all the responses it seeks, from feeding to coddling.

Kids sure in hell need love. They would drown and starve and wither away without it, and you will see them turn to ungraceful narcissism if it is withheld. They are like those creatures that pop up now and then in science fiction who feed off other people's emotions. Point is, it's damn good fun if you get it even half right.

Now I have the chance to tinker with my theory that the human being's formative views of the world arise in their first perceptions of it. That is, of you. I am Will's first world and he ought to know that if he wants love it is there for the asking, before anything else I may consider important such as discipline, deferred gratification, self-denial, learning to be a 'man', learning to eat without embarrassing the neighbours . . . None of which, incidentally, I give a tinker's damn about. I shall even leave his dreadfully insanitary habits unreproached, lest I consign him to a life of analism and hernial strain.

The first time you learn about something conditions all the other times you learn about the same thing. No doubt about it. Can't be any other way. I am going to base all of Will's first lessons in anything on love. With any luck, that will make all my mistakes small ones. If I start early enough, instead of trying to catch up with him later, it might be easier for both of us. Besides which, and as I say, it is much more fun this way. You can trust almost anything that feels good. No Pavlovian tricks, no bribery; lesson number one – teach him as little as possible. I am just going to have fun, because his biomystical programming will take care of the rest and if he learns the riches of being in love and having fun everything else will follow. I might even try to save him from education: no use attempting to preserve the angelic and then abandoning it to the dull machinations of the military-industrial complex. But such things are for the future, by which time Will and V and I will all be different people in whom nothing and everything has changed. At least we will not have been consistent.

At any rate, the Skydiver teaches me more than I can teach him. Physical patience; the patience of the body. He learns about the linear world from gravity, his great playmate and my great enemy. I have to bend over and pick things up four hundred times a day. My back begins to give, being the sedentary sort I am, incorrigibly. I look up my old yoga book for a cure. Meanwhile my ankles stiffen and twitch in the night. In the morning, I awake in the foetal position. A good joke: Will is turning me back on myself. Biomystically. Perhaps when I am sufficiently regressed I shall have the talent to save him from the staid assumption that gravity is a linear force.

Kfff.

He teaches me language, also, because he is not a slave to syntax and couldn't care less about the search for meaning. Meaning, after all, is boringly elusive and fickle. He assembles concepts at random and tells lies about the universe. I have to force him into occasional linearity so that basic routines are observed, else he may not eat or sleep for all we know; but I suspect that there might once have been a human rhythm to life that did not make unnecessary patterns of things. However, we live in this world. I force as little as possible, and V, being of the ilk, follows suit. His mind must light its own lights and come alive in its own time. The unfolding of genetic programmes, springing in and out of our temporal framework, creates his happenings for him. We shall not obstruct the unfolding. The child – all children – are sublimely equipped to apprehend and to create the world. V and I have merely to protect the equipment and allow him to place us in his universe as benign and constructive forces. I shall never have a single ambition for him. I hope he will equip himself with the power to make the choices. If God were not God, the first thing He would deprive us of is free will. Mind you, it would not trouble me in the least if he became a piano player.

Once we forget that language has origins at least partially outside the limits of meaning (imagine, it is programmed before it is spoken!), we betray the freedoms that the miraculously complex assembly we call throat, tongue, larynx, glottis and so on conveyed to us. That Will demonstrates the freedom of language is a clear indication of the human soul as an empowered participant in a connected universe. Such clues abound if we are focused enough to allow them into our normal awareness. Will's garbled syntax, in which semantic concepts will sit happily together without the merest reference to each other, does not reveal the child as ignorant of meaning, only as having – creating – meanings of its own.

When we treat the prelingual child as an insentient being, we steal it away from its comforts in the ineffable. We deprive it of one of the fundamental faculties of our species, perhaps of all species. Then we ask ourselves what went wrong in the depths of history. And we tinker with ideas to explain away what we have not yet defined. We speculate that dreams are a process akin to a computer's dumping of data. Hogwash. The child perceives a magical world; all we have left ourselves is a bunch of old mental encumbrances.

Hold me down slowly sleepy bathtime, Daddy.
Blue and white chair bus choo choo train finish.
Birdies have come out, dark Christmas Tree man gone.
Party do where caterpillar in green kitchen put it now.
Noise! Noise! Out there! Story bears laughing.
Will book! Will book! Have it now tired Mummy.
Happy time. Time, time. Bye bye bodies. Bye, bye!

Nonsense, isn't it?

And Will teaches me about delight – an acuity of emotion that I had largely forgotten. This is not a focused, causal phenomenon: Will can be delighted about something that has no laughter for us. To him, a dog is a hilarious object. A kite crashing to the ground is a cosmically enjoyable event. The way a train booms suddenly over a bridge doesn't merely surprise, it makes him manically ecstatic. The phenomenology of things and events is not prescribed for Will as it is for the rest of us, so there is freshness in all things. If we could preserve this unconditioned state for ourselves we might retain our faculties for learning. That is where I realize all Will's faculties take him. He accumulates, he adds layers to his memory, he is an entirely kinetic being; and the catalyst of this constant state of becoming is his delight.

There's the fun.

What have we lost? I cannot assume (because I have no proof, only cultural precedents) that some inexorable process of physical or mental entropy has caused me to lose a great part of my delight. I must conclude that it is only my belief in what to expect that has reduced it. But beliefs can change or be discarded. With my quantum licence, I have no need of them at all, and can choose from an infinite array of existences in every second. If I take away the conditioning, I am prepared to be delighted without casting things or events as delightful in themselves. I do not need my ontology sorted out before I can laugh. I have solved an existentialist puzzle. I can laugh my head off. I do.

Perhaps if we laughed off a few more of our prophylactic notions we would receive a profound education from our children. Renewal and continuity are in the genetic meaning of what we do when we bring children into this world. They are the renewing force that unlocks us from an entropic destiny, but we have let our poor understanding of time blind us to such gifts. We become endbeings, passing the theory and history of endbeings on to those who most palpably immortalize us. All good things must come to an end; by implication, all bad things must persist.

Kfff. Holdy pot nice do it good people come now later.

And thus, by extrapolation, Will teaches me about ageing. The entropic theory of ageing is based entirely on physical data, taking no account whatever of the biomystical. My old yoga teacher – whose presence was radioactive and whose voice carried over Alpine distances when he was seventy-eight years old – insisted that the process of ageing is a conditioned illusion. He admitted that changes take place, but swore that decrepitude was not inevitable. Bluntly put, the belief in – the fear of – old age, consumes us so entirely that we think ourselves into decay: we voodoo ourselves into the shambling and the senility. This would seem a logical fate for a species that cannot recognize its own gifts for renewal, forgets its capacity for miracles and brings up its offspring as if the end of the world is nigh.

Well, there's one in the eye for medical science. An empiricist might plead that the illusion is no different from the reality in its effects: we all stagger off to the grave anyway. I shall plead that transience does not necessarily indicate decay. We might as easily say that there is a growth or maturing towards a state that has its own validity. (Past societies have revered vintage people; ours does not.) For example, the changes in mentation that many vintage citizens achieve are often a progression into semi-mystical states. Why is this not a valid position? It's a free country, isn't it? The second childhood is a pejorative that betrays our prejudice against the very young and very old, as well as our idiotic, narrowly linear definition of sanity. For all we know, old age might be a condition of mortal apotheosis; given the right appreciation, we might discover a number of Buddhas among us. The capacity to be delighted is the one we should retain: all over South Asia the statues remind us that it is possible for the human being to make a habit of being delighted. The Buddha laughs; the scientist cooks up entropy. If the gods come down tomorrow, there's no question who gets the booby prize.

In quantum nontime, prowling around in your internal democracy, is the lame, leaky-eyed, mystic old coot, toothless as a baby, incontinent, incoherent, half here, half there, given to transports of delight, living in memories, knowing things for which he has forgotten the words.

Doesn't he scare the shit out of you?

Bbpp. Let me cast doubt upon all our assumptions, because doubt exists only where belief hangs out. Having thoroughly unbalanced ourselves we are forced to the extremes. In a quantum state I have no need of belief and doubt, no need of oppositions; they simply get in the way of delightful perception, of ontological being. I have no need of order and disorder, no need that is not capable of changing itself into another need. I am a child: my birthright is to be free from conditioned states, with faculties that equip me to enjoy that freedom. I am connected with the universe; to Will, I am God; I spring from nowhere; I am also a very old person. Finally, I may not even be the same person I was when I began this diatribe. I am in and out of time. I am and not am I.

How old does this make me?

I wonder why Picasso wanted to paint like a child.

I wonder why 90 per cent of the universe has recently been undiscovered.

I wonder what is intrinsically funny about the ontology of a dog.

I find the answers that suit me, and tomorrow I throw them to the four winds.

I am at play!

And Will teaches me how, naturally! We build a tunnel out of a cardboard box. This is alternately a house, a hideyhole, a transdimensional warp corridor, a dormitory, a refuge from existence, a rocking horse, a motor bike, a repository, an echo chamber and a foreign country. For now it is a tunnel and I have to adjust my sense of time in order to place myself at Will's disposal. This involves being selfless without the support of ideology, becoming something for someone else merely because they require it. Only the child can create the conditions in which you will unself yourself for no bargained reason. Imagine being told by another adult to be exactly as they wish you to be, for no reason other than they wish it! I resolve that V and I must experiment with this, if we haven't already.

Right! Having disengaged myself from myself, I am now ready to take orders from an authority that has no commitment to reason. Wonderful! Get down, Dad, push choo choo train, pick up phone! Noise! Noise! There's no phone in this tunnel, Will. Get phone! OK, I get phone. Put phone in house! OK – choochoophonetrain!

Will pushes the telephone through the tunnel-house timewarp. He has decided to see how a telephone would perform if it were a train. Tukka-tukka-tooo-tooo! Ring, ring! He puts the phonetrain to his ear and decides to talk to his grandmother. He tells her what he has had for lunch, his usual ploy to maintain conversations interminably. He is talking about his lunch to his grandmother, who is not on the other end of any line, using a teletrain. This is a perfect denial of the whole phenomenological basis of existence. Honest! If in a child's untrammelled perceptions phenomena are interchangeable, why do we grow up and invent phenomenology, ontology and entropy? If we are going to get so organized about things, why can't we take at least some account of our origins in the void?

Why *is* 90 per cent of the universe missing?

It is the faculty of play that keeps us free, allowing us to view things as one or another. This is not a useless, nonfunctional approach: we are better equipped to participate in the universe when we are unconditioned, when we are not so organized that we cannot find the exit into that half of ourselves in which definitions have no meaning.

The child slips away whenever it can, and so do we, as I have said, in our unguarded moments. It is a talent we are born with, but I get the impression, looking around, that a great many people work hard at playing. Work? My bank manager, until recently, has been comforted by the fact that I make the occasional foray into work. Will works hard at playing, but he doesn't know that he is working. There isn't a damned ounce of work worth doing unless it is indistinguishable from play. Any other work brings trouble. War is the hardest work there is.

'Rice, chops, chips, apples, oranges, jelly, chicken, biscuits, cucumber and sambitches,' says Will into the choochoophone. This bears no resemblance to the lunch he actually had, which he has digested not only metabolically but phenomenologically as well.

Tukka-tukka-tooo-tooo!

EIGHTEEN

The past, unrehabilitated, grows monstrous, coming out of the shadows to encompass us. (My debt is closing in on me.) I have become an entirely contemplative being, because that is my compulsion, and I had thought that to follow it might absolve me from . . . from what? What can save us?

It is touch and go now, old boy. How can an individual be judged who allows the monster to flourish as he contemplates the heavens? Stone me if I know; I have deprived myself of the instruments of judgement.

Late at night, to fend off the grizzlies of impending pauperhood, I force myself to deeper contemplation of the stars.

The carnivores congregate, but I have fun.

Will is fed, and V is tranquil. Mostly.

I do not know what will save us and this uncertainty I must accept for I do not prejudice my future. Is that a paradox? It might be simpler to take action to avoid disaster, but I can no longer retain a preference for any course of action.

V is braver than I am usually, but when she is not my world implodes. Temporarily, though; I am no longer a being concrete enough to implode with any lasting effect. I have unfixed myself so well that I can no longer grasp the nature of my enemy.

I have no enemy except myself, and I am unlocatable, multiple.

Sometimes, V's anguish exceeds mine and I am sorry that we ever collaborated in this folly. But it is not folly! says a better voice: You and V are braver than all of man and womankind before you; you have attempted to live out an emotion and an idea from beyond your time, attempted to get outside of time altogether.

Sleepytime, says Will.

Sleepytime.

This is a disjointed world for us. We wish that we could be where we really belong. Where have I come from? Some dim star in Cygnus where proud, silent, exoskeletal beings contemplate an unending universe? And V? The feminine spirit? From some unknown essence of the moon?

And Will? Will the angel?

You cannot bring Will up as a toy in your unfathomed universe, says a voice.

And I say, but my universe is better fathomed than yours and I have discerned that I am also a part of God or whatever originating force made the decision to place Will in my care. I live as I must. Will must live with the heaven or hell of his origins – and I think it is heaven.

You may choose, says the voice.

I may choose not to choose, say I.

Prepare to drown. Abandon ship. Women and children first.

But the spirit is not just renewable: it is indestructible.

Do I believe this? I believe nothing, I imagine all.

Is the imagining more important than the belief? I imagine it is. I imagine it is not. Find me the world where I may live with my imagination.

Or let me find it for myself.

Any moment now they will threaten to take the tower away from us. We are only commodities, after all. There hasn't been a chocolate fudge cake in the fridge for quite some time.

'Very dirty,' says Will, apropos of nothing. He is learning to abstract and has much fun making comparisons between things that have no remote relation to each other.

Except when we disagree, V and I avoid the subject of our imminent downfall. Our separate interpretation of our mutual history intervenes; depending on our mood we blame different events or past selves for the mess we're in. Sometimes we invent selves to blame; at other times we cook up sublimely pious and intrepid alter egos so we can indulge in mutual adoration. Neither of us has only one interpretation of the problem. Often, it doesn't exist.

Are we willing to believe that scars accumulate? The answer is no: we have arrived at the point where we may change the past simply by unbelieving it.

For the moment, though, not much is working. The holiday has taken a toll – in purely mundane terms, of course. Fortunately, Will is still young enough not to need the daft trappings of the consumerized kid entering society. I think of children in the Third World, so-called, who require only a pair of legs to walk to school, a chalk, a slate, a piece of unleavened bread and a pickled pepper. In the interconnected world, their predicament (which they may not recognize) is of the same order as Will's: insufficiency is only a matter of degree. In the West, children are a market segment; in the old world they are equipped with abilities to do without. One day I shall find the correct definition for the connection between Will and those children, and something wonderful might happen. Connect! One day we might all feel satisfied at having universalized our sentiments.

How else can one be human?

V is often tearful in the mornings. She dismisses it as hormonal and we check for pregnancy, though none is planned. For myself, I am still bred away from tears. There is a pain below my ribs where, biomystically, unshed tears may be stored away. I dream of carcinogens, but I shall not fix my fear long enough to allow them to take hold. Nor shall I consult a physician: I do not wish to be assaulted by a body of knowledge. If I drink any of the adulterated wines being flogged all over the Great White West, I experience a few moments of fibrillation. But I can afford wine less and less, or not at all, and I do not miss the booze. At any rate, I do not believe that I cannot cure myself.

When V and I fight, which is seldom now there is so much to fight over, we sometimes blame each other for our situation. I can duck and weave when the flak's flying my way, but the lingering male feels a tinge of regret at being now so completely defenceless. The barriers are down. One of the crowd in the internal democracy, a right little fascist, will not let me forget that once I would have deployed a whole armoury of tactical weapons. The democrat will defend his right to speak his bit, even if I disagree with the bloody lot of them. For now at least.

I am under siege, come to think of it. The internal Department of Disinformation and Propaganda fuels thoughts of leaving V. Being unfixed, I am acutely aware that I can abandon the road to heaven at a moment's notice. Marriages are dismantled for smaller reasons, for prurience or despair. Still, there are certain things that would simply make me feel uncomfortable. I need no more explicit morality than that. The absence of fun, temporary or not, shouldn't take one to extremes. That is just further discomfort. Rather than leave V and Will, I shall learn how to take them with me. This is not as egocentric as it sounds, for I am inconsistent enough not to fix myself in relation to them. They will always have the room to abandon or divert me if that is what it comes to. We cannot own each other.

I am alive. I can hope. I sleep well at night.

V, hormones, tears and all, is an even greater natural optimist than I. The hormones are part of her courage: acuity of emotions – a greater range of them – gives one strengths. She cooks up marvellous vistas of our apotheosis – mortal, of course, we are not ready to give up the ghost – and I am pieced back together again and again. This is what we do for each other, and what makes us, among other things, accomplices. The siege is always temporary, we tell each other; and when I compare us with the walking wounded I see that we have indeed arrived at a place where we will be for ever unassailable.

What is the worst thing that can happen to you?

V and I are unfixed enough in time as well, so our problems cannot impinge on us with any consistency. There are sanctuaries of peace everywhere. There is the feel of her hip under my hand at night. We have reduced ourselves so successfully to nothingness that every small connection with the texture of life is intense.

We burn bright. To reduce life to nothing is to get rid of the distractions that misinform us; then we are in absolute contact with all possibilities. This contact is a sufficient richness; it makes us universal participants. Once the distractions are removed, we discover our connection with *being*, we are in the first empty spaces of heaven.

People who come back from wars speak of such things. They see the rest of us as indolent and unfocused, refugees from what may be real. They have experienced the ultimate order – life reduced to only two choices: survive or perish.

There are easier ways to revive old faculties.

'Very dirty,' says Will.

I am making choo-choo-train calls and writing letters – very elegant letters – to the military-industrial complex that is hunting us down. They are occasionally diverted by my attempts at style. Meanwhile I beg from relatives and benefit from small windfalls. I wonder if the tribulations of the rich are of any significance compared with our prospects, but, of course, such comparisons are false and all woes, including the fiscal, are relative. The boy on his way to school at dawn in the rice paddies may be greatly concerned by the absence of a frog he is accustomed to playing with each morning. Existence engages us; beliefs disengage us; comparisons or oppositions undermine any integrity we might achieve for ourselves.

We must be what we are to ourselves and extend the same freedom to others.

Somewhere in history there must have been a society based on the precept of looking after each other.

And V and I, idiots that we are, still cannot behave as if the parachutes have failed. I take up the piano and pay for lessons from an invisible resource. V lapses into inconsequential bouts of wild consumerism, after which our larders and wardrobes are majestically stocked.

We do not know if we are winning. We do not know if there is such a thing as winning. Such a state also precludes the possibility of losing, and losing might have something indispensable to teach us. One thing is as good as another.

Kfff.

We *feel* good!

NINETEEN

In or out of time, I am forced to concede, at least when I am feeling prone to disaffection, that this world is not for me. The military-industrial complex forbids all ideologies except for the ideology of money, and this is hardly an ideology in the old Greek sense, it is merely a shoddy abstraction, merely the breaking of the First Commandment. I would rather, if I were to believe in time, belong to some future in which humans have returned to themselves and begun some real movement – steeped in chaos and change, in a forward momentum that is not encumbered by the corruptions of history.

Under siege, I feel at one with all those who have been exiled from sacred territory. I think of the Native Americans, whose culture was so advanced their conquerors mistook it for savagery. They will be back, once the rest of us have given up our mass abstractions. Like them, those who have attained the quantum state feel acutely connected with the past – with all the felicities and crimes of humanity. We are not separated from our history. The link in human consciousness is continuous and kinetic. Our awareness has among its components the internal screams of the Native American woman who sent her six-year-old daughter out waving a white flag to the US Cavalry, only to have her chopped down. Ta-ran-ta-raa! It is the same awareness and the same wound as that of the black men and women aboard the slave ships, clinging to what they could of their humanity by making love in the rancid darkness below decks. What desperate embraces the human being is capable of! It is the same memory that was blacked out in its mortal form among the peoples of East Timor and the Kurds of Iraq, among the Jews who lay in each other's excrement in the rattling trains of death, among the Kampucheans who found that you cannot recognize loved ones by the lineaments of their skulls.

It is the same incessant pain of all those people who, being of the lowest price in the commodity markets of our planet, have to sell whatever they can find in order to ... to what? Eat? Their children, their penises and vaginas, their kidneys, their eyes, their eye-hand co-ordination – fashioned over Darwin's eons; their scrawny legs and brittle backs; their mouths, as anuses for the feculence of demagogues or orifices for the post-Imperialist ghouls who still stalk this planet; their skin and hair, their chromosomes and genetic potential, and, when we have done with them, their corpses. Not a scrap is wasted.

Those of us who are connected across time will feel their pain; it is part of our consciousness and will be with us despite our detachment and our security in heaven. And those of us who are reluctant to make the mental space will be propelled towards this sharing of our narrow concerns, for we have created the means by which nothing can happen in our world without the information, true or false, leaking across to us, especially to our crazy Western world, where the distractions from our quaint discomfiture cannot silence the pain that shakes the hemispheres. It is no less audible whether it comes from present horrors or whether it is the cry of the Native American woman whose genitals were carved out of her, dried, tanned, polished and stretched across the saddle horns of the great liberators of the great American continent, the boys in blue. Come back John Wayne, all is forgiven.

Those of us who are connected will feel the pain and joy of whatever pain and joy takes place, or we shall be less than human. When called to account by some Galactic authority, we will be obliged to claim that the past is not immutable and none of us beyond salvation. We will have to forget all the theories and beliefs that have driven us to our atrocities and beg, instead, or barter, *parlez-vous*, pow-pow, swap and sell the one last part of ourselves that we still believe has any value. How shall we synthesize its essence and package it for the intergalactic commodity traders. Why, it is more than likely that they will be looking for the one thing that sustains us in all our turmoil!

I have no one word for it. It may be love, or kisses, laughter, weeping; it may be the way the Skydiver looks at me as I hold his head above water in the bath and he feels my soap caresses; it may be the thing that makes me hope he will always trust me so completely, but it is certainly this: it is certainly the connectedness that makes us feel the pain and joy of whatever pain and joy takes place. *Compassion*: a fine, high concept for the packaging and sale of the human essence in the steamy bazaars of the pangalactic multiconglomerate's far-flung mercantile outposts. Ninety-three cents worth of chemicals can take you a long, long way!

The quantum state is natural to us all; our smallest compassions confirm this and every new human being demonstrates its possibilities.

I am giving the Skydiver a bath and thinking about the Native Americans. There is an archetypal origin – a linkage across time – in every movement I make as I cradle and turn and jostle Will's little body; they are movements that have been repeated a billion times through our history. I would rather have a documented history of the archetypal significance of giving babies baths than the endless accounts of the selfish and downright fucking stupid wars and scandals and jealousies of a small number of death-bloated people who were a positive danger to everyday folk and who didn't bathe all that often either.

The holiday gives me a chance to do some *real* work, work that puts me in fleshly contact with the history of our species and in which I learn from the actions of billions before me. This is the way the chimp finds the club. My quantum imagination allows me the latitude for such speculation; it revels in the creation of a past which I know must have existed, documented or not. And it focuses me almost narcotically in the present. Were I van der Weyden, I might have to rush off and paint the fine juxtaposition of Will's hand and mine as I cup water in my palm and drip it over his splayed fingers. This he enjoys. This past, which is not fixed and may disappear from my memory by morning, I enjoy.

It makes me feel like a man.

More and more now, as I get in touch with Will and explore further intimacies with V, my mind is thrown open to inspiration

– to creating this world for myself. I am fully equipped with pain and joy, I am privileged to be a fugitive from the military-industrial complex; I have no immutable past and no future that is not tangible in every turning moment of the present; I have a quantum imagination that constructs freedoms and fantasies to dissolve the phenomenology of this world in which I cannot live. It never existed in the first place. It was always a matter of interpretation.

The truth is, I have rediscovered that childish sense that allows one to create the world. Everything I perceive, in the manner of children, is my own personal archetype; nothing happens but it is happening for the first time, because I have removed the conditioned mentality that transfigures and falsifies all events or phenomena with fixed belief. And the truth also is that I cannot see how this will go away, for I have transcended even the need to change. Let it all happen or not, I have distilled myself into a present that will last until I die, one long, extended moment always focused in the Now, undifferentiated by events, and in which qualities of some special order will always exist because I have cooked up for myself the kind of perception that makes all things special.

One thing is as *good* as another.

Even the pain and fear I feel when my courage quails is part of the phenomenology of a multiple being. The focus of the moment reacquaints one with the conditionless state in which everything has the right to exist and nothing is overwhelming: a state of invincibility and immortality.

I have arrived at a point of stillness. I am moving so fast that everything is simultaneous.

I have stopped the world, Don Juan.

TWENTY

On the drying-mat, Will, sprung back into the foetal position, clutches his toes and makes a complete circle of himself. He cuts out his extremities this way, gaining a proper hold of all his parts. Being only two, the proportion of his head to his body is still about one to five. An alien. Children are a species unto themselves and ought to be treated as such.

'Miwwa!' he demands. V and I have told him that he is handsome. When he is spruced up and ready for bed, he likes to confirm this for himself. I prop him up before the mirror. He does not look at his hair or teeth or his ruddy cheeks: he looks himself straight in the eye and smiles. He is altogether delighted at being *Will*, a friend who lives in the mirror, an intermediary between Sartre's phenomenological and ontological selves. Everything is possible until some meddler comes along and draws lines around you.

'Who's that?' I ask.

'Wiw!' he answers.

'And who're you?' I ask.

'Me!' he cries, making a sudden discovery.

'And who am I?' I cry.

'Me!' he answers.

'And who is V?' I ask.

'Me!' he cries.

And, by jingo, he might as well be right! Could it be that in a child's barely objectified, nonlinear world even our selves are interchangeable? Could it be that Will labours under the fine misconception that he is sometimes me or V or both – or all three? Naaaw. Let's stash that particular one away for a long and embroidered exposition one night after the sixth vodka, when we are in the company of people whose conversation is submerged in matters we would not grant a second thought – for which second thoughts do not exist! Then let's whip it out and brandish it, act as if we believe in it and be labelled cracked.

Will is cracked. There's no doubt about it; it is a prerequisite of being a child.

I wrap my arms around him and help him climb on to my shoulders. He has learnt to ride there, using his thighs and ankles to stay poised, tugging at my ears to steer. Robed and bearded patriarchs stagger under the burden of a thousand children held aloft from the burning sands of the Negev. I fly away to the pictures at every opportunity. De Mille has nothing on me.

Will steers me to the wall where I have nailed up a montage of all members of our family, living and dead. To each of these he bids a fond 'Noonight', then digs his spurs in to take me down the stairs of the tower to the living-room, where we will find V.

She is in her easy chair, staring into space like a person about to receive the full 20,000 volts.

'Where are you?' I ask.

'In the Dodecanese.'

'Say good-night to V, Will.'

'Noonight, V, huggy sleepytime.'

'See you luck!'

'Bye bye body!'

'Huggy huggy!'

'Sleep well, little boy.'

'Noonight! Noonight! Noonight choo-choo-train, noonight kitchen, noonight bicycle, noonight chocolate!'

To say goodnight to a forbidden bar of chocolate is a supremely nanometric act, especially since it is a ploy to make us relent and let him have it for a nightcap. He knows that we will fluctuate in our disciplines. I suppose it makes his life interesting to have a God that will stoop to negotiating. What the hell, do what feels good and work out the reasons not to do it later, after you've spread the fun around. Will isn't a docile, whingeing crank like some of his contemporaries. He's never hostile or unwilling to share, doesn't hoard and won't wail more than he needs to.

See you luck, bye bye body.

After a histrionic interpretation of tonight's selection from Will's library, I creep down the stairs, hopscotching to avoid groaning floorboards. V is still staring into space. I plant myself quietly on the sofa and make myself invisible. Intimacy, for all its liberations, is also sustained by great tact. Friends are often surprised to hear us speak to each other with the politeness of strangers. I wait.

'I was thinking,' she says, 'of all we have achieved . . . '

'An abundance of nothing,' I quip.

'Yet we feel so good so much of the time. My perceptions are so acute because we have nothing to distract us from ourselves . . . as if we're living off our imaginations . . . but when I'm feeling down the whole thing collapses and I wonder if we haven't made ourselves sick and mad. Then I have to pull myself up by my bootstraps and rebuild the whole . . . edifice . . . except that when I do that it's a different edifice each time, everything slipping away and coming back changed so that I don't know who I am and don't even know if I want to know who I am . . . and then, depending on my mood, this can be fun or bloody misery, like being on a ship and never being able to tell if you're anchored or adrift . . . and then realizing it doesn't matter because most of the time we feel so good.' She looks at me with the beginnings of a smile. 'Even when I'm feeling bad I am inspired. I could die any moment from the intensity of it.'

'Living off our imaginations – that's a good way to put it,' I say.

She laughs. 'And what imaginations! When you've nothing to grasp on the outside you invent everything on the inside. What things I come up with!'

'Sling me some, then . . . '

'Oh! Where would I start?'

'Hang in there, I'll get me a drink.' I settle in nicely. Where will we take each other tonight? The vodka is sparkling and the frost on the glass feels good.

'Working on the dream book opens my mind to all sorts of new things, and being tied to Will keeps me down to earth – so I'm stretched over a very long distance, part of me somewhere sublime and part of me right here; but the sublime part – that influences everything and makes it all special. The dream book makes me believe that anything is possible. It's as if all the limits of reason – of what one was taught to think – can be lifted – and not because they do not apply but because there is no real need for them to be imposed on the way I am. Do you follow me?'

'Always will. You tend to get there first.'

'I've been adding up the past, for instance: my feeling that there was always something more than the life we were given, with all its comforting assumptions and invisible restrictions . . . then shrugging off the past and assuming powers for myself – mental, physical, intuitive – the power of what we are – and coming up with a huge universe of possibilities where nothing is . . . inherently discouraging or negative . . . Now I am able to act as if this were true, which makes it true. No limits, preconceptions or preconditions to decide how I should react to anything at all. And the natural conclusion to all of that is an exploration of the sublime – psychic levels I've uncovered in myself which are now just another aspect of my being alive, another string to my bow . . . ' She closes her eyes and lies back, wrapped in smiles; then she squints at me and grimaces with an internal delight. 'Shit!' she whispers, 'I have progressed by doing absolutely nothing!'

'Everyone should take a holiday,' I say.

She sits up and wags a finger at me. 'And I have liberated myself to the extent that I can explore anything that comes up. I can question things more acutely, but without scepticism or the dismissiveness one has when one's reactions are limited to the rational – Akashic records, underground tunnels, visualization, visiting my own body, talking to Will's unconscious, finding out how telepathic you and I are . . . knowing that I have a direct link to some higher knowledge while knowing that it could all originate in me and then deciding that there's no difference between inside and outside . . . fancy that! Fancy discovering that one is . . . emotionally linked to a source of higher knowledge . . . and that the link is so strong that there is no real separation between it and me!'

'It's the kind of knowledge available when one is free of rational thinking,' I say.

'Don't interrupt, I'm in full flow.'

'Yes, missy!'

'The point is I can consult my source of knowledge for anything I need to know. The word "psychic" is meaningless because it's a knowledge that comes naturally from . . . from a unity of the self – all one's faculties working together to provide a sublime talent for deduction. As I go along I pick up hints of all sorts of other things . . . the significance of events and how they originate in mass fantasies, for example . . . and the visions I have! . . . aliens, God – again and again – presences, parallel spirits . . . Jung's archetypes, perhaps, or the things themselves – no difference . . . God isn't supposed to be within reach of our rational senses in any case! . . . and intimations of other lives, too: being a man in a medieval seaside town in the English West Country . . . a very direct sense of being there, of past and future selves . . . an accumulation of selves focused in the present so that our normal awareness is only partial, filtering out the other lives . . . I can't connect it all and express it to you in a sentence because these things aren't *connected*, they are the one thing . . . But, with all that, there's also Will and all the problems and the trivia and the nonsense – and the fun . . . I know! I think what is happening is that I am finding out how to pull the two worlds together, changing my own consciousness so that I can approach everything from the level of the sublime . . . the sheer momentousness of just *being*. It fills me with anguish when we try to deal with this world using only the rational tools that we were given, like hopping through life on one leg and getting so used to the discomfort that you don't notice it any more. When you get rid of that, you can be anyone you like. There, I've finished!'

'Do you know the Catholic prayer, I can't remember the name – "Hail Mary! Full of grace, Blessed art thou among women . . ."?'

'We were right, you know . . . in the beginning . . . when we said that if we pooled our resources we could be gods and goddesses.'

'The trick is to internalize everything,' I say, 'until one realizes that all things are possible because they are internal anyway, and that the internal world is a world of flux. Nothing is fixed. Sooner or later, everyone will come to the same freedom. It's the freedom to interpret everything for oneself, without the restrictions of history or psychology or the deference to one authorized version of the way things are. One day people will feel it in their bones and wonder what all the fuss was about.'

She leaps up, drains my vodka and staggers around the room, miming a retch. 'I can't think about the future any more, unless I'm being a prole or I fantasize about it. Funny thing is, when I fantasize I can't help feeling that there is a connection between that kind of projected dreaming – a state where I am completely absorbed and transport myself to the future – and what I actually become. It is a sort of template on which the surface of the future is marked out, and a version of the dreamed event almost always occurs, even if only by making us expect it. We condition ourselves, predispose ourselves to the happening, so we create the future. Bugger me, I knew it all along!'

'I'll drink to that as well!'

'The dream isn't so solid that it fixes us in our approach to what might happen ... Blast! How can I put this without it sounding like nonsense? ... I think the dream opens us to the possibilities of what might occur and also makes us capable of appreciating the random effects that will alter events so that they disguise themselves and surprise us. They become symbols of what we expected in the first place. Either way we create the events! We can't lose!'

'Yep, one thing is as good as another,' I say, suavely.

'The beauty of it is that one can dispense with faith! All you need is a certain openness to change and the recognition of your ability to influence it. We invent a new way of believing which doesn't involve faith!'

I jump in. 'Which doesn't involve fixed belief. Believing in not believing, a quantum paradox, but only a paradox in language.'

'It isn't possible!' she cries. 'What if we change our minds tomorrow? Ah, I know! We can! This kind of belief doesn't prevent it. Yes, that is exactly what I feel. I don't have to maintain any kind of position. But wait a minute – I always knew that!'

'Yeah, women know it more than men.'

'What?'

'I said women know it more than men.'

'Well stone the fucking crows! Why didn't you tell me that before?'

'I thought you knew.'

'I did! I just needed the confirmation!'

'Well, there you are, then. Look, women are more of a piece; they haven't sold out completely and they can't because of their biological imperatives. They have to belong to two worlds, so they become infinitely adaptable. When they are intact they are quantum beings, which to me is the natural state of our species. I don't know what happened with men. They chickened out. Or maybe we're just drones gone mad. Dunno. I'll figure it out one day.'

'Jesus, that explains everything. Women are infinitely more loving than men are, and it isn't just a biological imperative: it's because you can't be adaptable without the motivation, and the essential motivation is love. Love is the controlling factor, the interplay between what does and does not exist, which is why we can create the future. Men misuse the power, while women sustain it. *Ergo*, we couldn't exist without the sustaining powers of women – not just their ability to propagate but their power to use love to create the world!'

'Seems pretty watertight to me,' I say. 'Love: that's probably who or what or why God is.'

She laughs. 'God is love!'

'Silly old coot!'

'Yeah, the patriarch – the male version!' She steams into the kitchen. I hear the sounds of knife and chopping board. 'You want a peanut-butter sandwich?'

'Not with vodka, thanks.'

She pops her head around the door. 'What if it's all hogwash?'

'What if it is!'

'You didn't mention that before either.'

'Mention what?'

'That it doesn't matter a damn if it is hogwash.'

I sip my vodka long and slow. Who am I? Humphrey Bogart or John Wayne? 'Waaal,' I drawl, 'I only just created the possibility!'

*

I am sitting alone with my glass while V throws another sandwich together. I am fifteen billion light years from head to toe. This sense of limits we live with is like a dark sixth sense, conditioning us without our knowledge. What is it for? If it is a cautionary response, it is based in fear and ought to be defunct; if it is the reasonableness that warns us off great expectations then it belittles us. What is the worst thing that can happen to you? Life could not be worse than it is if every week we took a pill to prevent undue enthusiasm.

Once we have discarded our unfixed selves, we take precautions against their reemergence. Even in those who profess power over their destinies, or over the destinies of others, real freedoms are subverted. I'll figure it out one day. Perhaps they function from the old internal dialectic, pitting themselves against limits they deem inherent in man's nature, setting up the tension of further challenges where there could be a simple participation in the flux. Another set of oppositions; another fight to fight.

Well, here we are, V and you and I, trying to formulate a new fundament for creation itself, one without the oppositions, a life unashamedly of wishful thinking and the highest possible expectations for each of us. Who cares if they are attainable? That is to precondition them, take all the wonder and surprise away and learn nothing in the process. To assume that all things are possible and behave as if there is no limit to what we are: what can this be but a kind of duty, a final, overdue leap into the potential of the human being! As quantum personalities we may experiment with dreams, wishes, aspirations, fantasies and even just our passing thoughts to see how they can interact with chance and destiny, with this external world which is also our creation. We may then produce, in the same way that particles emerge from virtual states to become fleetingly real, a universe that is a fine approximation of ourselves. This is a reciprocal act of creation, and an act – inescapably – of love. There may be no greater infinity of riches that awaits us. Look into the face of your child and remember how once you felt.

V returns with her sandwich and is quiet. She has a knack for retreating suddenly into her privacy that leaves me unsettled. 'So what have you achieved?' I ask.

She eyes me absently between mouthfuls and answers matter-of-factly, 'I've danced, chatted up a few leprechauns and extraterrestrials, immersed myself in light, sensed events from unrecorded history, swapped my dream world for my waking world, called down our son from heaven, confirmed the existence of my kindred spirit, rescued my past and flown missions into the future so that I can have news of what I was when I arrive there. That,' she says, brandishing her sandwich, 'is the whole point.'

I am lying back with my eyes closed hearing V's voice as my own. I might as well be floating in Andromeda. Somewhere in the desert, the first V and that version of myself that knew the meaning of loneliness are meeting again, splitting into parallel realities and meeting again and again. One moment will suffice to raise the dust of ten thousand years. I am spread across my past and future; I can feel the subliminal hum of the universe in the pit of my stomach, which is chilled with the cold sluicing of vodka.

Thank you, God, you silly old coot.

TWENTY-ONE

With her flawed female spatial sense, V has never learnt how to avoid our creaky floorboards. We creak up the stairs of the tower in darkness and Will, with his immaculate timing, is there at the top, waiting for us. We get into bed together, V and I crammed into the two-thirds of it Will does not occupy. I think of the films of wildlife I have seen where the big cats pad around and squeeze into minuscule spaces in deference to their sleeping cubs. Lying between V and Will, I feel like a lion. Will's poky knees dig into my side; the length of V's thighs are against the length of mine. I can hear from V's breathing that she is almost asleep. The three of us are like one flesh.

In the darkness I fly away to Deneb and survey the ferric plains of an M-class planet that swoops about it, the home of my exo-skeletal alter ego. Back on earth, I am a wheeling dot, affixed to this planet spinning round at a thousand miles an hour in this solar system humming round the edge of the galaxy which is hurtling through space with Doppler-screaming momentum. I become unfixed, travelling through immeasurable distances in a medium where no straight lines exist and time ticks only once. The whole thing is crazy, of course: some fevered dream of God; God dreaming that He is falling. When He wakes up with a start we shall all vanish and even He will never know that we existed but for a queer, metallic taste on his cetacean tongue. He gets up to raid the fridge, the dear old coot. His knees creak because he is so old, and his lungs rattle for fifteen billion years of nuclear chain-smoking.

I have forgotten my body now, encased in the flesh of my loved ones, and become one-pointed, a spark in the Third Eye.

Ah, what else is there? The bank manager, who is now a great friend and solicitous of my welfare. My quantum persona walks past the bank the other day, and there he is, the bank manager, being carted off to an ambulance with the faintly embarrassed look of someone who has just had a cardio-vascular hiccup. What do you say to a dying man to whom you owe money? I give him a thumbs-up and a cracked smile without breaking my stride. Later he tells me he felt terribly alone and my interfaceable digit practically saved his life. I think I revived his unwounded self just when he needed it.

And Rostand, now an oilman, I hear, with a brood of kids. Those bills shoved away in a corner downstairs. Tomorrow, more phone calls and letters in which I plead with some ceremony. I put it all out of my mind; I run away. This is not the time, now I am wrapped in the flesh of V and Will. This is all there is, all there ever shall be. If we survive this process, V and I, and go on to create a succession of worlds, each happier and more felicitous than the other, they shall not have a single spot more pleasant than this. There is only this feeling and the attempt to recreate it in other forms. Like the orgasm: single moments between which there is only the work of life to be done, graft and tears, or, if my luck holds, just a straying of the imagination from here to there like a dumb animal after the scent of water. This is all there is. I am dead. I have died and gone to a blackness where only my last memory persists – of this resting place between Will and V. With this feeling an entire system of virtual particles has collapsed and I have died into nowhere.

I am certain that the last illusion of a final and material death is only one of the deaths we experience. There is death in joy and pain, and in every moment of the past retreating from us. It is absurd to think of this life as a continual progression of a single individual with a single coherent memory and immutable past. The only me that has ever existed is the me right here in this present, and that me has also just kicked the bucket. He is decidedly late. The final death of the body is merely the consummation of a multiplicity of existences and nothingness. Cop that, Mr Sartre. You had no idea at all. You lacked the soul of the poet, that is, of the melancholic who feels death in every moment. Fortunately, Monsieur, I am something of a reprobate and can exorcize this melancholy by unfixing myself; I cannot maintain my affection for such an overweaning character as the moribund poet. You got caught up with one of your characters, me old *légume*! Just one, when you could have had the lot! Must have been your rotten childhood; a bunch of pretty sinister personal archetypes! Mental guillotines, old toot!

Me? I am free. I don't exist. There is a huge crowd here in bed, sandwiched between V and Will. Old cronies and down-in-the-mouths; self-flagellants and wild epicureans – a Brueghelian fest booming away beneath my ribs, the whole swag of them leaking away into oblivion, dying like flies and popping up anew just as fast as they fall. Know thyself, ha! Know that thou are multiple and that the reflexive pronoun is only a matter of convenience – of appellation. Rejoice! Die rejoicing!

What else is there before the little death? Ah, there is the Painter. He is a character in the crowd I must endure. I came across him after my father's death, churning out canvases of horror. A dark imaginer. Gervase said he was the dark side, but that is too definitive for me. The dark night of the soul, said Gervase, assuring me that Christ had survived it. Some reassurance! My father died and woke up the Painter. Goya, I think he is, in the last mad period. Horrors! Decapitations, disembowelments, devaginations, the peeling away of skin and the pouring of boiling oil into opened veins.

He is let loose on V and Will sometimes, exploring the possibilities of horror to their logical conclusion. Too often I have asked myself what is the worst that can happen? The Painter is there to provide the answers. Were I evangelical I might see him as the Devil and externalize his existence; then the terror would destroy me. As one of the crowd he has his place, though he makes me think of the murder of children in favelas, of the passing round of babies on Japanese bayonets in World War Two, and the burial alive of pregnant mothers, who, when disinterred, were found to have miscarried. The Painter draws these pictures for me and I do not yet know if there is anything I can learn from him, but he is not the better of me; I can send him away most of the time with a slow repetition of The Lord's Prayer. It is astonishing to contemplate there might have been human beings born in the grave. These mad memories we shall carry with us until they force us to abandon belief, until we are unfixed and liberated from even the smallest presumption of a universe conceived in death and entropy. I do not know.

Our Father who art in Heaven.

Will might remember me in ways I cannot recall for myself when I am old. He will have stored away versions of me that have long died in my memory and whose existence I may even deny. As he neared his death, my father shared little of the fine memories I had of him. I remember all the films he ever took me to, all the jokes he ever cracked, and the way, when he took a siesta, he would lie on his side, propped against folded arms so that he looked belligerent. I remember the smell of him, the feel of his flesh, the way his limbs fell and the sounds of him going to the toilet. I remember that we only ever embraced once I had grown up, when he was beginning to go and I felt sure enough of myself to breach the gap. By then, the feel of his flesh had changed. The love of a man for his father is the only permissible tenderness between heterosexual males, but even that must be disguised or constricted by the small norms of male culture. The loss of the father is always a loss of opportunities and a recounting of things that ought to have been said or done. If I do not fix myself I may not leave Will with such a melancholy retrospective. I must constitute myself so that . . . But what of the future can I fix for Will?

V makes little clicking sounds in the back of her throat. Every night her infant self emerges and has a round at the breast, the uvula flying up and down to co-ordinate breath, the palatal vacuum and the flow of milk. A simultaneous being. Watch someone asleep and you can see the unfixed person, the ontological presence unencumbered by intervening perceptions. These suckling forms we can love without question. This is the V I love especially: the V in whose eyes I first detected the unencumbered being. Perhaps I shall find a way to hold on to that for Will, so however I look to him he can see – in the eyes – some sign of the person intact beneath them. Remember my eyes, Will, and you can see whatever pleases you in your memories of them. I leave you with your own freedom.

When my father hadn't long to live, he spent much time looking at me, but he never said what he thought and I never asked him.

The future! The future! I am dying now in every second, while plummeting towards the illusion of a final death. Enveloped in bliss, I have the freedom to speculate, journeying warmly with the essence of V and Will, to whom I have given birth and who gave birth to me. I am a wheeling dot with no existence but for the slight pressure between the brows.

The time of the quantum will come, though it may not be known as such. Some expansion of our selves will take place once we have disencumbered each other – a reunification of selves and sexes, a living off the gifts of internal being, a rediscovery of nothingness. Kind chaos!

This nostalgia for the future – this sense of what we can be . . . it arises from somewhere; we have a precedent knowledge that there is more to what we are; I call it the ineffable because only words have betrayed us into thinking that all can be grasped and held in a certain way – into distrusting what we cannot define.

The linearity of language filters the world, letting it through in thin streams which we must watch go by. But now we are reaching the stage where some critical mass that has accumulated begins to stir. The ineffable selves we keep dormant will be pushed to the surface; they will change our perceptions from the sequential and fragmented to the whole, our knowledge from the reductive to the instantaneous and connected – because we ourselves will be whole and connected with the streams that run through us. Knowledge will become a *sense*, an intrinsic faculty rather than something strange to our inner being, something objectified and lodged in decaying memory.

For what do I hope? An apotheosis? How many generations of our descendants will have spun back into the earth before such things can be contemplated? We must ride the neutrino and obliterate the boson. How can we not be a part of some exponential process? How can we possibly be isolated from the dynamics of this universe if we cannot find what separates us from it?

The child, still blind and arriving with no knowledge we can define, knows what to look for.

Time does not exist except as a framework imposed by our sense of order, itself temporary and spasmodic. Will it not be dismantled?

How is it possible for us to say we have integrity if we fix ourselves in a single place while the very universe draws away from us at speed, creating distances we will refuse to explore? Once these fixed positions have gone there may be a better chance for men and women to get through to the core of each other and see that only love exists there. Only love recreates us in every second. Only love accounts for nothingness.

When we have found these unencumbered selves, will we not perceive that this is how the children were – we were – all along? Then can we not begin to treat them to the freedoms we have discovered in ourselves?

The reductionists would separate us from the universe; the impossibility of this shows the scale of their illusions. They would separate us also from our genes. They have defined the universe as progressing towards death; even if that were true, it is an assumption tenable only in linear time, and they themselves have discovered that linear time does not exist. Do they lie, are they mad, or have they merely fallen into a fixed position? (Answers on a postcard, addressed to the late great Akoond of Swat, please.)

Why should I kill myself before I die?

Even in the progress of the mundane – if you detach yourself from the drag of the past and the pull of the future – you gain the momentary focus that connects you. This equips you for any task and allows you any patience you may need. It brings you the absorption that unites all your faculties and drives you ahead in the full power of yourself. You create your world and participate in it. This isn't hard work at all. It is fun. Perhaps they forgot.

What is left for us to define? Evil? Disease? War?

I am falling into a dream. It is nightfall in paradise. I have arrived in heaven, just in time for a nap. Good-night! Good-night! Sleepytime . . .

TWENTY-TWO

'This is Wahida,' says Rostand, standing at my door. He is so eager to make introductions that he has forgotten to come in. Beside him is a small, bright-eyed woman covered from neck to toe in yards of flowing black silk.

'How do you do,' she says, in a studiously enunciated accent. Her palms are filigreed with *mehndi*.

Rostand has arrived unannounced. I haven't heard from him in what must be eight or nine years. A girl and boy of perhaps five and six years peer at me from behind Wahida's ample skirts, as if confronting a friendly ogre. Rostand has planted himself outside my front door with his hands in his pockets. There is a calculated air about him; he has planned this moment for some time and is determined to extract the maximum from it. I can expect nothing less from Rostand. He mutters to Wahida in Arabic. It has the tone of, This is the bastard I've been telling you about.

'Wahida,' says Rostand, looking me pointedly in the eye, 'is my wife.'

I rummage around for an appropriate response, then abandon the mission. 'Well, stone me, you old reprobate! Very pleased to meet you, Wahida. Do please come in.'

He stands his ground, rooting his wife and children to the spot. 'And these are my children, Pierre-Ahab and Nasreen-Juliette.'

The boy disappears behind his mother, but the girl takes my extended hand and speaks with an American twang.

'Pleased ta meetcha.'

'Do come in,' I repeat. I am so taken aback that I am being rather ceremonious. I do not know whether Rostand is pompous because he sees I am being affected.

192

He squares his shoulders. 'We will come in on one condition; you have a son, do you not?'

'Will, two and a half.'

'And he is the son of the girl you spoke of when we were in the desert, and she is your wife now, is she not?'

I imitate his patriarchal tone inadvertently. 'Indeed! I have been greatly fortuitous!'

He gives Wahida the nod and from under the copious rustling of silk she produces a very large bottle of Scotch. 'Then,' he roars, 'let us celebrate!'

Wahida is bemused by V, whose every move she follows and whose hands she has clutched with touching affection after Rostand has kissed them comprehensively, addressing her knuckles in English, French and Arabic. V whisks out biscuits and orange juice for the children. They sit where they are told, keep their eyes down and do not move unless they have consulted Wahida in whispers. It is a visit from the Magi. V disappears upstairs and returns with a large bottle of vodka, which she places alongside Rostand's large bottle of Scotch. I fetch glasses while Rostand sits and surveys the ceiling, his thumbs hooked in his waistcoat. I remember that he has never had a social persona; it would not be unlike him to clam up for the rest of the evening, having done us the honour of presenting his wife.

But he is at great pains to explain. 'Wahida has little English, though you may speak to her directly if you wish; she has a sort of sixth sense to understand what you say.' He rises and helps himself to the glasses and whisky, pouring a small, neat one which he hands to Wahida and repeating the process for V. He clinks glasses sombrely with each of us and with the children as well, then he cracks a smile for the first time. 'Ask me how I met her,' he booms. He seems to have abandoned his European side, displaying only his patrician Arab manners. There is a pause while V and I reel under the impact.

V chimes in. 'Oh, do tell! How did you meet Wahida?'

'She gave me a lift!'

'She did what?' I remember that Arab women do not drive,

legally or otherwise; at least not normally in the postbedouin countries.

'Do you remember the old Alhamra cinema? I fell asleep outside it after James Bond – have you seen the latest? Brilliant bastard! I'm afraid I was drunk at the time. I wake up at two, maybe three o'clock with no way to get home except to walk. Where is my car? I do not know. I start walking and this taxi pulls up with two men in *dishdasha* sitting in it: they say you want a lift, I think they are secret police so I dare not say no. One man gets out and sits in the back and I have to sit in front with the driver, and when I look under the *dishdasha* I see Wahida!'

'Good grief!' I say. I sneak a look at V. It would be unseemly to ask what Wahida was doing dressed as a man, picking up strangers in a taxi at three in the morning in a country where purdah is still observed. Wahida giggles, jingling her own weight in concealed jewellery.

'Wahida wants to learn to drive so she gets out of the harem in the middle of the night with her eunuch. She takes fifty or sixty lessons until she is Stirling Moss and picks men off the street for her eunuch, who is a very large black man with the face of an old houri. This she tells me quite frankly and also asks if I would like to go home with the eunuch. She says he will be *gentle* with me!' Convulsed with laughter, Rostand discovers that he is uncomfortable in my rattan chair and slides to the floor.

'Don't mind me,' he says to V. 'I never sat on a chair until I was sixteen, and then I was forced. Anyway, I start to explain to Wahida that my sexual preferences do not extend to very large men with no' – he glances at V – 'with no pudenda; but then I get a better idea. You see, I took one look at Wahida and I thought: This is the one. So I decide to play the game and say that I might consider the proposition but that I do not form liaisons of such an intimate nature without becoming better acquainted with the, er, suitor. Wahida is somewhat surprised at this and I notice a glint in her eye and know she has seen me in the same way, but now I have ruined everything by allowing her to think I am a homosexual, or at least – what do the Americans say? – AC-DC! So we arrange to meet in the same way the next night and the next, and all the time the man in the back is drooling and moaning. Wahida tells me he has not been with a man for at least a month and he is getting the terrific hots for me, but every night I get busy chatting her up and she begins to realize why I come night after night. I tell her to lose the eunuch but he is like a leech, so I say to him I will do a trade: I wish for one night alone with his mistress before I surrender to his weeping and gnashing of teeth. He has to agree. The next night Wahida and I catch a plane to Libya!'

'Incredible!' cries V. 'Like something out of Valentino!'

Wahida asks Rostand a question in Arabic. At the end of it I catch the name 'Valentino'. She has been studying V's reaction to their tale and doesn't seem much interested in me. I get the feeling she knows all there is to know about me from her husband. V is the curiosity.

But Rostand has already changed tack. 'You are *good*!' he says to V. 'You take people as you find them, not like this man here. He is too finick-finick-finickity. He thinks he is the intellectual but he has less brains than the backside of a she-camel — not enough brains to take people as he finds them. If I had not kicked his backside all over the desert he would not have found his balls and proposed to you. You do not mind my language, please; Wahida does not mind, she has a few words of her own which I will translate for you later! But your husband, he is a sheep in wolf's clothing!'

'That's what I liked about him,' V replies, good-naturedly.

Rostand picks himself off the floor, flicks specks from his trousers and sits down again. 'Now! Where is your son?'

'I'm afraid he's fast asleep. It's past his bedtime.'

'Aha! I forget, the West has a time for everything. Bedtime, lunchtime, dinnertime, notime! But you will please do us the honour of waking him up. He is the brother to my two children. I have brought them seven thousand miles to see their brother. They will be going soon.'

Will throws a fit when I wake him, but calms down when he realizes we have company. Rostand's kids erupt when they see him. The girl clutches him and won't let go. The boy plucks at his clothing and rubs the back of his neck. The three of them run around in small circles. Pandemonium. Wahida silently mimics

V's boyish mannerisms, slapping her knees and tossing her head back to laugh. V giggles madly; she can stand no more than one drink these days. My head is reeling.

The doorbell rings. Rostand says, 'Ah, that will be Bilal. You will please now excuse Wahida and the children. She has taken it into her head to visit four beauty salons and Bilal will accompany the children to the ice rink. They have never seen an ice rink. I will stay and talk with you about the old time. Is this convenient?'

It is two in the morning. V has taken herself off to bed and Rostand and I have been jawing about the desert days. I discover those times were rather desperate after all; much of the fun of young men is edged with aggression.

Rostand has become immensely rich. I surmise that he has his hands in the coffers of some political organization in the Islamic world, though he swears he is a middle-man in oil rigs and drilling implements. He has brought Wahida over for an inspection of her waterworks at some clinic where there are always fresh flowers in the foyer. He hints that all expenses will be met with funds he has expropriated from a certain Arab pressure group. He is half rueful, half boastful, and dying to tell me what he cannot. But he does not expect me to be curious about his mercenary side. He has always looked to me to liberate the poetic part of his nature, which emerges after a few drinks and is sentimental in the way of the old Arab, with much pledging of friendship and blood-brotherhood. This return to his Islamic roots has removed what there was of the European in him. His manners have changed from those of the decadent young French colonial to the budding Nasser – the haute-bourgeois Arab in the waistcoat and Italian shoes. Even his accent has changed.

Out of courtesy, he compliments me about V. 'Very pretty, *mon ami*, and with kindness you do not often find in your women, if I may say. Much laughter, too, but not polite in the Western way.' He seems to be suffering from the illusion that he was always the old Ottoman, appreciative of white women but disapproving at the same time. Perhaps he was: one cannot tell how people really see themselves until they have gone through the process of being fixed. Rostand was now a man who had taken on the airs of his age and status in the world. I hope that he sees me unchanged.

'I'm glad I took your advice, old boy,' I say. 'Only piece of advice you ever gave me that didn't lead to some kind of retribution!'

'What have you been up to, bastard? I have heard nothing of you – not even from my spies.'

'You hear nothing because I do nothing.'

'Fucker! How do you survive? You and your wife work?'

'Not at all. V and I are both busily engaged in doing nothing. And doing it very well, I might add.'

He eyes me with the same weary irritation that suggests he is going to have to kick my backside once more. 'How do you *eat*? You have an inheritance? Are you well or are you as desperate as usual?'

'It's a matter of interpretation, Rostand. I have other rewards. I live and think exactly as I wish.'

'So how does this put food in your boy's mouth?'

'Drink up, Rostand. Cool down and have another. There's no need to interrogate me; I was doing pretty badly until I decided to go my own way. I'm still doing badly but I've learnt a few things. I just wanted to make room in my head for something other than work. I took some time off to find myself.'

'What have you found? You look like shit! Pretty wife, beautiful son – intellectual shit in slippers with holes, too lazy to get off his intellectual arsehole. I see your car parked outside – the itty-bitty red one? Shitmobile!'

'Fuck off, Rostand! You're in no position to judge me! I had to take a risk because I needed to find out about certain things. And that's a simplification. I couldn't begin to tell you why we live the way we do. Ask me about my soul, not about my car! You never used to be so shallow!'

Now he is rueful again. 'I got wise. I kicked some arse. Remember how we used to say "Do unto others before they do it to you"? I got wise. You got your arse kicked.'

'You're wrong, you know. You're judging from appearances. Nobody kicked my arse. I'm a moving target, you old shit.'

Abruptly his mood changes and there are tears in his eyes. He is getting swiftly drunk – and so am I. 'A moving target, eh? Maybe you've got something there. Bastard! The truth is I fucked myself. I did myself before anyone could do me.'

'I thought you were rich, Rostand.'

'Now who's judging by appearances! Rich, ha!' He sinks to the floor, flat out, his tie askew and waistcoat open. Tears stream down the side of his face. I kneel beside him and loosen his tie. His eyes are closed. I think about going to bed. He clutches my hand. 'Don't go, bastard, I'm not asleep.' He puts my hand against his forehead and cries loudly. I dab at his face with my free hand. He collects himself and rises stiffly.

'It's been a long time since I drank this way. You understand? It brings out the old person in me, the one you knew. Rich? I am not rich, I beg just like you, but I beg for bigger sums and I take money from people who ask a great price in return. I would give it all up for the old days. When I had nothing, I was free. Now, even the people who love me put me inside a prison.'

It wouldn't surprise me if he was in some kind of trouble. He comes from a feudal world where favours and promises are often called in on pain of death. 'Is somebody after you?' I ask.

'Many people are after me and I am after many people. I play the game I never wanted to play, the one I went to the desert to escape. The arse-licking, the bowing and scraping, the sharks and devils ... I have never been one of them but now they have swallowed me up. Wahida knows nothing of this, by the way; we protect our women, we don't send them out to work like you. I long for just one evening when I can let my guard down and sit with old friends – real friends – and talk of dreams or of nothing, make music or speak poetry. Do you remember how you used to read to me? The Jesuit! Read me the Jesuit!'

I laugh in his face. 'Where's the old spirit? You've been in greater trouble. Why don't you make a run for it?'

'Read me the Jesuit!'

I quote from Gerald Manley Hopkins' 'Carrion Comfort':

–

Not, I'll not, carrion comfort, Despair, not feast on thee;
Not untwist – slack they may be – these last strands of man
In me or, most weary, cry *I can no more*. I can;
Can something, hope, wish day come, not choose not to be.

'Ah . . . ' He dabs his eyes. ' "Not choose not to be!" '

I am levelling off at cruising altitude with the vodka. 'Will Wahida follow you wherever you go?'

He rouses himself from his reverie. 'Don't ask me fucking stupid questions. I'm not a half-arsed Western shit like you.'

Tactics, now. 'Good! If you were, the subtlety of it would kill you, old boy. Do you know what your problem is? You imagine that your spirit is too fragile for the shit you have heaped on yourself. Some arsehole inside you has sold you a lot of crap. You're still here, are you not? No one has swallowed you up! You remember the poetry, don't you? You still know how to drink a bottle of whisky before bed! So why have you turned into a whinger? There was a time you would kick my arse and call me a fairy for giving up hope – well, kick your own arse now, or ask me to do it for you!'

I don't mean to sound quite so aggressive; I had in mind just the right blend of sympathy and scorn, but the vodka has pried my tongue loose. At any rate, I think I may be having the desired effect.

Rostand rises quietly, taking off his tie and waistcoat. He opens his shirt, stands wide-legged before me and points at a spot just below his sternum. 'Hit me here,' he says. He has decided to prove his invulnerability.

'Don't be bloody silly. I never allow any kind of violence in my home.'

'This is not violence, this is love. I love you, I love your V, I love your boy. You are my family. Make a fist and hit me here. It will give me the cure you speak of.'

'Don't be a fucking dickhead. Besides, you could get hurt.'

'I won't get hurt. This is the cure.'

I am pretty drunk by now and don't trust myself to respond without histrionics. If I hit him it could turn into a fully fledged brawl. I'm not sure how he would react after nine years of not knowing him. Still, I remember his craziness: he would burn his fingers over candle-flames and exult in the catharsis. Everything he did when I knew him was a flight from some anaesthetized part of himself. I was the ticket.

I get an idea. 'Tell you what, if you still think I'm a shit maybe I need a cure too. I'll hit you if you hit me. Fair trade!' The more I think about it, the more I like the idea. I haven't been this drunk for a long time. Where did V get the vodka from? I feel like nothing can hurt me.

'You are a shit, you always were. But I'm a bigger shit. You hit first.'

This is grand fun and fine drama. I won't lean back and put my weight behind the punch, I'll bring it up from the hip, so fast he won't see it coming. A right jab, not hard enough to do damage but painful for it.

I lash out. Rostand's rib-cage is surprisingly soft. I expected to hit bone and feel my fists sting. He had braced himself. He rocks back on his heels but doesn't need any legwork. The punch is harder than I intend because he doesn't roll with it. There is a red welt on his chest, blooming under the tangle of curly black hair. He draws his breath in slowly, feeling the pain. I don't think I have broken anything.

He measures me up carefully by placing his fist against my chest, pulls his arm back rigidly and lets fly. I forget to put one foot behind the other and the blow knocks me off balance. I reel backwards and crash into the furniture, ending up flat on my back. The pain is far away, but I cannot get my breath. I have smashed my elbow against something; there are two epicentres of pain cancelling each other out. I am winded but I feel grand. Some stale breath I haven't been able to shift for years has been punched out of me.

Rostand hauls me up. 'Let's eat. I need chunks of meat.'

'I can rustle something up,' I gasp.

'Fuck cooking. I need air.'

I leave a note for V and we stagger down to the main street. I take him to an all-night burger joint run by a slab-faced old crock who won't hire a waitress unless she's under nineteen and undulates when she walks. A couple of old men in overalls are sipping coffee loudly at the other end from where we sit. Rostand is drumming on the table and whistling an Arabic song. The crockery rattles.

A waitress meanders over. She wears a long black apron which looks as if there's nothing on behind it. Rostand curses in Arabic. 'Merchandise,' he says. 'Ask her if she fucks.'

'Don't be ridiculous, this is civilization, *mon ami*.'

'You call it civilization where women work in bars at four in the morning? Hullo, missy; two of your largest burgers with plenty of everything and two cold bottles of beer.'

'I'm sorry, sir. The cook is off-duty now. We serve only coffee and cakes until six o'clock.'

I can tell he is going to embarrass us. 'What! No chunks of meat! Nothing to eat? Not even one little . . . !'

'Rostand! You will forgive my friend, miss. We'll be on our way.'

'Never! You brought me here to eat and eat we shall! Go and wake up the cook!'

'I'm sorry, sir. The cook is not on the premises. You can have coffee.'

'You can have coffee! You can have coffee!' he simpers, mimicking her. 'Like Marie Antoinette! You can have cake! Let them eat cake! No food, huh? Then sit on my knee and entertain us!'

I haul him out before the waitress calls for reinforcements. Dawn. A warm rain is falling. 'Let's go back to my place, Rostand. I'm sure I can find something in the fridge if you're desperate.'

'I'm off. I have a plane to catch.'

We call a cab from a phone booth and shelter in a doorway waiting for it to arrive. Rostand is writing something in what looks like a notebook he has pulled from his breastpocket. I cannot tell in the dark, but I have my suspicions. He tears a slip of paper out and hands it to me. It is a cheque. I look at it; I say nothing. 'We have the cure between us,' he says very quietly. 'I will get away, and you and your family will come with us.'

'Don't be bloody daft. I don't need your money.'

'What do you have to keep you here? Your Shitmobile? Debts?

This hellhole where women work in the dead of night?'

'Keep the cheque. I'll get by under my own steam, thank you.'

'You'll sell out and become a turd.'

'I thought I was one already.'

'I don't give money to turds, I just borrow it from them.'

He snatches the cheque from my hand and rams it into my pocket. His knuckles graze the welt from the blow. The pain makes my eyes water. He peers at my face in the light of the streetlamp. 'Cry, bastard, it's your turn.'

'Fuck off. I'm not crying. I'm not a blubbering Arab like you.'

He falls silent. I take the cheque out of my pocket and throw it in his lap. He rams it back into the pocket, knocking me off balance again so I hit my head in the doorway. By morning I'm going to be a mass of bruises. Down the end of the main street a milk van rattles and wheezes. The sky is lightening and the streetlamps take on a green hue.

The taxi pulls up. Rostand has a word with the driver, then comes over and sits by me again. He seems to have sobered up. 'Wahida, the children and I are going to visit her people in India. She's half Indian, you know, half Indian, half Yemeni and half Saudi. A woman and a half. I think I will take your advice and disappear. Maybe in India, maybe somewhere I can get away and think and work something out. I can have some fun. Now, you and V and the boy, you come with us. You use this money to get away. You need the cure, too. You can give it back when you're rich if you're too proud – it's a small payment for all the poems. Fuck your debts – they can wait. I have bigger debts than you will ever earn in your whole half-arsed life. You give me courage but you can't find your own balls. So you get into some more debt and so do I, but we don't do it sitting here in a basin of piss, paying off the turds who make money from the likes of you and me. You come with us! My phone number's on the back of the cheque.'

He dives into the cab and it pulls away. I am still sitting in the doorway. Faintly, from a hundred yards away, I hear Rostand's voice like a siren in the morning air. 'I love you!' he bawls. Then, perhaps another twenty yards on, 'Bastard!'

In the doorway, just above my head, there is an aluminium plaque. It reads: 'The National Schizophrenia Fellowship'.

TWENTY-THREE

I have never seen the sun so large as it looks when it sets off the south-western tip of the Malabar Coast. Across from where I sit is an outcrop of rock on which the local people gather each evening with their children. They stand shielding their eyes against the sun, as if saluting it. When the last sliver of it steams and hisses into the Arabian Sea, they applaud. Night drops down like a visor and the Square of Pegasus looms large overhead, marking off the heat-scented sky like the four holes in a square tent.

My bags are packed, said V, when I told her I couldn't think of an earthly reason why we shouldn't accept Rostand's generosity. We had a shoulder bag for each of us and a knapsack for Will's indispensable trinkets. The rest of our possessions, books, mainly, and a few worthless items of sentimental value, we lodged with our relations. I sold the piano and left the tower to the repo man. The debts would have to wait. I decided to let them track me down, leaving a forwarding address and some vague but carefully composed excuses about having to retire to the Tropics to avoid death from an obscure disease. I invented a name, Hartmann's Calorific Syndrome, tying in something recognizably German with implications of a faulty metabolism and immune system.

That should confuse their mechanoid minds, and I shall deflect any threat of legal action by stating categorically my intention to make all necessary arrangements to pay up, but at such a time as my health allows the resumption of gainful employment. They will have to balance their own priorities with regard to clobbering me or letting the interest mount; that should take them a good six months. Who or what will eventually save me, I do not know. If they require the confirmation of a physician, I shall plead religious exemptions. Ha, ha! One thing at a time.

Arriving in India, we were surprised to learn that Rostand's money would probably last as much as a year, even after a good chunk of it had paid for an escape route back to the Great Wild West. I calculated that the interest and penalties I would have to pay on my return would add a third to the debt I left behind, but would still amount to less than the additional borrowings we would have needed had we stayed.

Then I stopped calculating.

The Great Western Post-Colonial City of Bombay – Heptanesia to Ptolemy – was given to Charles II of England as part of the dowry of Catherine of Braganza. That was in 1661, when to the local people it was still the fishing village of Mumbai or Mumba-Bai, seven islands afloat in malarial swamp, redolent with the utterly rank odour of *bombeel*, a sun-rotted fish laid in great array on the shorelines and sold as a condiment.

Six hundred billion years later, the smell of the past lingers after the departed British and Portuguese. As V and Will and I step out of the plane we are enveloped in thick, soupy air – a tureen of swamp water and piscine decomposition.

The light is refracted differently here, there being no shadows to speak of; and there is a different sun in the sky. A journey sheds a multitude of one's characters. I am convinced by this surrogate of Sol that we are not the same people who embarked in the West. Then I realize also that we have not simply left the West, we have arrived on an alien planet. I search the sky for the additional sun that consumes the shadows, perhaps a small red twin in wobbly orbit. There is something in the air here besides soup and dried fish: it is definitely a planet where conflicting hemispheres have been inseparably united. If it is not so then I have just named it so. For me, a liberated quantum being whose realities are all conditional and who is on the run from debt, that is as good as anything.

The White House is a yellowing edifice of nondescript architecture, set in the midst of slums in the city's northern Muslim quarter. To this redoubtable refuge V and Will and I are whisked, through seas of brown people, most of whom appear to be taking their leisure on the kerb or in roadside cafés. The White House is Wahida's ancestral home, three storeys, six apartments, all save one occupied by Wahida's relations and the spare one designated for us. Nothing is recognizable; I have never seen furnishings or interiors as strange, nor smelt air or squinted at skies so unearthly, nor heard such a storm of human and mechanical sound, nor lived ever in such disproportionate spaces as these.

V and I stand dazed, looking down from a wrought-iron balcony at a crowd of street urchins staring back at us. There are people living under shreds of sacking, mangled tin and slivers of rubber tyre in the shanty directly opposite the White House. Everybody talks animatedly to everybody else. I can see no despair, though this might be a Western city bombed back to medievalism and crammed full with a postnuclear diaspora. And the palpable air is a medium for omnipresent, alien sound, a greater density of sound than can ever be produced in the cities of the earth. There is a demonic, open-throated roar that is allegedly of traffic, but it does not drown the rustle of thirteen million whispers, and the whole is melded by a black and raucous sheet of sound that never stops but for a few sinister hours before the dawn – the endless rasping of a hundred billion black crows.

It is also the monsoon, with rain that leaves one choking at the bottom of an ocean. The population gasps and gags but hurries about its business nonetheless. A multitude of rats is drowned in a trice, some as big as Chihuahuas.

It is bliss. V and I are delirious. The discomforts of an alien world are a catharsis of the first order, assaulting all the senses at once. The first few nights are sleepless for the noise. The food is utterly strange, filled with things we cannot identify. We have been three days without any air that does not turn our lungs to lead. But we are finely tuned.

I think it is the planet Chaos. I think I have been justified in my quantum supposition of chaos as a benign force. This is a benign planet, given over to the life and death of each of its organisms. It may be a fictional place that really exists, a place to make a home that will never rest at a fixed point, for, as I look about me, I can find nothing that is not in an intense state of flux. Some might call it decay.

I have seen nothing of Rostand since our schizophrenic night. A young nephew of Wahida's, seeing us into our quarters, mentions that Rostand has booked us on a train south, where he has a surprise for us. We will spend three weeks in the city, acclimatizing ourselves. Our fate has been decided. This suits my inertia well.

Each evening, Wahida's father, a widower, holds court in the apartment below us. A servant, a voluminous woman of great age, is sent upstairs to babysit Will, who loses himself in the grimy expanses of her sari, while V and I dine with the family. It seems to be taken for granted that we will congregate in this way every evening. This, I learn, is not a matter of hospitality, though that is not in short supply, but of the family's consuming curiosity: they insist on learning all they can of us before we go south. It dawns on me that they have no better way to pass their time. Our evenings are all booked up, and Wahida's father, Salim, has a vested interest in the painstaking welcome we receive, each time with more surprise than if we had dropped in unannounced from a passing Zeppelin: he has a few things he wants to say to all Westerners.

An underground river of booze flows below the White House, for, in the course of an evening, stocks are constantly replenished by trains of servants who canter up the iron fire escapes at the rear laden with unmarked bottles. There seems to be no middle generation here, all of it probably having gone West to plunder more opulent economies. The apartments are occupied by a variety of ancient aunts and uncles and by scores of children with servants in tow. The ancient ones appear to be much devoted to the consumption of hard liquors, but I do not see any of them get drunk.

Wahida's father dominates the centre of a room hung with cobwebbed chandeliers and crowded with furniture of the kind that has animals carved into the legs. I have the feeling of being inside an atrophied menagerie of inscrutable gryphons, cockatoos, lions and jaguars. Around the father, other elders arrange themselves in reserved spaces, with the children spread out between cloth-covered stools and rattan mats. Each evening, there must be twenty-five people in the room.

'You Vesterners,' proclaims Salim, whose accent is thick and flat with a Victorian ring in the *r*s, rolled like a sergeant major's, 'think that your culture will remain for ever youthful . . . ' He pauses to take a great swill of the local grog, which is somewhere unknown between gin and vodka, with a dash of kerosene and rubber solution thrown in. I am getting to like it quite a lot, though it has turned V into a teetotaller. ' . . . and that the older cultures have nothing to offer the vorld: you make the mistake – in fact, you are the first culture in the history of the vorld to make the *greevious* error of thinking that life is a downvard progression, that age is the same thing as decay. But vhat this shows – ' and here he saws the air, leaning forward with great deliberation to make his point to his audience – 'is that your culture is not – has never been – may not ever be – a fully fledged culture at all. Not at *all*!'

There is a titter around the room. I cannot tell whether they are applauding his haranguing of Westerners or whether they are embarrassed by the rude histrionics. However, it is not really rudeness: the speech is delivered in the spirit of debate, of a proposition, and I can see that I am expected to challenge him.

'A fully fledged culture,' he adds, waggling a finger at me, 'is one that understands the potential of each individual, regardless of their age, size, caste, colour, creed or financial status.' He resorts once more to his glass, leaning back in his chair a little breathless and lowering his eyes as if to say, Well, go on, get out of that one, see how much I care!

I look at V and she reads my thoughts. We decide to play along, to see if we can convince this whiskered patriarch that we are Easterners at heart, subverting his tactics by defecting to his camp. Are we Easterners? I do not know. Perhaps on every alternate month of the year, depending on the state of the world's economies.

V speaks up. 'We couldn't agree with you more. Not only is Western culture, if it exists, in its infancy, it has also made the mistake of thinking that it has already aged enough and so seeks a noble sort of death, a dramatic exit, taking everybody else along with it.'

I cannot imagine what this statement of V's means. Perhaps the food or the weather have got to her. Salim has drawn himself even further back into his armchair, which is fashioned like a palanquin that has been set down by its bearers. I can see that he is not accustomed to being challenged by women, even if his ancient sisters scold and cajole him constantly. In his day, Western women were probably memsahibs cracking under the strain of marshalling servants and keeping antimacassars unsoiled. I decide to be difficult.

'Well, as a matter of fact, Salim, I don't agree at all. Western culture is as old now – if you count it as going back to, say, Anaxagoras or Heraclitus, as the Eastern cultures were when they began to show their age. However, I don't subscribe to a linear growth in cultures or civilizations. I think that's an illusion of history.'

Salim is not going to be deterred by the need for any kind of logical development to this conversation. 'Aha!' he yells, pouncing, 'but it is Vestern culture that invented history and the whole ethos of age and youth in historico-cultural terms, and the Vestern culture vhich is dominant – the Anglo-Saxon Protestant culture – has commandeered the Greeks for its own purposes. The Greece of Pericles and Socrates is as far away from today's Vest as the Persians of Darius are from Khomeini's Iran.'

V attempts to salvage her part in the proceedings. 'What I was trying to say, and not very succinctly, was that Westerners imagine they are an old culture, but their obsession with materialism proves they are culturally infantile. Even our philosophies are modelled on structured assumptions, the structures being an analogy for material order. We are still stupid enough to imagine that there is an essentially material explanation for everything.'

Now I am lost. Salim hops on to V's bandwagon. 'Yes, yes,' he says animatedly, 'Vesterners think that their culture grows old prematurely because they are obsessed vith the machine and use it as the model for everything. Because they build obsolescence into their machines, they imagine that their culture vill also run down like clockvork. They have no experience of the East, vhere our cultures are not thought of in terms of young or old, but as a continuum of the people. As long as the people survive, culture survives. They confuse culture and heritage. Heritage is vhat dies and becomes the same for everyone. They do not see that it is the people who make up the culture and that culture is reborn every day. Vhy, in the South ve have the Tamils, who have spoken the same language and vorshipped the same gods for at least four thousand years. Ask them about culture and they von't say a thing about it is dying because it is very old. They might even have been the same people as the Aborigines of Australia vhen all the continents vere joined up in one big cake.'

'Ah, the Aborigines,' I say, abandoning myself to the continental drift, 'now they will have some interesting things to tell us when we are ready to listen – if they survive to tell the tale . . . '

Salim picks up the torch. 'Yes, but the Aborigines vere overvhelmed by heartless Europeans who thought their own culture vas older and more authoritative than that of the indigenous Australians. They viped them out and then showed them how to drink, or how not to drink! They never got avay with that here! In India, our culture has alvays svallowed up whole the culture of the invaders. This is because until the Vesterners come, ve did not even talk of culture; ve had only the persistence of the vill of the people. That vas our culture. The Vesterners point out that there vas no India before the Britishers came, but who *vanted* an India? Ve had a dynamic collection of states vhich had their differences but also had the vill of their peoples. Our Emperor Asoka, he invented the velfare state, do you know; our Akbar vas the first to embrace religious tolerance among the vorld's rulers. There vere many, many things that happened here first.'

This is not the history of India I am acquainted with, but I sympathize with Salim's indignation. However, I am at a loss as to how to reply without reeling off offensive facts about caste, feudalism and bonded labour. Since arriving I have noticed that Indians take every opportunity to insert lists of their country's historical achievements into the conversation; this is a touching ingenuousness, when, for the likes of me, it is nothing less than the planet Chaos, benign and living proof of the success of an abandonment of an ordered way of life. I try this tack on Salim.

'Do you know, the thing that has struck me most about India since we landed is that it is a place of benign chaos. Things seem to work, to get done, somehow, even in the face of terrible odds.

I've never seen people so adjusted to their lives and so kindly by nature. I can't describe it any other way, and you will forgive me if my impressions seem naive to an Indian.'

Salim is not convinced. 'That is a typical Vestern assumption. You use it as an excuse. It makes you think people here can do vithout the luxuries and riches of the Vest, just because they know how to be happy. Vhy, they vill be even happier *vith* them! Ve shall show the Vest how to be happy and to have everything and not to think the culture is running down like a vobbly top. You vait and see!'

I think I may have offended Salim, though it is difficult to tell what he really feels. The people too, are from another planet. I notice that they do not have the same recourse to logic, arid and sterile as it may be, that Westerners assume as the basis for certain exchanges. Arguments are not constructed on the logic of pro-position and refutation: that is the structured Western way. Here there are bargains and red herrings. I discover with some delight that nothing is approached from a fixed point; your protagonist may abandon an initial position simply to gain the upper hand. It is all allusive, and one can lose oneself in streams of conversation, leaping in and out of smaller tributaries if the original flow has lost its momentum. I can see the scope for almost any kind of talk except small talk. These people get right to the point naturally, kneading and tossing you until you are pliant enough to reveal something of your interior. To find a place where there is no small talk! I have come to the Mecca of my soul!

Rumi Junior mutters under his breath. He is twenty years old or so, a gaunt man of tubercular appearance who wears only one item of upper apparel, a black T-shirt emblazoned with a drawing of a white coffin and the words: 'Fully Biodegradable'. I catch the last few sentences. 'You oldies are all spaced-out people, man. You think you can sit here and discuss which culture is dying and which is not. The fact is there are starving people all over the world, man, and the whole world is dying. The planet has entered its last phase. The astrologers know it and the politicians know it. Only people like you sit around and make useless noises about culture. No personal offence, see, but it is pathetic!'

I can no longer take this seriously. 'I agree with you absolutely,

Rumi. I was merely trying to understand your grandfather's point of view.'

'Don't patronize me, man. You honkies think you have something to say to us that we want to hear. We get along fine without you.'

I fail to see the connection once again. And Chaos is making me exceptionally meek. 'No offence meant, I assure you. I certainly didn't mean any personal slight. If I've made a, er, cultural *faux pas* please accept my apologies.'

Rumi's mother, a Parsee memsahib in a spectral sari of white chiffon with gold borders, breaks in gently. 'See, Rumi, he is a humble man. You can learn from humble people no matter what colour they are, white, brown or purple.'

Rumi is incensed. 'Shut up, *Mamaji*! What do you know about it! You haven't spoken to a foreigner since bloody Jim Corbett was decimating tigers in Bengal!'

V steps in in her granny mode. 'Well, if you're an example of the young India then the West certainly has a lot it can teach you. Manners, for a start!'

Rumi's face falls. He is not accustomed to being smacked about the chops by youngish honkie women. Salim roars with laughter. 'Young vippersnapper! You vill have to learn your manners from the Vest!' He turns to V. 'Ah, but sadly, young voman, the Vest has always been reluctant to learn anything of vhat ve have to teach.'

'That is our loss, Salim. It will come right one day.'

Salim leans out of his palanquin and chucks V's cheeks. 'Such firmness and visdom! Vestern vomen haven't lost their spirit!'

I am still smarting from not having stamped on Rumi.

Salim changes tack abruptly, addressing Rumi's mother. 'Sonia, play! Play for our guests! Play "It Had To Be You"! Play some Victor Sylvester!'

Rumi's mother wafts over to a baby grand with snarling lions for legs. She plays an up-tempo version of 'It Had To Be You' in stride, banging the left hand rigidly up and down so that the song acquires an oom-pah-pah feel, even in four-four. Salim thrusts several of his grandchildren into my arms and commands a dance. Rumi, who has recovered sufficiently from his battering to lech after V, asks her for a dance. They embark on a faltering quickstep. Two of the elderly aunts dance with each other. The doorways fill with servants, who have come to spectate. I have a child on each hip, one hung around my neck and two clutching my ankles. Salim himself has picked up one of his teenage nieces and is hurling her the length of the room in an amazing approximation of the tango, which, executed at quickstep time, threatens a perilous collision.

Suddenly, everybody in the room seems to be whirling around, and I have the distinct impression that some of the atrophied menagerie have joined in. Outside, it is late evening. I can still hear the scream of traffic and the unremitting caw of the crows. Sonia runs seamlessly through Broadway and Hollywood: the planet Chaos pays tribute to Fred and Ginger. Lions, jaguars and cockatoos leap and prance in the magic-lantern light of the ghostly chandeliers.

'Louder, Sonia, faster! I can't hear if you play like a bloody cissy!' roars Salim.

The noise is so great that we almost do not hear the tremendous, splintering crash. A massive rock glides in through the frosted glass of a window overlooking the street.

'The Hindus!' Salim bawls. 'Attack! Attack! Give the bastards hell!'

Sonia switches to a breakneck rendition of 'The Star-Spangled Banner'. The younger children disappear, the servants scurry off and reappear with an assortment of bric-à-brac. Everyone joins in hurling it out of windows and balconies on to the street below. Ashtrays, chair legs, broken toasters, cutlery, coat-hangers, books, bath-taps and shards of old tiling cascade from the first floor of the White House as the aunts, uncles and servants are mobilized in rapid attack lines.

V and I nip smartly into an adjoining room to see what is happening on the street. There is a crowd of perhaps fifty people hurling stones back up at the building. In their midst, set down in the middle of the street, is a wizened figure on a stretcher. We are being attacked by mourners. The figure on the stretcher, covered in jasmines and wearing a white skull cap, is a corpse.

A rock whizzes over our head and slams into a bookcase behind us. I cradle V's head. She kisses me. 'Christ,' she hisses, 'where have we been all our lives!'

Salim bursts in. 'Come on, you two, this is no time for lovey-doveys! Join the fun!' He thrusts a heavy round ashtray into my hand and drags us to the main theatre of battle. The ashtray is a fine onyx piece, hand-lettered with a poem from Kipling. I set it down on the piano and select the most innocuous missiles I can find, pitching them hard over the street so that I hit the walls on the opposite side. For all I know I might brain some poor Hindu who has been rudely diverted on his way to inter a loved one. Then, suddenly, the whole thing dies down and Sonia, like an old-time piano player in a silent cinema, shifts to 'Beautiful Dreamer', *legato con espressivo*, without breaking stride.

Salim peers out of the window, ducking and weaving. 'The bastards are going or they'll miss their crematorium. Good riddance!' He hurls a bath tap after them for good measure. Miraculously, no one has been hurt. It seems there has been an acceptable display of public temper. The Hindus had taken Sonia's thunderous revivals and their accompanying pandemonium personally. The servants pick up unused ammunition.

Salim is clutching V around the shoulders attempting a two-step to 'Beautiful Dreamer', but the tempo defeats him. He claps his hands. 'What bloody good fun! Nothing like a good tussle to stir up the appetite! Dinnertime! Bring food! Bring food! Our guests are famished! If we eat and finish before eight o'clock ve'll catch the bastards on the vay back! Pardon my French, Mrs V!'

And so the evenings go.

There is a subculture of children here, with a social life quite separate from the devices of adults. Will is constantly visited by his contemporaries and we have hardly to lift a finger to take care of him. Salim's retinue of servants has also adopted him as their charge and he is walked, watered and fed too frequently. One of them has been appointed our guide and takes us around the city whenever we ask. It is unremarkable but for its people. Amidst the dilapidation there are a few colonial monoliths of defunct grandeur and some astonishingly garish skyscraper hotels. The Mumbaians have a proper disregard for both, antiquity and modernity. To our delight, the people are always to be found in the eating houses, the fashionable ones thronged with students who are at pains to ignore us and the slummy ones with ragged, loud people who spit and hawk constantly to get the leaden air out of their lungs, and eat their food with gusto, in the manner of Doc.

They stare at V relentlessly, having first sized me up as not being particularly threatening. They do not imagine that their curiosity is offensive, and they are right. We stare back, at the diners, and out on the streets at people who accost you with their disfigurements and madnesses. On the planet Chaos, there is the overwhelming fact of humanity; nothing is hidden which is not also revealed; no abstraction can cover up the godawful misery and the exultant laughter of these people. In the face of this, the order and similitude of the West seem like an immense, carefully wrought illusion. If the Western edifices of constraint, decency and organization crumble, this is what we shall come to: one vast, exposed wound of suffering and of triumph.

In the nights, V and I chatter endlessly. There is a huge open window beside our bed, two storeys up, letting out directly on to the upper fronds of a coconut palm. This rustles all night and is a haven for the crows of the morning, who wake us with their sawing and cawing. V has lost a good stone since our arrival and the bones of her shoulders have begun to stick out. She has also tanned a smooth bronze; the new colouring makes highlights on all her curves.

She is saying, 'My God, if we had come here a year or two ago we would never have survived!'

'What's the difference? We were probably tougher then.'

'You have to have the right mental equipment to appreciate this place. You have to be so sophisticated that you can forget what it is like to be sophisticated.'

'Like the old British explorers, perhaps. Just take people as you find them.'

'And the place as well,' she says. 'The filth! It shows a sublime disregard for their surroundings, as if they're just passing through in some sort of dream. They're the happiest people I've ever seen!'

'With the most cause for misery! Perhaps the dream is a happy one.'

'There is the chance we're being naive tourists!'

'You have to believe what you see. Perhaps the medieval West was like this: the pagans and druids, the Wiccans, Brueghel's revellers, the same collection of misfits and endomorphs, amputees and wide-eyed infants . . . '

'We have to go back to Madrid and look again at all those Hieronymus Bosch paintings,' she says. 'There's something about the condition of hell we haven't grasped.'

'Hell, or heaven?'

'Nothing here makes any sense!'

'Maybe that's the secret. Remember how long they've been around, Salim's old culture. They've found out that nothing makes any sense anyway, so they live and die and have what fun they can in between. Have you ever seen such masses of people living with such horrors? But it doesn't show in their faces . . . '

'They've brought heaven and hell down on themselves and decided to ignore both!'

'I think we may never be the same again,' I say.

V is silent for a moment. It has been a while since we thought of ourselves, those selves we have left behind. 'I think we passed the point of no return long ago. This place is somehow a reflection of what we are. I'm terrified, but I've never felt so at home.'

'We had discovered Chaos before we left. This is just the materialization of – of our desperate dreams!'

'Yeah. Where the hell will we wake up!'

She is reading my mind, as usual. 'Well,' I say, 'perhaps we may never have to leave here. Perhaps we may never get out.'

She searches my eyes. 'You're serious, aren't you? I feel exactly the same way, as if I've finally found a place that isn't full of ghosts. This is the only place I've seen where it is impossible to doubt the spiritual existence of human beings – that's it! Everything is in sharp focus; there is too much going on, too many stimuli for our senses. People like us are blinded until we develop the extra sense they seem to have, a sense of dreaming that deflects the awful materiality of the place. That's what we've come here for – to acquire that extra sense. That's what we've been missing!'

I think of Rostand's cure and the last stale breath he knocked out of me. 'It's jet-lag and dysentery!' I say.

'Oh, don't be so prosaic! If we let our imaginations run away we might develop mentalities large enough for us to be able to live here.'

'You've made a decision, then?'

'One place is as good as another! There! Have I put it well enough in your language to convince you?'

'What makes you think I needed convincing?'

I am so infatuated with this woman who can uncover a mission in her own mind and then speak mine as well. I cup my palm around the back of her neck and draw her to me. A lone insomniac crow cackles in the night. In this embrace begins our season of comfort. It is the embrace of Chaos.

I am idling. Waiting for something new to break. Rumi, the little snerp, has unsettled my theory about this place being a haven for dreamers. He has been infected by the Vest, and rightly so, for only a synthesis of politics will do, if we must have politics. It is a small world, after all, a global hamlet.

Rumi pays us call grudgingly, turning up at mid-morning and staying till well after lunch. He is on some mission I cannot detect, probably to ogle V as much as is humanly possible. Rumi Ogilvy, the Harpo of Heptanesia, the Akoond of Aches, in his biodissemblable polo-neck. Rumi the Ruminator.

He has the awkward silences of his compatriots, seeing it rightly pointless to fill gaps with small talk. I'd rather have the silence, but V is pressing him about the slums opposite the White House. He looks at her dolefully.

'Why do you need to know? Look at them. Everything you see is authentic. You Westerners think of it as theatre, the theatre of poverty and degradation, man. That is your way of explaining it to yourselves. Simply look at what is there and you will have the authentic answers.'

I haven't a clue what this means. The three of us sit in silence. Salim's cook presented herself at the back door early this morning, teetering horrifically on the fire escape with a vast covered tray. 'Break please fast,' she intoned, sidling past me and laying a table

without warning. 'South Indian phwawourite, werry phwolesome.'
I have been examining the alphabet of Hindustani: it does not
have a labio-dental *f*; the swastika-shaped letter that is the
equivalent is pronounced as an aspirated 'phw', like someone
blowing specks off their cuffs. Likewise, the *w* is blown out
between protruding lips, and in English replaces the *v* mysteriously, though they have a perfectly serviceable *v* sound. This
accounts for Salim's Sam Wellerisms.

V, seldom undiplomatic, cracks up when the old lady whisks
off the covers to reveal two cylindrical objects about fifteen inches
long. These turn out to be rice and lentil pancakes with a potato
filling. '*Ghee masala rocket dosa*,' says the old lady, admonishing
V incomprehensibly.

By mid-morning they have induced a languid narcosis in me,
and I sit here impatient with Rumi Junior. 'I thought,' I urge
sleepily, 'that you might have some insights on the situation that
we do not.'

Rumi ignores me. He is one of those geezers who will consist-
ently address only one of two people in his company. Turning to
V he says, 'None of your fancy notions from the West will define
India. It is about failure, loss and death. You are in a society that
is already dead. Even its energy is corrupt. There is no pride in
survival if you can only purchase your survival.'

V seems to understand this. She is dismissive. 'Does no one here
have any hope? Do they all feel the same way you do? I've never
seen so many smiling faces . . . '

'When you have nothing it is easy to smile. Depending on their
politics, foreigners mistake the smile for colonial grovelling, man;
or if they are romantics like you, they think it is touching bravery.
But it is the smile of submission and failure. The world's largest
destitute population has nothing left but its smiles. The smile of
the beggar.'

V isn't buying any of it. 'There's a lot of degradation and
poverty in the West, too. No different from here. What we see
here is people making an effort to be human, but the West has
gone the other way. There, people's emotions have begun to die.
Their sense of what life is – the quality of it – has been trivialized.
They don't even know their own children any more. Here I see

people who love their children, no matter if they live in the gutter.'

'Yes, here you also have people who *sell* their children.'

I can see that this is going to get combative. V is bristling. She hates negativity. She spits in the eye of the cynic. 'People commit the same sins everywhere, for God's sake! I think the sense of shame that you are implying is your own. You make a mistake attributing it to the rest of your compatriots. I think you are transferring your own hopelessness to them because you cannot stand the thought that they may cope with life better than you. They are people, for God's sake, not just a premise for an argument! And even if they are depraved and corrupt, that doesn't mean they cannot hope for deliverance. Nobody lives and breathes who doesn't hope for better things. Hope is a kind of wisdom, and that's the wisdom we see in your people.'

'Very well,' says Rumi.

'Very well, what?'

Rumi heads for the door. 'Very well, you have changed my mind. You are right. I have abandoned hope. I will go away and think about all this again.'

He is halfway out the door. V looks at me, astonished. I think I am about to fall asleep. 'Bye bye, Rumi,' says V.

Rumi pauses at the door. Finally he looks at me, cracking a smile that makes his face sheepish. 'You haven't got fifty rupees I could borrow, have you?'

I am trying to think of a response other than total and immediate capitulation. V leaps from her chair and confronts him. 'Rumi,' she hisses, 'bugger off! Bugger off!' And she slams the door in his face.

'Ingratiating little bastard!' she says. 'All that philosophy because he wanted to touch us for money. And then pretending that I had converted him!'

I am ruminating and belching up cumin from my *ghee masala rocket dosa.* 'A ghoulie from the corridors of Chaos,' I mumble.

But what Rumi has done is to remind me once more how easy it is to fall asleep on the job. At every turn there is something that will try to fix you. Fix you good. I had had a romantic notion that this place would fit the bill as Chaos, but I should have known that Chaos has no geographical purchase. I shall instead console myself with the thought that it is part of my condition to be periodically overwhelmed by a romantic notion. What elements of perception shall we rule out without denying ourselves great streams of probability? I will be taken for a fool now and then, but the priorities and perspectives of a fool are also a part of the internal democracy. What else are we given minds for?

At any rate, V is in love with this place, and that is good enough for me. We have come from a place where there is the illusion of progress and order; here they are only two ingredients in a morass. It is beyond definition. Phwabulous! Definitions are for dodos. The moment I make up my mind about something I put aside all the virtual possibilities of what I am and what the world is, and I close off so much of that world that I might as well be lying in my grave watching an unchanging patch of sky. People here do not seem to try to make sense of their lives; they have more important pursuits than the formulation of mass abstractions. Nothing is fixed, because nothing *is* fixed! I have come to a place that will allow me to begin reinventing the world as I wish, but which will always be more than I can create. It is incomparably richer than great parts of the West, where, until one learns that places do not matter, life is lived in opposition to one's surroundings.

Now I am shrugging off that oldest of male imperatives: the right of territory. The lessons of V and Will have enabled me to renounce the male in favour of a more coherent and yet diverse personality for whom territory of any sort is an encumbrance; first the mental territory, renounced because it is antithetical to the quantum state; then the emotional territory, because maleness excludes too much of human potential; then the sexual territory, because men have politicized it and disenfranchised their own emotions; then the philosophical territory, because it refuses the ineffable even when it transcends dogma; then the territory of power, which has stolen the real powers of the individual male and female with its pursuit of order and its obligation to fix oneself ineluctably ... but now, in India, finally, I am able to renounce *territorial* territory, the sense of a geographical destiny which still makes us carve up the globe, the sense of being locative.

I think I have uncovered some old human allegiance to the state of the nomad, the physical equivalent of being unfixed and unconditioned, but also a greater allegiance to a greater state, in which I am free to roam. An endless territory, internal and sacred. Its vastness is there to be explored. We cannot do it justice with our minds closed or our eyes on the clock. And to approach it, we must forget who we think we are.

TWENTY-FOUR

And so we have arrived, under the Square of Pegasus, on the tip of the promontory that is the hanging, drifting lingam of the Indian subcontinent. We were guided here by a cryptic telegram from Rostand, who is up to no good in Singapore, and not in the south as Rumi had implied:

> Dear N
> The Home of the Rock Stop Your new home if you like it Stop Take the train to Trivandrum Stop Telephone Vasudevan 41252 to meet at station Stop Go exclamation Stop
> Rostand

Salim, with typical flair, has chosen a most circuitous route for us; but I am in no hurry. Over the Western Ghats we go, katankachank, katankachank, in a toy train on the medium gauge, rocking and rocking on perilous heights, over and under the primeval rainforest where the silent monad lives, in the dark shadows of the canopy. At every station, V wanders off the train, leaving me nervous that we will depart without her. We are calling at places never known to exist on the planet Earth: Lonavla and Kolhapur, Belgaum and Hubli, Davangere, Arsikere, Udagaman-galam and Coimbatore; places beyond history which will survive any of the holocausts of the self-centred West, with its small, cramped purchase on survival.

Passing one village after another, I discover a universe asleep. Nothing has stirred here for millennia, though the Raj might have dispatched the odd boxwallah to strip away its idols. There are none of the marks of history: I see dams and tractors, technology swallowed whole without the heritage of conflict that is its ethos in the West, familiar objects in an alien landscape, in the midst of unidentifiable monuments and aimless collocations of people.

I am witnessing the unfolding of a scene in which there are no references; yes, there are trees and hills and plains, but they are meaningless; there are villages where the movement of people is arrested by parallax, but I cannot assume that the people were in motion. We may be traversing a land of statues where the movements of generations of inhabitants – ploughing fields, drawing water, driving cattle, dandling children – are merely the repetition, in simultaneous time, of an endless series of poses. It is a virtual landscape; its ontology is perfect.

This is what I came for. At dawn in Hubli Station I watch four men who have been commissioned with the repainting of a station bench. The train has stopped for breakfast and now that the scene outside the window has ceased to creep forward, a complex pastiche of order and disorder comes alive on the platform. In the foreground, an invisible procession of people moves to and fro, but my eye is caught by the stillness of the four men. They have approached the bench and stand before it bewildered. They are staggered by the momentousness of an impending and required action. Their inertia is temporarily undermined.

Finally, one of them takes up a spanner and uproots the bench from the platform. Once he has accomplished this, he retreats to the position of a detached spectator and lights up a cheroot. Another man comes forward tentatively and dusts the bench with a rag; then another scrapes it with an assortment of tools, none of them fitted to the job. He does this with an air of condescension, giving up halfway and leaving large flakes of the old green paint that could be pulled off with his fingers, but are not. They now have a dappled bench and reach an unspoken agreement that it is ready for new paint. There is hierarchy as well as division of labour here, for the fourth man, who is about to paint the bench, has obviously pulled the senior job. He summons the first man to hold it in various positions while he applies the paint. This he does with incredible speed and despatch, until the bench is covered haphazardly with new green paint that is indistinguishable from the old. It looks as if it has been lightly cleansed rather than newly painted. The four men then settle down on the floor beside the bench, smoking cheroots and talking animatedly.

I have never before encountered such a perfect belief in the absurdity of action. Everywhere else in the world groups of men carry out their tasks with the same reluctance, hierarchical deference, uncooperativeness, disaffection, expediency and stupidity, but these men actually believe in the futility of their mission. They have no illusions.

Now I understand why this place is beyond history, and, like V, I begin to feel at home. Action requires commitment, but for commitment to last it must become fixed; however, our enthusiasm for any consistent course of action is always encompassed in the flux of what we are, and we become separated from our selves by this conflicting state – by this counterposing of momentum and inertia. No matter which of the two we choose, we become like the bench-painters: inert, even as we act. The trick is to avoid the singular commitment and to abandon oneself, or, more properly, to direct oneself to the momentum of the flux. The flux is enough of a force within our natures to guide us through successive actions without disaffection. To have no commitment is to be inert; to be committed is to deny the value of inertia, but to be a participant within the flux of action and decision, of will and event, of chance and destiny, is to be wholly alive and able to act.

Sartre never painted a bench in Southern India.

I am not proposing the abandonment of will – or of the great enterprises of humankind; I suspect, at any rate, that they were all initiated by single human beings who had found sufficient freedoms within themselves to be able to affect events momentously. Chimps with clubs. But randomness, disorder and inertia are adjuncts to the human spirit. The final marriage of order and chaos – of the spontaneous and unfixed aspects of our being with our tendency to symmetry and linear organization – can take us beyond the arid evolution of the Darwinists. And if any theory is capable of absolving us from this useless dualism it is quantum theory, the first empirical and living embodiment of the ineffable that our civilization has produced, and the first perceptions of phenomena that glide into the ontological, moving beyond words.

There will be more, of course, because the ineffable will bring new ways of perceiving, new faculties with which to explore what might turn out to be heaven and to learn what parts of it we may design to our own ends. It is there for us to create it: our participation in it is now a palpable fact, no longer a matter of faith, and therefore I propound not the cessation of action but a much larger and infinitely enriched choice of action that will be taken in a wholeness only just out of our reach. We must abandon ship to keep from drowning.

When we look at the child, we find the wholeness intact and are reminded of the potential that we have ordered out of ourselves because we could not see the value of our childlike imaginations – our original faculty for participating in chaos. There is less of this constriction in women, which is why this is an issue also of gender, and why V and I were led to explore a synthesis of our natures. The beauty of it is that in this repossession of our essential selves, which we can accomplish quite simply in our everyday lives, an infinity of secrets is revealed. We have only to move away from fixedness, from the opinions which we hope will make us coherent, but only bring us an early death.

The male nature has been driven far enough away from itself by empiricism, by the acceptance of history, by the absence of men from the firesides by which their children play; it has been subverted by the shallow and dispensable culture of misogyny in societies where men may not love each other and where love itself is subsumed by the sexual act; it has been buried under territorial imperatives which assumed, unlike the native Americans, that portions of the earth could be 'owned', and by generations of cold patriarchies who monopolized history even as they did not constitute it – for if it had been left only to them none of us would have survived.

Now, in a world where information assails us from all angles, the truth is no longer definitive or captive. Men will lose their grip of the certainties that sustained their folly. A great planetary revolution may be taking place, with information too voluminous to be the property of anyone and the authority of science diminished by the discovery of the ineffable. Whether these conditions are revolutionary or evolutionary, men will have to develop a new definition of themselves, and because the ineffable is reestablished in their lives this will be no fixed definition at all, but an equivalent of the unfixedness that women have preserved in their natures.

Men will become the undiscovered sex: they will finally arrive at the point where they will find women waiting for them. At that point of meeting is the arrival in heaven; the unification of our faculties will equip us for mental, psychic and even bodily expansion into a universe we participate in creating. Then we shall begin to traverse the distances of heaven.

Something will happen in our minds that will enable us to exceed the speed of light, as a mental or physical barrier – it will not matter. The states of uncertainty generated by the quantum will send us all into the momentum of the flux: time and distance, trajectory and momentum, inertia and force, order and chaos will no longer be perceived as external laws, conditioning us and forcing us to moribund ideologies, but as counterbalancing entities in a universe where the force of our imagination gives us our rightful place – each one of us, the woman, the man and the child. We shall think our wider universe into being, then step out into its beguiling distances.

Love, consciousness and imagination are human forces that equate with the forces of the universe – that *are* its forces embodied in us. Once we have realized this, all our journeys might bring us to that fortuitous arrival which presents us with a further infinity of choices. How can we be bound for only one destination? And the quality of being that this infinity bestows is the same quality we have forgotten, which reveals itself in its potential state in our childhoods and our unguarded moments.

To deny it now is to deny the renewal that each new human being brings to this planet. I can see no other course which promises such riches, and none for which we are so naturally endowed, whether we are beggars in the shadow of degradation or adulated patriarchs.

We all have our unguarded moments.

And to deny it is also to deny that there is anything for us but the path of entropy, which says we will come to an end, unfulfilled in all our enterprises, for whatever span of time we have endured, for all the effort we have made. Better, if we are to create a universe of the imagination, to imagine one in which there are endless possibilities, to recall that everything around us gives evidence of this, and to remember that there will always be the undefined beckoning and sustaining us. Nothing we perceive with only our empirical senses, with their division of the numinous and the material, can lead anywhere but to an end.

It is an end imagined and so made true: a surrogate heaven to which we defer our peace.

Renounce it! You have only your death to lose!

Trivandrum: the train stops. I look out of the window and there is vestigial movement, a scene of stillness being pulled slowly backwards by my own vision. Continuing the line of trajectory that has blended the movement of the train with the movement of my imagination, I am launched into a possible future of mine. Here, one future self, rummaging among rocks by the seashore, has uncovered an edict from the past. This edict was written by a man who has tried to prophecy the one particular future in which his future self exists. It says:

> The love of chaos in the year 2047 will have rendered the human species into a collection of anarchic beings. This will be to the good. After generations in pursuit of order, men and women will have discovered the pleasures and gifts of nonlinearity; that is to say, they will have renounced time. They will have understood that it had been, all along, an enslaving concept. They will have left far behind the need for conflict within, among, themselves.

It is the last year in the life of this future version of myself, who will have spent, in all, ninety-five years looking for this confirmation of what he had always suspected. He shall find it under an outgrowth of rock on a south Indian beach, where, in the very near future, I will have planted it.

Simultaneously – for it is all simultaneously: our tenses betray us, our language will have to encompass this renunciation of time, even if it makes us speechless – there is a version of myself in the past which is just beginning to understand that only his imagination will ever liberate him. He is the machinist of fake Wedgwood bowls and garden pots who stands at his injection moulder through the night on a twelve-hour shift, infected by despair. He places a filigree of white polystyrene, cut out in the shape of an idyllic scene of classical Greece, on the nipple of the mould. Waiting for the mould cycle to start, he looks at the figure of Apollo and wonders about the potential of men. The machine hisses and the spur of the mould closes in on the white polystyrene, then it disengages and he plucks off the completed bowl, snipping away the stem of plastic blown out by the mould-hole. It is just past midnight. He has another seventy-four bowls to make.

When he cannot free his imagination enough to think about the potential of men, he sings. He makes up songs with convoluted melodies to engage his mind. The machine battles for his attention, and when it wins, he cries. Behind the machine, none of the other machinists on the shopfloor can see that he is crying. But every now and then, he manages to transpose himself to another place, a place that he can barely discern in its features, but where there is silence.

In the simultaneity in which I exist, I can reach back to him and find he is still there, warbling on the shopfloor. From here, on the platform of Trivandrum Station, disembarking with V and Will, I can say to him, I have just written in my mind, in the same imagination which you tried to free, these few words; you may find them of some comfort. I shall show him the edict. Perhaps the first inklings of what it means will surface in his mind.

I begin, in retrospect, the process of liberating myself. The past can be rehabilitated. Those small refuges of imagination which he created I shall bring to him in full, announcing the arrival in heaven and beginning the process which rescued him.

I shall loop the loop in time!

TWENTY-FIVE

The Home of the Rock is aptly named for the large outcrop of pitch-black gneiss on which it sits, some thirty or forty feet above a precipitous drop into the Lakshadweep Sea. We have come to the precipice.

Below the rock is a small beach, the first of many leading off to the southern tip of India, from which smaller crops of gneiss jut out like beached black whales. In one of these, which I have carefully marked on a map of my own, I have interred the edict.

The Home of the Rock began life as a small seminary for novitiates of the Mar Thoma, a sect of the Malabar Christians, who were converted by St Thomas the Apostle, Doubting Thomas, no less. I am pleased to be associated with an historic line of questioners. He presented himself at the court of King Guduphara, was martyred forthwith, buried somewhere near Madras, then disinterred and carted off to the West. This despite the fact that, according to the *Acta Thomae* in the Apocrypha, it was his express mission to evangelize India, and his church grew up separately from that of the boys in Rome.

The Home of the Rock, at any rate, is now a hotel, derelict but for a few months in the boiling winter, when Westerners off the beaten track find it an adequate refuge.

Vasudevan, an intense and serious man who is studying to become a scientist at the rocket station up the coast, runs the hotel for Rostand in his spare time, keeping a casual roster of staff who disperse when the winter months are over. Arriving at the hotel, Vasudevan unlocks a safe and hands me another cryptic note from Rostand:

228